I0104875

The Taming of Nan

The Taming of Nan

Ethel Holdsworth

With an Introduction by
Pat Johnson

K&B

Kennedy & Boyd
an imprint of
Zeticula Ltd
Unit 13,
196 Rose Street,
Edinburgh,
EH2 4AT.

http://www.kennedyandboyd.co.uk
admin@kennedyandboyd.co.uk

First published 1919. This text follows the original US edition, published in 1919 by E.P. Dutton.

Introduction and notes © Pat Johnson 2023

This edition © Zeticula Ltd 2023

Ethel Carnie Holdsworth published under her maiden name (Ethel Carnie) and with various versions of her married name.

Front cover image: Ethel Carnie Holdsworth.
Reproduced with kind permission from Helen Brown.

ISBN 978-1-84921-236-6

All rights reserved. No part of this publication may be reproduced, stored in a retrieval system, or transmitted in any form or by any means, electronic, mechanical, photocopying, recording or otherwise, without the prior permission of the publishers.

To
Edwin Holdsworth
in appreciation
of sterling worth

Contents

Introduction

In 1919 Ethel Carnie Holdsworth published her third novel, *The Taming of Nan.* At this point in her career, Carnie Holdsworth was an established author with one notable success, *Helen of Four Gates* (1917), to her credit. As was typical of her, she did not try to replicate her recent success; instead, *The Taming of Nan* explored new territory, addressing the issues of fair compensation for a workplace injury and working-class domestic violence. In addition to addressing these societal problems, *The Taming of Nan*'s central family grouping consists of three original characters that reinterpret accepted working-class tropes: Nan Cherry, a working-class virago; her husband Bill, a stolid family man; and their daughter, Polly, a teenaged mill girl who wants nothing more than to have a good time. These characters develop in a context of intergenerational family ties as well as a widespread community whose advice and traditions provide a fertile context for their family drama.

Biographical Background

Ethel Carnie Holdsworth was born in 1886 to working-class parents and first attracted attention as a mill girl poet. In 1909, after a decade of factory work, she briefly served as editor of socialist Robert Blatchford's the *Woman Worker*, producing editorials based on her experience of the lives of factory workers and working-class women. Fired by Blatchford because of her radicalism, she went on to become the first British working-class woman from an industrial background to publish a novel, *Miss Nobody* (1913), and the first to have a successful novel adapted to the screen (*Helen of Four Gates*, 1917).[1]

The years leading up to the publication of *The Taming of Nan* were tumultuous ones in Carnie Holdsworth's private life. In 1915, she married Alfred Holdsworth, a fellow writer and working-class radical. Their first child, a daughter, was born in May 1916. Although they were strongly opposed to the WWI war fever that gripped the U.K. and to military conscription and Alfred Holdsworth registered as a conscientious objector, he was conscripted in 1917 and sent to the Western front in a non-combatant role. Then, in 1918, he was reported missing in action, presumed dead, and, for a year, Carnie Holdsworth believed she was a widow. When the war ended, Alfred was found in a hospital and it was discovered that he had spent months in a German POW camp. He returned home in 1919.

This period was a financial roller-coaster for Carnie Holdsworth as she struggled to provide for herself and her child on a soldier's wife's—and then widow's—pay. Even the publication of her second novel, *Helen of Four Gates*, brought no relief, and she and her daughter were reduced to near destitution, boarding with a family in Blackburn in 1918. Then, suddenly, the tide turned. The war was over, Alfred came home, and, as Helen was made into a silent film, the Holdsworths' financial fortunes improved. Carnie Holdsworth went from near destitution in 1918 to being able to buy a small farm for £100 in 1919. This is as financially secure as she and her family would ever be.

Novelistic Experimentations

As a writer, Carnie Holdsworth was committed to using her abilities to challenge the political and economic status quo and to voice working-class concerns and perspectives. She shaped a wide variety of genres to reach her audience, beginning with poetry, published in working-class newspapers in the early 1900s, and then in three books. In 1911, she began experimenting with fairy tales as a genre, producing four collections in as many years.

The same type of experimentation with form can be seen in her novels. Her first novel, *Miss Nobody*, is a *Bildungsroman*, focused on its working-class heroine's, Carrie Brown's, struggle to find a rewarding life. The novel traces her journey from a working woman living in industrial Manchester to, after many struggles, a married woman settled in a nearby farming community. Carnie Holdsworth's second novel, *Helen of Four Gates*, is also the story of a working-class woman, but its setting and tone are radically different. Helen's story takes place on an isolated farm and, contrasting *Miss Nobody*'s everyday realism, is written in a Gothic style that many critics have compared to *Wuthering Heights*.

The Taming of Nan, published in 1919, addresses still different themes and uses the genre of the novel in a different way. The setting is the first difference. The action takes place in the small industrial town of Narrowfields and its surrounding countryside. Narrowfields is described as "the body of a long dragon, from whose back rose half a hundred chimney stacks" (1). The ugly town, however, "could not wholly hide the beauty of gleaming Cherrydale," the surrounding countryside, to which the town dwellers can escape (15). The novel centres on the lives of the three distinctive characters who make up the Cherry family but extends to include neighbours, friends, family members, and the surrounding farming community. In other words, this is a far more peopled novel than either *Miss Nobody* or *Helen of Four Gates*. *The Taming of Nan* contains multiple story lines, but, in all of them, both the harsh realities of working-class life and the strength and resilience of working-class community and culture are evident. The novel starts with the social problems of domestic violence and workplace injury but then expands to cover a broad landscape of working-class life.

Social Problems in *The Taming of Nan*

Through the Cherrys' tumultuous marriage, Carnie Holdsworth dramatizes two concerns, domestic violence and fair compensation for a workplace injury. Domestic violence as an issue in working-class households appears frequently in both 19th- and 20th-century historical sources, and, while scholars now debate how widespread it was, it was an accepted part of working-class culture.[2] Carnie Holdsworth had experienced it in her own family life [in 1901 her mother separated from her father because of it] and her previous novel, *Helen of Four Gates*, provided a hellish example. *The Taming of Nan*, like many of her novels, supports the idea that domestic violence was widespread.[3] The local policeman makes regular visits to the Cherry household and a neighbour comments on what he would do to Nan: "At it again, By th' Mass, if she were mine— !" (9). The Cherry household is not the only instance of violence as a constant presence in the working-class home. Nan's mother, Granny Harker, has "her 'gammy' leg (souvenir from Pa Harker, defunct)" (35) and the charwoman, Jane, is regularly beaten by her husband and appears midway through the novel with a black eye.

Before the passage of the Workmen's Compensation Acts of 1897 and 1906, workmen had to prove employer negligence in order to receive compensation for a workplace injury. Carnie Holdsworth had direct knowledge of the resulting injustices in the life of a local labour leader, Dan Irving. In the 1870s, Irving lost a leg in a shunting accident while working for the railway in Bristol, and the company refused to compensate him adequately. An exemplar of working-class resiliency, Irving went on to become a socialist and labour organizer and leader of the Burnley branch of the Social Democratic Federation (SDF) when Carnie Holdsworth was a teenager.[4] In 1918, the year before *The Taming of Nan* was published, Irving was elected Burnley's first Labour M.P. Even though the passage of the Workmen's Compensation Acts of 1897 and 1906 improved the situation, major problems remained, such as the facts that compensation could be offered in a lump sum and no provision was made for retraining the injured workers. Although domestic violence and workplace injury are not unique topics, Carnie Holdsworth's approach to them is. In both cases, by dramatising their impact on the very particular personalities of Nan and Bill Cherry, she provides fresh perspectives.

The Stories of Nan and Bill Cherry

Nan and Bill live in a constant battle of the sexes, marked by "cyclones" of domestic violence so regular that Bill tracks them on a calendar. But the source of the violence is not Bill, huge and immovable as he is. He longs to live in peace, but Nan demands violence from him, physically attacking him until he gives in and responds. She screams, "Hit me, Bill! Hit me! For God in heaven's sake, hit me. I can fight. I'm not a toffee doll. Hit me. An' let me hit back" (7). Described as savage and "untamable" (2), Nan, in outline, fits the late Victorian stereotype of a slum shrew, violent and drunken. For example, in George Gissing's *The Nether World* (1889), the character Clementina Peckover wreaks havoc wherever she goes. Like Nan, she gets into physical battles and goes on drinking sprees. Similarly, Clem is described as a savage; Gissing's narrator states, "Civilisation could bring no charge against this young woman; it and she had no common criterion".[5] This comment parallels this description of Nan: "She was the untamable hooligan—the Stone Age hidden under the veneer of Civilisation" (2)

But other details separate Nan from this monster. She is not a sadist or a seductress, as Clementina is. While Gissing's narrator ponders whether the source of Clementina's evil is slum conditions or whether she is an evolutionary throwback to an earlier precivilised world, the origins of Nan's anger and behaviour can be explained. On the most basic level, she is raging against male dominance and women's entrapment in marriage. She is described as trapped in "a cage she was flinging herself against" (6).

However extreme her behaviour, this anger resonates with Carnie Holdsworth's own views of marriage. In *Home in British Working-Class Fiction*, Nicola Wilson states, "Carnie Holdsworth's writing consistently exposes the home as a gilded cage for women."[6] As the reader learns more about Nan's life, more is revealed about the sources of her behaviour. She was raised in a violent household in Narrowfields' worst slum and, late in the novel, her mother-in-law refers to the fact that she was a "pit girl," someone who worked picking coal at the surface of a mine, a job considered rough and brutalising (116).[7] Five of her children died in infancy, and she is shocked to learn that many people blame her for that. Her mother-in-law, however, points out that Nan had wanted to care for her infants but never had been taught how. Finally, Nan is redeemable. In the second half of the novel, Nan comes to terms with her anger and redirects her enormous energy into fighting for her family. Nan cannot be tamed by others; she tames herself.

Bill's catastrophic work injury, losing both his legs in a railway accident, both changes his home life and underscores the untrustworthiness of the legal system when it comes to justice for the working class. At the same time, although struggling to recover a sense of identity, which before his injury was based on being "the Big Porter" (3), he firmly and repeatedly stands for his rights in the face of the railroad company's malfeasance. The company first determines it will pay him only his nominal regular wages, ignoring the fact that, as a porter, he more than doubled his wages with what he would earn in tips. Bill files against the railroad in court, but he finds the proceedings an unforgettable "ordeal" (124). He and his fellow workman, Billy, who is testifying for him, are uncomfortable with court procedures and feel completely unheard and out of place. Exposed and humiliated, Bill is seized by "the burning thought that they were being treated like children" (100). This court rules against him. When he decides, with the Union's approval, to appeal the court decision, the company sends a negotiator to him with an offer of a one-time payment of thirty half sovereigns. But, even under severe economic pressure, he refuses. Eventually, he wins his case, but this underscores, not the system's fairness, so much as Bill's determination to get his rights. Not only that but he draws something positive from his tragedy.   "[F]eminise[d]" by his injury, Bill begins to understand Nan's unhappiness because now he is trapped at home (103). In the end, he rehabilitates himself as a successful fent (clothing) dealer and makes Nan his business partner.

Polly, a Working-Class Flapper

In the interstices of her parents' violent drama, seventeen-year-old Polly flits about the countryside, pursuing her own interests and amusements, and, through her, different streams of working-class life enter the novel. Polly Cherry is another fresh character in both the Carnie Holdsworth canon and generally: a working-class flapper. Polly has no interest in politics or in working-class debates, but her character indirectly comments on contemporary changes in women's behaviour. In the 19th century, cultural critics had fretted about mill girls who strolled the streets with their friends and spent their pocket money on clothes. In the 1910s, a new societal bugbear emerged and newspapers began to publish horrified stories about "flappers," restless, irresponsible young girls who might also be sexually immoral.[8] Polly is repeatedly described as a representative of "flapperdom," with one character even providing an etymology for the word flapper, explaining that it means "a young duck" (53). Later in the 20th century, Polly would be recognized as a typical teenager, undergoing the "transition from girlhood to womanhood ... that awkward, moody, dangerous age" (39). Carnie Holdsworth is prescient here about changing mores and roles for women.

Polly is represented with a refreshing lack of moral judgment and her desire for some fun is seen as natural and often celebrated by the novel. In her 1909 editorial "Our Right to Play," Carnie Holdsworth had begged, "For God's sake, women, go out and play".[9] And Polly does. On a Saturday night, she stays out well beyond her coming-home time, gets in trouble for trespassing, and is kissed by two possible boyfriends. But, unrepentantly, she tells her Granny Harker, "I don't care for aught but—dancin' an' lads, I don't" (35). Through Polly, the novel provides instances of working-class celebrations and love of music. She goes to an annual event, half fair and half circus, called the Cherrydale Tide, where she sees a lion tamer and rides on a swing boat. She has a lovely voice which she likes to show off at church, eventually competing in a local singing competition called the Charity, with her debut advertised throughout the neighborhood on a pink bill that announces "Soprano: Miss Cherry of Narrowfields" (73).

Importantly, this theme of "play" appears in other characters' lives as working-class love of music and communal celebrations provide them with respite and renewal. Music is a presence throughout the novel and the working-class repertoire is all inclusive, from popular contemporary tunes to traditional ballads, and from hymns to classical arias from *Faust* and *Rigoletto*. Bill whistles "Home, Sweet Home" when he gets up in the morning (2); the charwoman Jane performs "Burlington Bertie from Bow" (56) while she cleans; and Polly will spend her honeymoon going to operas. Gatherings of family and friends to mark important occasions are frequent. Although some fail to lighten the characters' burdens, such as the Cheer-up Party that greets Bill when he returns from hospital (58), many others are successful. Thus it can be seen that, while there are literally life and death struggles going on in the characters' lives, there are also working-class customs and celebrations and family and communal ties. *The Taming of Nan* concludes by uniting all its characters and themes at Polly's wedding. This celebration features plentiful food, drink, and dancing while Bill Cherry acts as M.C. for a song contest "where people had to sing whether they would or not" (191).

While the first part of *The Taming of Nan* shows the Cherry family sliding deeper into disfunction and despair, the second half reverses their decline. One factor in this reversal is that each character learns from his or her experiences. In *The Taming of Nan* the characters are not tamed by others or by circumstance. Instead, they learn from their experience how to improve their lives. This optimism reflects Carnie Holdsworth's personal history in 1919. She and her husband had a second daughter in 1920, and she entered a very productive period professionally, publishing two novels in 1920 (*The*

Marriage of Elizabeth and *The House That Jill Built*) and seeing *Helen of Four Gates* made into a film. More significantly, the optimism represented her hopes for the future of the working class, not just in Britain, but worldwide, where she had faith in the growth of the international socialist movement. The conclusion of *The Taming of Nan* comes at this dawn of brightness as the Cherrys resolve their troubles and the novel celebrates working-class communal culture.

Notes

1 Biographical information is from Roger Smalley, *The Life and Work of Ethel Carnie Holdsworth, with particular reference to the period 1907 to 1931* (PhD thesis, University of Central Lancaster, 2006).
2 See Anna Clark, *The Struggle for the Breeches: Gender and the Making of the British Working Class*, (Berkeley: California UP, 1995).
3 Nicola Wilson, *Home in British Working-Class Fiction* (Farnham: Ashgate, 2015), p. 74.
4 See Roger Smalley, *Dan Irving Socialist* (Nelson: Scotforth Books, 2021).
5 George Gissing, *The Nether World* (New York: Oxford UP, 1992), p. 6.
6 Wilson, p. 74.
7 See Angela V. John, *Coalmining Women: Victorian Lives and Campaigns* (Cambridge UP, 1984).
8 Richard A. Voeltz, "The Antidote to 'Khaki Fever'? The Expansion of the British Girl Guides during the First World War, *Journal of Contemporary History*, Vol. 27.4 (Oct., 1992) pp. 632-633.
9 Ethel Carnie, "Our Right to Play," *The Woman Worker*, 14 April 1909, p. 342.

The Taming of Nan

Chapter 1

The sweeping out

The voice of Nan Cherry, shrill and aggressive, sounded its war alarm on the quiet, dawn-glimmering street. Whereupon a crowd of sparrows, busy picking up from before that door of the unluckiest of unlucky numbers what looked like a supper flung out the night before, flew away with great commotion. Their panicky flight made a cloud of wings against a long white cloud, behind which boiled the gold of a September morn ready to overflow the world of Narrowfields. The town lay in a hollow below the little street. In the imperfect light it appeared as the body of a long dragon, from whose back rose half a hundred chimney stacks. These stacks pricked into the opaline glimmer of the sky like the charred fingers of some underworld giant, thrust smoking through the earth to grab at sun, moon and stars.

The bent figure of an old man who could toil no more, crept from little door to little door, rousing others to toil, then disappeared from the street. Through it all the voice went on.

A child's rebellious cry rose sharply as it was roused to be carried out to nurse — quavering away into little exhausted, sob-calmed murmurs of acquiescence. Whilst the sound of a poker rattling the bars of a fire that did not realise it must boil a kettle within ten minutes; the banging of a door; the barking of a dog; were the first signs of industrial Lancashire waking up.

Unawed by the echoes that shrilled back her voice, in the mocking way of echoes, the shrew carried on her tongue-onslaught. To all its fire, no defence answered.

According to Scripture a soft answer turns away wrath. But the man who wrote the proverb had not met Nan Cherry. Possibly, as Granny Harker said, Nan was familiar with that provincialism which states that nothing said often means quite a lot.

Be that as it may — the fact has to be recorded that her rage leaped the higher for not being fanned by back-words.

Her voice became such as only a man deaf and dumb, dead drunk, or a philosopher could hear without a human desire to choke it into human decency.

"Thee! As calls thysel' a 'usband. Tha lazy son of a whilk! Thy tay's brewed. Mun I sup it for thee? Th' world's aired. An' thee — our Polly, if I come up to thee, bitch, I'll scalp thee. Folk doesn't know what I go through. I don't shout *my* troubles off the housetops. For you never get pity if you carry colour in your face."

Then silence fell once more. The sparrows returned to their feast. The sound of a woman beating carpets two streets away woke dolorous echoes.

Within the Cherry castle a chair was rocking. The sound suggested gritted teeth.

A mighty yawn from an upper room was followed by a shower of ceiling-plaster in the room below as a number eleven foot touched the bedroom floor.

The shower fell on the head of a dark-haired, comely-featured, blue-aproned woman rocking in the ingle-nook. Her body had a crouching attitude. Day-light streaming through a red blind just behind her spattered crimson bars and blotches over her.

Nature had given her a pleasant exterior. Her chin might thrust itself out too prominently, but she did not look anything that could demoralise ninety-nine men out of the hundred. Only as she turned her face to the fire, under that pattering shower of plaster, an expression crossed her face which stamped it. She was the untamable hooligan — the Stone Age hidden under the veneer of Civilisation. She had neither humour, imagination, nor protectiveness. She should have been an apache's mate. She had married a porter who gave her a pound a week and bought his own clothes. With that look upon her it seemed miraculous that this cramped, drab kitchen could hold her.

A jocular whistling of "Home Sweet Home" filtered down into the place that was mainly wash-boiler, table and chairs — four badly blistered, dun-painted walls, and a phonograph.

On the very first sound of the big voice there was a response of doggy delight from the yard, which taken in conjunction with unframed pictures from "Our Dogs" and a couple of framed pedigree forms hung over a pipe-rack holding pipes mostly crippled, told its own story of man's ancient love for dogs.

Then more plaster fell.

The look cast upwards at the ceiling, just at the centre of its trembling, was rapier-like enough to have made a hole — if a look could. The boss of the show was hitching up his braces. Innumerable bumpings, on the same spot, at the same tick of the clock, week in, week out, had first shaken the ceiling.

Bump!

It really seemed as if the roof must give way at this last assault. He was crossing the room.

His weight was set upon the stairs. They creaked under his fourteen stone. Two steps were followed by a longer pause, as the man dodged an angle of a dark staircase built for lesser men. On an after-thought he called to the sleeper in the other room.

"Polly!"

The word was at once a caress and an apology.

"I'm up."

Muffled as it was by bedclothes the voice had all the Harker euphony — that curious, bird-like sound come down from generations that had sung in choirs — and sometimes in pubs.

"Lyin' little hell-cat!"

The viciousness from the one member of the Harker stock who had been given no singing voice, was of the quality which only one female can mete out to another.

"I thought I was up."

A girlish giggle ended the admission.

It was a gush of light in a dark place, that trickle of laughter from a little white feather-heart that might blow anywhere. It became a symbol of the tenacity of youth to turn to the sun of life — to have its day — in the mire of the pit, or on a cinder-heap of hell.

"Tha's only once to get up," said the big voice of the man on the stairs, and he bumped down another step.

The reply was curious, the voice more bird-like on account of bedclothes no longer muting it.

"Oh — some gets up twice," was the remark on which her father pondered as he went down the stairs. Had the tone not been so utterly frivolous the words might have been interpreted into some dark hint of discontent.

"Bump — bump."

There were thirteen bumps in all. Their steady way of coming on gave no clue that Cherry wished to dodge the storm waiting for him. He must pay this morning for that ten minutes game at draughts he played last night with Billy Breeze, after which he had returned to find his shirt on the doorstep, his supper laid out on the pavement.

"The Big Porter," as he was known to Lancashire and Yorkshire passengers, bent a massive head and passed into the drab cage of a kitchen. He was almost a giant of a man, fair-haired, dangling in his left hand a pair of boots ridiculously large in this world of dwindling manhood. A stump-end of a cigarette was stuck in his close-shaven mouth — a cigarette being economised to the last shred thereof. It was a mouth that did not need covering up. Under it was a great depth of chin. His blue eyes were of the sleepy order that Granny Harker had once defined as being able "to see without looking".

His first action was to spit out the cigarette a couple of seconds before it would burn his mouth.

His second was to blow out the smoky lamp — with a saving instinct to burn daylight.

The glance he had cast at the woman in the chair was one of affectionate tolerance, mingled with that of a man who has lost all illusions, but knows that he has his feet, if the worst comes to the worst.

The woman returned the look with one only explainable by the fact that this was the man who had married her — who, for twenty years, by the aid of Laughter and of Feet, was still unvanquished, yet outside what he sarcastically termed "th' Henpeck Club".

With the persistency that is the virtue of the savage, she still maintained her attacks, whilst with the patient geniality of a Yorkshireman he as stubbornly resisted.

"Top o' the mornin'," was his greeting. His attempt at the brogue would have turned an Irishman sick.

"Jesus wept!" was the response of the woman in the chair.

It would be impossible to say how this shortest verse in the Bible became in Nan's mouth a challenge, anathema, and war-cry. The tone of the delivery was utterly divorced from the subject-matter. It had passed into a new language.

The big man sat down and laced his boots, thrusting the holes in his socks respectably out of sight — his bending position showing a neck like a gladiator's and the great back of him that carried more boxes than any other man's on the Lancashire and Yorkshire Railway.

There was a magnanimity about him only to be compared with that shown by a big dog attacked by a little one.

He went off into the scullery, where his rendering of "Queen of the Earth" sounded through a great and cheerful splashing, combined with a blowing against the water.

Whilst from a kennel in the yard came a pandemonium of undisciplined dog-emotions which broke off the song into short ejaculations of "Good little dog, Rag — " "Goin' to show 'em what tha are, Rag, eh?" "Top of the mornin', Rag" — whilst the scratching at the kennel door, the barking delirium of worship, grew more frenzied.

When it could no longer be withstood, Cherry went out, opened the kennel-door, and out blundered the pedigree dog — one ear cocked at its top-notch of joy, its body rolling along, its great feet making the slipper-like sound, as it trotted before him utterly unconscious that it was not the finest dog in the world. Perfect in colour, a good head on it, its overlarge ears that could perform weird gymnastics, its legs defined by a small boy as "bow-legged in front, knocker-kneed behind, an' walks like Charley Chaplin" — for some mysterious reason, Rag had got rickets and fallen short of his glorious ancestry. That it was a dog of spirit no man could have denied. There was no cringing sense of its own long short-comings.

Cherry sang out in full voice as he watched Rag trot before him. His face was softly paternal. It had upon it the faith in its regeneration which made him the unconscious laughing stock of the whole street on his Sunday morning parades, to straighten Rag's legs.

"That dog'll come into its own, yet," he observed to the shrew. Whilst he rolled shirt-sleeves over muscles that might have been used as art photographs.

Nan's look was aimed at shattering his morale.

Cherry met without blinking the super-contempt that would have submerged the insensibility of a brass monkey.

More than that, as it maintained its steady, shrewish attack, he winked, with the query as to whether he was not a good-looking man when he was scraped.

Ominous silence greeted these overtures at friendship.

Chirping to the pup he wound up the blind. The sordid untidiness of the kitchen lay bare under the eye of day. Cherry looked out on another row of houses, and behind them the stone-yard with its stone-piles that almost blocked out the sky.

"Everything in th' garden's lovely," he remarked, genially sarcastic, after his survey.

Nan's language in reply to this was fitted for the apache's mate.

The big man, hands in pocket, turned round from the window. Without appearing to do so he was staring across at a railway almanac on the wall opposite. At various intervals on the date-margin were little black crosses. These were the marks he had set to mark the epochs of their domestic cyclones.

There was quite a big gap between the last cross and the present date. Therefore ——

His shoulders squared themselves.

He hurried to get down bite and sup — before the burst.

"Tha greedy devil! Tha's ta'en th' biggest cake," shouted the woman in the chair, as he took one of three pieces from a plate with a snip in it, set on a table that appeared none too friendly to soap and brush.

Cherry made no answer to this mis-statement.

He sat down, eating quietly; the pup settled down also, looking expectantly for crumbs.

Arguments, the porter had long since discovered, were of no avail.

Best to keep quiet — whilst the tide came on and up, and then to breast it at its flood.

As he licked his fingers clean of the cake, the massiveness, the placidity of this half-literate British workman lent to him a paradoxical, fleeting resemblance to the gods in statued galleries.

The shrill clapper of the woman's tongue raged against him. A chant-like rhythm sounded in her voice. Her breast heaved. She spat out vicious, corrosive words interspersed with oaths selected specially to attack his Yorkshire pride in coming of respectable folk.

"A pound a week, to be a slave for a b——y Yorkshire tyke!"

With this exclamation she rose from her chair.

5

The sound of Polly Cherry overturning a chair in her hurry to get dressed and out of the house before the storm came on, was heard from above — a protesting, youthful nervousness in the incident.

Cherry was watching his mate closely now. Out of one of these lulls would come the attack.

But she went on again, hurling mud on his family, his living mother, his dead father — the respectability of the whole lot of them — the hooligan flood rising, shouting, shrieking, roaring, bursting down the barriers, until a hoarse raven note sounded in her voice, her face showed whitely instead of its high colour, the kitchen dwindled and became a cage she was flinging herself against, this Amazon, nursing in her breast the unquenchable desire to get him down — yet.

Even as his eyelid flicked expectantly she rushed at the table — seized something — hurled it.

He ducked his head with the easy skill of long use.

A swift glance revealed that the thing sent was the milk-jug with Disraeli painted on it. A long china splinter had impinged itself in the nose of the prophet Moses, still, however, surveying the Promised Land through a baptism of milk, very steadily. Grandma Cherry's wedding-present had witnessed many of these scenes.

"Bad shot, Nan," was his comment.

Another woman would have collapsed and wept at his cheery ignoring of her attempt to quarrel with him.

Nan usually began where other women left off.

"Ooo! — At it again?" came from the doorway.

A big fair girl, whose colouring lent her a likeness to the porter which her vivacity of expression tended to destroy, was looking in on them.

Her parents were too engrossed to hear the disrespect in her tone.

She regarded them both out of eyes yet sleep-heavy — a look of youthful antagonism, mingled with something despairing. Then, with a certain callousness of demeanour, a movement of detachment from the house altogether, she edged away from them, and took up her pot of tea. Being too hot to drink she blew it, with an over-full indeterminate little mouth that seemed hard to close. The dog came tugging at her blue mill-apron. After picking Rag up her face wore another look. She was divided between shielding the dog and the task of sipping her tea. Indeed, her face had as many swift expressions as a piano has keys. She was too childish or too careless to try and disguise them, as yet.

"I don't want to bother wi' thee," said the Yorkshire man, in genial tones. "So — cheese it."

He might as well have tried to stem the sea.

Apparently this was his usual preliminary, to keep a clean conscience.

"Polly," he said suddenly, without turning his head. "Lap my best clothes up — everything — my tie wi' th' blue spots."

A glance at his mate's face told him that he had put his finger on the motive for this row before breakfast. She had hoped he would forget his clothes in the chaos. She wanted to pawn them, and have a holiday down in Tanner Fold with the hooligan folk of Fiddle Row.

Polly went off, dog in arms, her back expressive of flapper patience taxed to its utmost.

Cherry did not notice it.

He was watching.

Even as Polly gained the threshold of the parlour Nan rushed upon him.

He reeled, despite his size.

Her head only reached his top buttonhole.

But her strength was a wild cat's.

"Cheese it, Nan," he said calmly.

One great hand loosed her from him, put her gently away, in masculine reverence for woman. His tone had the jesting ease of a man who knows he is top-dog.

As if this magnanimity of his enraged her beyond endurance the shrew came on again. And again, with a show of fierceness that half-covered the determination not to hurt her, he threw her off.

"Hit me, Bill! Hit me!" she screamed at him. "For God in heaven's sake, hit me. I can fight. I'm not a toffee doll. Hit me. An' let me hit back. Beat me, if tha can, beat me. Oh — hit me. Like I were a pal. Hit me. Jesus wept! Hit me."

The motive of her attacking him was now forgotten. The rage in her sprung now from a deeper source, the source of all human drama — character.

The rising flood was bearing her away. She was conscious of nothing but the desire to goad this cold-blooded, commonplace Yorkshireman near to murdering her, to break up the alien, quiet reserve that divided him from her. She wanted to wake devils in him, to make him like the mate she should have had.

Protected by the tolerant chivalry in his blue eye — she attacked his manhood — driven on by the irresistible desire to draw some big danger into this monotonous, skimpy life.

"Cheese it," he warned her again.

Her nails had come perilously near his eyes.

"Hit me," she almost sobbed.

"Look here," he asked mildly, seizing her wrists, "What's it all about?" Then he added, whilst she struggled, "When are we goin' to live like other folk?"

7

A faint note of exasperation sounded in his voice on the last words. Before breakfast! To start on a man before breakfast!

He flung her away a little more roughly, yet with the same iron control.

But for the whiteness of her face, its vicious menace, and a certain weariness on the face of the big porter, an onlooker could have taken it for a friendly marlock between husband and wife who were yet something of children.

"Like other folk," echoed the shrew. "Jesus wept! Do I care for other folk?"

Standing there, as she spoke these words, they became not so much individual antagonists, as two opposite clans. A blaze of intense passion on the woman's face gave it a momentary beauty, a bigness not seen in her before. She rushed at him again.

"Hit me," she persisted. "Forget I'm a b——y woman. Fight——"

It was the cry of an Amazon pinned down in a narrow world she was not made for.

Whilst the man's frown was growing as he threw her from him again. He was regarding her much as a tamer keeps his eye on a savage thing that may tear him. The thought that she had started on a man before breakfast became more intolerable.

"Ooo!" exclaimed Polly.

Parcel in hand she had reached the threshold just in time to see Nan apparently bury her teeth in the man's arm. He jerked his arm. A long tatter was suspended from his elbow.

"Another job for th' lad to do," he said calmly.

His incorrigible common sense drove the woman frantic.

She came on again.

As she did so she met the full glance of his eye.

With a swift movement he locked his hand round her jaw. She had seen him handle Rag so when he didn't want it to bite him as he looked at the progress of its feet Her eyes expressed the indignity she felt.

"One of these days — one of, us will get hurt," he warned her placidly. "It's a long run has no turnin', they say."

The shrew could make no answer.

He was letting her feel how easily he could hold her so — what an atom she was — how little he feared for the worst she could do — a giant with a giant's strength, pitiful for her futile attempts to oust him from his rightful position in the household.

Then he let her go.

Her hooligan laughter filled the house.

There was the sound of a pair of clogs pausing outside the little door.

At that sound the face of the man changed.

Half his placidity fled, pell-mell.

A light was kindled in his eyes.

"Shut thy mouth. Afore I shut it for thee!" he breathed.

The vulnerable spot had been touched — his hatred of them opening their mouths to fill everybody's.

Myriads of well-conducted ancestors clamoured against her loud laughter, her shout to the whole world, and he turned his head involuntarily, listening disgustedly to the sound of a second pair of clogs stopping outside his castle walls.

As he half turned back, swiftly, some instinct warning him, her teeth caught his hand. He made no sound, but gave his first blow — a smart, light cuff that toppled her hair down and did little more.

"Shut that," he asked of Polly, nodding towards the inner door.

The girl shut it.

Her look of dark dissatisfaction had deepened.

"Shut up," the porter commanded his wife.

There was a white restraint on his face.

"Let 'em listen! Penny a week to bury theirsels, Christian cats, let 'em listen," shrilled the shrew.

"At it again," came ironically from the street. "By th' Mass, if she were mine——!"

What she was going to say in answer to that other male Cherry could only guess. Before it could be said, he had taken her by the throat. He had cast off his robe of restraint, now, save for a few patches.

The big fair girl standing with her back against the door, the dog held in her arms again, had a help-less, forlorn look.

"When are we goin' to live like other folk," he asked the shrew.

"Nev-er!"

The little indomitable word came chokily.

The Yorkshireman tossed her away from him in disgust.

"What does ta live wi' me for, then?" she asked, in a loud, hysterical voice.

It was the query the street had asked itself a thousand times since their coming there.

Cherry ignored it utterly, as outside the question.

As he saw her coming on again, heard her burst of laughter that was purposely to draw a crowd round their door, a resolve leapt into his face.

His eyes became terrible in their quiet smiling.

He allowed her to get quite close to him, then his great arm shot out. He handled her as if she had been a dumb-bell. Up and up she went, into mid-air, to Polly's shriek of terror. Whereupon there was quite a patter of clogs, running, running.

"Drop that din," commanded Polly's father to the shrieking girl.

He had become a resolute giant, with great knitted brows.

"Murder! Help! He's killin' me," screamed Nan.

She almost touched the ceiling.

The floor had become a dizzy thing far below her.

She could hear the creaking of the mighty muscles.

Whilst looking down she saw his upturned face, white in its effort not to dash her to the ground, this thing that had been a thorn in his flesh for twenty years.

"Help! Murder!"

Her appeal rang out again.

Some one shook the door gently.

Panic was in her cry now — but away down under the panic hooligan malice, proud triumph that she had got a crowd round, scorn of it and of him who cared for it, consciousness that every one of her cries was a stab at his Yorkshireman's pride.

He merely raised her several inches.

Her hair brushed a dangling cobweb on the ceiling.

Beneath her she could feel the great strength of him — the Stone Age man she had evoked from the genial, prudent, rational being whose meals she prepared.

He did not look unlike an apache now.

Whilst as he looked back at her she saw his look of scorn that this was the only force she recognised — brute force.

"B — Bill," she ejaculated. "Set me down."

His great forehead was still knit in that magnificent frown of disdain.

He did not answer that appeal.

"Dad——" said Polly.

He did not hear her.

"An' to think," he murmured, that puzzled frown upon him, that searching for reasons why, "better women nor thee are murdered — every week".

In a sudden reaction from his rage, he set her down on her feet, still giddy, blanched to the lips — apparently tamed. A half sigh of relief escaped him. He imagined that it was going to blow over without him having to give her a licking. Even as he sighed, she wavered towards him — her expression unmistakable.

She had not had enough.

With his old calm upon him once more he put her from him, again, again, and again. He parried her blows with a natural ju-jitsu learnt by trying to stop her from marking him without hurting her. She was laughing again, laughing and coming on time after time, tirelessly, indomitably, towards his face, with the old rational look she hated, his face with the deep chin that counterbalanced the brute passion that had flashed in his eyes — his chin that divided him from her by thousands of years, proclaiming him her better.

Polly made little helpless cries and occasionally told them she would have to go, though she did not move an inch. She had put on her factory shawl.

"Whatever I do, you can't blame me," she said vaguely to the combatants, once. But they did not hear her.

Cherry was flinging Nan off every few seconds now.

The moment came when his heaviness was beaten by her cat-like suddenness. Her nail flayed his fore-head, scrawked its way down to his eye-corner, made as though to plough through his eye-ball.

At that moment the devils woke in him.

Yet though they woke he gave them only so much leash. With a minimum of passion and the maximum of reason, he thrashed her.

Whilst the girl in the shawl circled round them now, saying babyishly, "Mam! Dad!" the dog under her shawl adding to the general din.

She was crying — crying easy, girlish tears, and rubbing them away with her shawl-fringe.

Then she sat down disconsolately in a chair, stroking Rag, and waited until it was over.

A great quiet fell upon the house.

The shrew was sobbing in her chair — subdued, ready to carry out his every wish now.

But Cherry's face had all the demoralisation of a man who has thrashed a lesser man than himself.

He moved about the house; put on his coat; fed the dog; drank up his tea, picked up the dog again, as one who intends to leave nothing behind for revenge to work on, and with his nebbed cap on jauntily to show the crowd outside that his manhood was intact, he strode up the passage.

It was then that the shrew ran after him.

Tear-blurred, penitent, her face asked him to — forgive.

He looked at her fixedly.

Then he turned back, into the kitchen.

But it was for no reconciliation.

Three days was his usual time for becoming his genial self again after these frays. There was no mercury in his make-up.

The shrew watched him approach the almanac, take out a pencil, wet it — and add another to the number of crosses.

"Happen," he observed, "we'se ha' peace for a bit."

He went down the passage again, Polly taking the tea-can with her. Cherry still held the dog. Nan followed them again.

"Bill!" she said.

On the doormat Cherry turned.

11

"Wants to lick my boots, because I thumped thee," he said disgustedly. Then, "No — a!"

A hearty force was in the negative.

He pushed Polly gently out before him.

The crowd edged away as he appeared unto them.

But it cast a furtive, interested look at his face.

It was not the face of a humiliated man.

Polly hurried on. She was too young to stand the staring so well as Cherry. Her head was high, but her cheeks burnt. She walked a little unevenly.

"Mornin', Polly," said Cherry.

"Mornin', Dad," she replied.

"Not after ten o'clock, Polly," he said gently.

She nodded obedience, and went off sharply.

But the dark look of dissatisfaction had returned.

She was wondering, and quite reasonably, what there was to come home early for.

Whilst Cherry was thinking that ten o'clock of a Saturday night was quite late enough for any girl of seventeen — particularly for one who couldn't fight her way out of a sugar-bag.

He opened the door of the last house in the street.

"Billy!" he shouted.

Billy came, took in the parcel of clothes, the pup, and assured some person within that everything was all right.

"Best keep the door locked, though," warned Cherry.

Whereupon an old man came out, a gentle-faced, docile creature with white hair and a long pipe.

"If she were mine, lad," he said in a voice like a drowning kitten's. "If she were mine——"

Billy and Cherry looked at Grandad Breeze contemplatively. The jaunty air shed itself from Cherry as he looked. The man of humour appeared again. Billy also was trying not to laugh.

"Tha couldn't tame a louse," indignantly cried out Grandma Breeze, and followed her voice.

Grandad Breeze looked darkly across the street as much as to say what he'd have done with Nan Cherry.

Cherry slapped him on the back.

"There's only two things I haven't tried, Dad," hie said.

"Ay. What's them?" he was asked, curiously.

Cherry pulled Billy by the sleeve.

"Hypnotism an' — chloroform," he said gravely.

Then they heard the signal drop — and set out at a mighty run, seeing Grandad Breeze dragged inside the house by Grandma Breeze, lest the vixen should come and besiege the house in an attempt to get Cherry's clothes.

During the running Cherry's face gradually became that of a man who had come down the stairs.

His sense of moral loss cast no shadow over him.

"Billy," he said, as they ran along, like two lads, "I've a lot to be thankful for. After a', a chap on our job doesn't need to be much at hoam."

Billy nodded.

"From now — till neet — I work on the finest job on earth," he said reflectively, keeping pace with Billy. "Ay. Thank God for trains."

Billy nodded.

He could understand that.

"An' — for feet, Billy — feet," said the porter. He looked reflectively at his own, as he ran. Then he said, "Where would I ha' bin, Billy, but for — Feet?"

There was a gratitude in his big voice.

Then they saw Mr. Menser.

"You'll report yourselves for lateness — write it out and hand it in to me to-night," he said.

"My wife," said Cherry, in a trembling voice, "has had a fit".

"Oh — in that case," said the stationmaster.

Cherry winked at Billy.

Billy grinned admiringly.

"It isn't as if we get paid for that sort o' overtime," said Cherry. "I'm not a bloomin' clerk. I'm a porter."

Whistling a sea-chantey he passed into the porters' room with Billy.

A minute later he was rushing along by the train — swinging himself on the footboard — transposed into the man who took the most tips on the Narrowfields line.

Grandma Breeze, stepping out to sweep her flags, with a great show of courage that covered a quaking heart, saw that the shrew also was sweeping out. Something white had evidently been spilt upon the flags. The mouth of the shrew was moving — then the words stopped. Her lips thinned out. Grandma could see the flash of her eyes, and wondered for the thousandth time why suchlike were born.

But seeing Nan look in her direction, she finished hastily.

"She didn't say aught, did she?" asked Grandad Breeze, puffing at his pipe in the yellow-stoned kitchen where Billy's books were the chief feature.

"If she said aught to me——" said Grandma, like a Spartan.

Then Grandad Breeze said, between the puffs, "I've sometimes thought our Billy were a bit sweet on Polly."

Grandma drew herself up angrily, at the idea.

Part of her apron-string showed itself as she did this — emerging from the crevasses where it was usually buried deep, too deep to be seen.

"Naught at a' of th' sort," she snapped.

"She might take after her father," said old Breeze. "He's a daycent lad."

"If yonder lass lands herself where lasses should," she prophesied, "it'll be more luck nor management".

"She's a nice lass——" said Grandad Breeze.

"Ay. A bit o' rosy cheek an' breet eye — that's a' chaps cares," said Grandma. "An' after a' — beauty only goes skin-deep."

Grandad looked at her slyly.

"But ugliness goes to t' boan," he finished neatly.

There was coldness between them for a full minute and a half.

Then Grandad Breeze said, "Tha allus ware jealous," and puffed his pipe in great enjoyment

Which Grandma repudiated indignantly.

She returned to the subject of the shrew.

"Somebody's spilt either flour or saut on yon flags of hers," she said. "An' she's sweepin' away on it like it were poison."

"Eh — if I had her!" said Grandad.

"She'd ha' put three o' thy sort into th' grave long sin'," said Grandma.

Grandad Breeze's love of posing as a wolf in sheep's clothing always amused and made her cross, at the same time.

"I wonder," she said, after a long pause, "if it were flour or saut were spilt".

In the full light of day in Christian England Nan was performing a rite from the Dark Ages. She was sweeping her husband out, with salt, sweeping him, according to the black wish, out of her life, whilst the Lord's prayer, chanted backwards, made the spell efficient. Even so, as a wide-eyed child, in Tanner Fold, those slums where Granny Harker had lived for some years, she remembered a drink-sodden Irish-woman sweeping out a lazy husband who would not keep her in home comforts.

Pat O'Brian had come home despite the spell, it is true. But Nan reiterated hers three times over, to make quite sure. The moment of her turning to go within, broom in hand, synchronised with that whereon Cherry remarked to his pal, "Thank God for feet, Billy". Which, after all, says nothing at all. Life is full of coincidences.

Chapter 2

Trespass

The hour the porter had set as the one beyond towards Narrowfields and Cherrydale — places which Polly must not transgress, was creeping so near, yet far from each other. Narrowfields could not wholly hide the beauty of the gleaming Cherrydale!

Cherrydale, at this hour of transition, oozed sweetness from its pores, turning into a great, dark flower, palpitating between silence and the few sounds of the autumn night.

Adam Wild's upland field of wheat, valued by the farmers around as worth forty English sovereigns, became an altar of mystery. The wind whispered over it of primal beauty, primal pain, primal gladness. Bread of life! Life that was so beautiful, holding things like Adam Wild's perseverance against terrible odds; holding Susan Thorpe, with her quiet eyes and heart of country faith; holding Polly Cherry, with her baby ways and baby habit of clutching at things, without knowing whether or not they would hurt. But when the dark shadows went over the field, and the wind felt chill, and the faithless swallows made their crave for the south — the wheatfield, food for the bodies that hold the souls of men, said that life held also sordid things like the mortgagee of the Wilds' farm, weak things like Adam's father, who had given way to inertia since his wife died — inertia that is said to mark men with the sign of the ape.

The swaying field of wheat became a paean of life — wherein many voices battled with each other, with the issue yet indistinct

A black gate at the top of the field showed its five bars against a sky filling with silver as the west filled with fire of gold. Between east and west rolled broken country, with few trees, saving those seven beeches that made sooty blurs against that spreading silver that would soon take definite shape as a moon, an impatient moon that Adams had made to refect his haste to gather in the wheat, whenever he saw her like a sickle bending down towards it. To the left of his field was a great bump of hill like that of a dromedary humped under bronze velvet. Down below this, lay the Narrowfields' road.

At the foot of his field was the round stone that had taken his fancy as a step to his stile. He had carried it half a mile and laid it down proudly as any woman adds something to her house comfort. Before he had ventured into wheat growing in a grass-county as a last throw of the dice against that townster who held the mortgage deeds, lovers had found this stone very convenient to climb up to sit on the stile; a high, uncertain, involved country stile enough.

Since the wheat growing, there was ever a man prowling in the field — a fanatical man whose old hat the scarecrow had worn when the wheat was green, a man whom Cherrydale said was gifted with a wonderful head-piece, had the perseverance his whole family could have done with dividing up between them, but withal a man who couldn't see for looking — meaning Susan Thorpe.

On the other side the stile were the three steps leading down upon the road that ran glimmeringly, now, between holly hedges.

To the left from the stile, this road ran to the village, which only showed now a church spire, gleaming with some reflection from the light of the fire of gold in the west. The right of it led to Narrowfields — as did that upper road now hidden beyond the topmost glory of Adam's triumphant field of wheat, that paragon standing exultant over the shaven fields around.

Men's voices sounded from the heart of its glory — its forty pounds, that was to put confusion into that dried soul of the yellow-faced man who said this was to be his — his, by divine right of paper deeds as against Adam's willingness to spill his blood to keep it.

A sudden blaze from an uplifted lantern showed the crest of an old billycock hat with hawksbit and purple scabious thrust through a slit in the side — then, a ruddy, credulous country face and a pair of squat shoulders, whilst alongside was the taller form of a young man, without hat, the shadow making his eye-sockets deep caverns, his brow a cloud, and accentuating the horizontal line running down the deep upper lip — the lip that according to Cherrydalers stamped a man as of the old yeomanry, the "potato-faces".

"It's a seet for sore e'en," said the voice of the older man. "I couldn't ha' thowt it could be done, hereabouts. 'If at first you don't succeed, try, try, try again.' Ay. A good motta. Though my Aunt Bethsheba——" He broke off suddenly. "By th' Mass, I nearly went then," he added. He had stumbled.

"Better let me go in front," said the young farmer.

There was a wincing tone in the voice as if he had felt human pain for the wheat touched by his god-father's hobnailed boots.

"Ay. It'd happen be better, Addy," said the other. "I'm not seein' so weel these days. We noan on us mend wi' keepin'."

Adam Wild did not answer.

The lantern rays flashed once across his countenance, as he led the way along the narrow path through his wheat.

It was smiling.

It had all the kindly tolerance of a man who does not come of a talking-stock, being entertained by the childish frankness of a man who would talk till the cows came up. He might have stood as the type of the old yeomanry, with their strong bodies, and equally strong, if narrow minds. Short, dark hair almost stood erect as he walked against the wind.

"I'd like to hear thee courtin' a lass, Addy," said his companion, droll humour in his voice.

"How's that, Uncle Nat," he asked, and laughed.

His laughter was whole-hearted.

"Thy words might be tuppence apiece," said the other. "But then — tha wert born in th' neet, an' them as is born in th' neet is mostly o' that mak. An' thy mother went out without sayin' a word!"

In the way of the north country he referred to death as a light going out.

Silence fell again — through which came the sea-like sighing of the wheat.

"Tha'll shake thysd' free o' yon chap wi' th' papers," said Uncle Nat, with faith. "Eh, it's bonnie wheat. What put it in thy heyd to try grow wheat on grassland? Eh, ay, it'll be a rare lift to 'art thy gettin' free. For I'll never believe 'at th' Wilds 'at as lived on that land a hundred and fifty years, — to my grandfather's countin', — is goin' to be pushed off it by a chap as yellow as his own papers, an' e'en like he stops up a' neet."

Silence fell once more.

"Tha'rt fain o' thy wheat, aren't ta?" asked Nat.

"Ay," answered Adam.

"Well, happen tha'rt reight not to brag on it," said the old man. "For we never know what's comin' next, in this world, as my Aunt Bethsheba said. Eh, she were a queer un, my Aunt Bethsheba. But — tha didn't tell me what made thee think to grow wheat on grassland."

"There's bin wheat grown there before," said Adam. "Ay, before the Wilds had it. I read it in an old book."

"To think a chap like thee, wi' a' that in thy heyd, should be content to muck fields," said Nat, in innocent wonder.

"I'll pay the mortgage off out of th' land itself," said the young man, in a tone of almost fanatical fervour. "I'll tear our freedom up out o' the ground where it was lost. Look out, Uncle Nat — the stone."

They had reached the stile, the stone acting as a step up to it. Down below was the road.

Uncle Nat squeezed himself through the stile.

"Three steps down," Adam warned him.

"Ay, I know there's three," said Uncle Nat "There were allus three. I daresay, Adam, tha's often wondered why I took an interest in thee. Well, I'll tell thee. Forty year sin', to-neet, I axed thy mother if she thought she could fancy me — at this stile. And she said 'No — a.' She'd a reight on it, lad. But I think she made a mistake a' th' same. Safely down, now, Addy. Lad, if I were thee I'd not trust that wheat long afore gettin' it in. My bunion says 'rain.' Eh. Ay, she told me 'No-a' reight enough, An' I felt sure she'd made a mistake. But it weren't for me to point it out to her. Not likely. An' tha'rt as like her as if she'd spit thee out o' her mouth. An' *tha'rt* goin' to mak a mistake."

They were walking along the road now.

"How's that, Uncle Nat?"

Adam's query was in a tone that said he guessed what track Uncle Nat was on. Though, to be sure, his mind had never been so impudently broad before.

"Work's a good thing, Adam," said the other. "An' I can understand thee bein' ta'en up in this feight to keep th' old farm. But, lad, tha'd feight a' th' better — for not lettin' luv go a-beggin'. It's a sad thing to turn luv a-beggin', Adam. My Aunt Bethsheba, she said we were born for it, an' a chap 'at hadn't bin made miserable ower a woman didn't know he were born, an' a woman — well, she said she'd no right to be born if she were goin' through life like a statoo, for it were a waste o' good blood, an' she might as weel ha' ban made o' plaister o' Paris."

Adam walked steadily on.

The old man cast sly glances at his face, but the lantern-bearer manoeuvered to keep the darkness on his own face, the light full on his "Uncle" Nat's. Though the only feeling Adam's face showed was a shrinking embarrassment at what he rightly judged the old man was leading up to.

"I don't know aught sweeter than freedom, an' th' earth," he avowed, sincerely. "An' I don't want to, Uncle Nat. I'm a mean man. I'd liefer buy oats an' rye an' barley to put into th' ground, than spend money buyin' bonnets. You should look on me as wedded — to th' Earth. She's a splendid bride. Worth dressin'. No, Uncle Nat." It was as if he jestingly pushed away an unwanted article.

"She could buy her own bonnets!" declared Uncle Nat.

Whereupon Adam groaned inwardly.

He was sure now that it was Susan Uncle Nat meant.

"Her mother heard her a-prayin' for thy field o' wheat, Addy. Tha could fare to th' ends o' the yeth, an' tha'd not find a tenderer, lovinger, purer heart than our little Susan's got. An' th' right mate for a farmer. What is there she can't do? Eh, Addy — tha'rt makin' a mistake. She'll be snapped up in no time."

Adam Wild walked steadily on.

"Come — Adam," asked Nat, as if asking him to bid for something under the hammer.

"Do — do you mean to say — that — Sue — likes me?" queried a voice out of the darkness.

Had he not been so eager to delude himself Uncle Nat would have heard the naked horror in the tones.

"She were prayin' for thy wheat," answered Uncle Nat in a voice that said that was enough for anybody. "In the middle o' th' neet when she thought everybody were asleep. Coom — Adam."

"There's a shrew mouse," cried Adam, eagerly.'

He lifted up his lantern, following the flight of the little creature into the grasses edging a ditch. The light blazed on an autumn hedge, with scarlet hips flashing amidst the gold of fading leaves. Uncle Nat noticed that Adam's ear-tips were almost as red as the hips. He took this for a good sign.

"Gone," said the young man, alluding to the shrew mouse.

"What says ta, Adam?" went on Uncle Nat as though the shrew mouse had not been trailed across his path.

"I never thought on it before," confessed Adam. "An' I'm sure I've never given reason——"

"There's no reason in it," laughed Uncle Nat. "Now — tha's hit the nail on th' head, there, lad. But — she's a nice lass, isn't she, lad?"

"Very," said Adam with sincerity. Then, "I think women haven't as much wit as hens, Uncle Nat. An' you've kept hens".

The hard gaiety of his tone had an under-current of perplexity.

"She's as much common sense as a policeman, our Susan," said Uncle Nat, indignantly. "Anyhow — I can drop her mother a hint as tha'rt not smitten. Tha can't ha' a young woman prayin' for thy wheat, on false pretences."

Which upset Adam's gravity at the situation arising.

His laughter rolled out into the night, waking the echoes.

After a short pause, Uncle Nat joined in it, though uneasily at first.

They had reached a long, uneven wall, dry-built, and with blacker patches in its darkness showing where the sheep-gaps were. Nat's hand touched a gate. The barking of dogs arose.

"Comin' in, Addy?" asked Uncle Nat.

Before the man could reply a thin thread of light widened into a flood. A farmhouse door had opened, with a black figure like a fat marionette's stuck out against the light, with something decisive in it, even though it was two fields' distance away.

"She's sin thee," said Uncle Nat, blithely, as if that settled the question of Adam's going in to supper.

"Now then. Don't let him go. He only wants pressin'," came a voice anything but marionette-like. Withal the voice of an elderly female it had a hearty lustiness, and even the distance could not steal away altogether the humorous double-meaning the speaker insinuated into the word 'pressin'.

Nat nudged him slyly.

"Did ta hear her?" he asked with droll pride. "She said tha' only wanted *pressin'*."

His laughter rang out.

Adam did not answer him directly.

"Not this time, Aunt Sarah," shouted Adam, genially.

His shoulders made a resolute square of blackness.

"Neet, Adam," said Uncle Nat, stung at last, "I reckon tha'll go through t' wood an' through t' wood an' get a crooked stick at th' finish——"

But Adam had already taken some paces away.

He was restlessly eager to get away from that farm — uneasily afraid of that cherry-lipped damsel who might be peering out towards them from behind her mother — little Susan Thorpe, laughing, industrious, modest as a daisy, who played Ludo with Uncle Nat, till she almost fell off her chair asleep, and for whom Uncle Nat had never lost a chance of putting in a good word. Little Susan — little Susan, who, according to the village gossips, would one day have a pot of money and wear silk every day. .

"Good-night, Uncle Nat," he called.

Uncle Nat walked on in grim silence, never turning his head, for quite half a dozen paces.

Then he came back to the gate to which Adam had also returned.

"Tak' no gaum o' my gruntlin', Addy," asked Uncle Nat. "I get like a bear wi' a sore back. We noan on us mend wi' keepin'. An' — next to havin' had thy mother say 'Ay' to me, I'd have chosen thee to have our Susan. But — tak' no heed on me, lad. Tha'rt not mad, arta?"

There was so tender an anxiety in the question, so noble a lack of pride, so much revelation of the way the rat-catching old bachelor clung to the approval of this son of his soul, that Adam felt ashamed of having been mentally setting the old man down as a meddling old fool who was getting him, Adam Wild, into an awkward corner.

He gave Uncle Nat a slap on the shoulder that made him cry out.

"There's naught could come between you an' me, Uncle Nat," he said with earnest conviction.

Then he added, feeling the old man's gaze upon him, expectantly, "I'll drop in an' have a game at Ludo with you before you go back to Ashdale. By th' way, not a word of this".

For quite suddenly it had struck him, that to definitely say that Susan Thorpe would never be Mrs. Wild, was to be unnecessarily insulting. There was something flattering in the thought of her praying for his field of wheat. The picture haunted him. Susan was pretty. Moreover — he had remembered the pot of money that could purchase the freedom of Sagg Farm, if the worst came to the worst.

"Not a word, lad," said Uncle Nat, laying his finger across his nose; as if that was the usual way of taking solemn oath.

The silence that fell between them had something guilty in it.

"Good-neet, lad," called Uncle Nat, blithely, when half-way across the field.

But Adam was already out of earshot.

Whilst as Nat's shoes made a soft "prop-plop" over the ground between him and his youngest sister's farm, he was telling himself that it was impossible for any young man who was right in his head to go on seeing his niece as often as Adam did — all the modest, innocent ways, and sitting in that house of cleanly pride, and even walking home from church with the quiet-eyed young creature with one little hand holding her prayer-book, the other dangling at her side, a Sabbath look in her eyes — without falling in love with her. So that when he got inside, and Susan poured out his porridge and blue milk, and set his slippers in the fender, the oath of the finger across the nose clean went out of his head. He believed that he spoke the truth, as he heard himself say that Adam had literally torn himself away — that they had been having a very important conversation — his knowing look bringing a pleased light to his sister's eye, a blush to the little Susan's, and a laugh from the gawky man who was sitting scraping manure from great boots so that it fell on a sheet of newspaper spread inside the fender. Which method of self-delusion is not unknown to men in higher walks of life than Uncle Nat's, more clever meddlers in other people's destinies.

His godson, meanwhile, was standing looking down on the broad stream that flowed under the old, one-railed wishing-bridge. He held the lantern so that the light trembled down upon the water — showing with the fantasy of a will-o'-th'-wisp, now a great stone fringed with foam, ghostly branches of willow and their shadows in some illumined stone-locked pool, whilst, conscious of the beauty of the whole, his eye was seeking out any new detail since he had passed a few days ago. He discovered the appearance of a herb that made a splendid autumn-cup, according to old Culpepper, and had an impulse to clamber down the bank, and gather it by the light of his lantern. The impulse passed as suddenly as it had come. The thought of Susan Thorpe — in love with him — had come upon him, bewildering him into unhappy despondence.

He passed slowly forwards, missing the holes made by rain-rot, his hand feeling the chill dews on the shaky rail with an intense delight for the soil in which he had grown. Whilst the thought that before giving that up, he would be glad to marry old Mother Green Teeth herself, throbbed in his brain.

From a small knoll that met the bridge he looked upwards at a black blotch against the sky — Sagg Farm, its two illumined windows and the chink of light escaping from its hollowed threshold giving it a subtle resemblance to a square-jowled ebon face with two wide-open fiery eyes, a thin mouth spitting flame. As he looked, the only passion of his rational life threw its spell over him. His father had given up the ghost so far as the old place went, when Ellen Wild went out without a word. Adam knew that even now his father would be stretched on the settle, mumbling drunken incoherencies. As for him — it was as though the indomitable soul of the silent mother who had died seven years ago had passed into him. In all the world nothing mattered except that Bob, Sary, and he should not be driven forth from the place that had sheltered four generations of Wilds.

He brooded on the last interview with the man who held the deeds — and walked fiercely into two gelder-rose bushes. They dashed a baptism of dews on his stormy young face. As he disentangled himself he caught a sight of the moon, that topaz tenderness a magic now.

At this moment, whilst freeing his coat from the innumerable invisible fingers that seemed to cling to him out of the bushes, he heard an echo — laughter, ghostlike, from the old Narrowfields road. Such laughter was common to it on a Saturday night.

The thought that Uncle Nat had not closed the gate at the top of the field haunted him. He became an irritable Fear, lamp in hand, listening, the scorn he had of these town fools glowering from his brow.

The laughter throbbed unashamedly upon the air, nearer, yet nearer, as he listened.

In that quiet place it had an unholy sound.

It was the town, come for sport, into the unobserved country places.

Adam's head was up like a dog on the scent now.

With an unintelligible jumble of words he re-crossed the bridge.

Once upon the road he raced along — whilst ever the laughter met him. In a lull, once, he heard voices, and could distinguish above the rest a feminine one which even affectation could not make hideous. It broke into a snatch of song, whereupon the affectation was shed immediately, and it became only the fresh voice of youth, singing under the moon, because the world was so fair, and to walk through the dews with a white dress rustling and one's hair up for the very first time, sub rosa, too, demands some escape for the joy of the heart.

Adam was intent on that voice.

He found it useful to locate the intruders by.

The race had become a set one, between that voice and the young farmer's fear.

Even as his feet touched that round stone Nat had stumbled over, he heard the bang of his gate. It always gave a long-drawn-out groan, like the thunder-notes in "Judas Maccabeus".

They were in the field!

Yet they must have noticed the trespass-board.

Stealthily he crept along, the lantern blussed by his coat, his free hands touching the stalks of the wheat to guide himself along the sinuous path.

Silence had fallen on the intruders as they entered the wheat-field. A girlish giggle trickled somewhat nervously once, followed by a girlish voice wondering what time it was. To which a youth's voice answered that it was too early for two pretty girls to go home.

Townsters!

The man creeping along muttered the word as some faint expression of his scorn, his prejudice of the clan to whom belonged the yellow-faced man who held the deeds of Sagg Farm.

Even as it left his lips he caught the flash of a girl's white hat — then a white bust, and around the waist a black sleeve. There was a jumble of other figures behind these two. But it was on this first couple that the antipathy of his gaze turned itself.

The wheat was swaying to and fro before their progress.

Quite suddenly the girl began to sing again.

She was singing "He shall feed His flock," her head flung back. There was no thought of faith, or religious fervour in the way she sang. Had she sung a rag-time she would have sung it with the same fine quality of ecstasy. The wheat-field had suggested it to her irresponsible mind. The wheat-field took on a new significance as she sang — and as she sang her feet trampled it thoughtlessly down. Through the surging sea of the wheat she sang — as though she were the only person the globe had been made for. The wheat tossed stormily as she endeavoured to free herself from the thralldom of that black sleeve. She stopped suddenly in the middle of a bar, with an almost peevish, "Let go, Peter! I can't bear to be held — when I'm singing."

"Amen. Sister Becky will go round with the hat," said the voice that had previously said the hour was early for two pretty girls.

Adam, creeping up, his underlip bitten, perceived by the motion of the wheat a movement on the girl's part to shake off the arm.

Quite suddenly, a flapperish scream arose, the two young men guffawed, and the unmusical laughter of another girl rang out. The group had come to a standstill, the wheat tossing all about them. This was town horse-play.

"Becky!" called the girl in the white dress, imploringly.

"Kiss her, Peter. Kiss her! She told me herself. Sweet seventeen, an' never been kissed. I'll hold her——"

Whereupon the flapper's scream arose once more, and the wheat made a great murmur.

"Stop that!" said Adam, springing up, and flashing his lantern on the group, hypnotised into stillness by his sudden appearance.

The first movement came from a little wiry girl with dark eyes, assisting a youth with receding chin and weak, blue eyes, to hold the girl, whilst a hand-some lad, with a dare-devil countenance not without some nobility in it, was trying to kiss the girl — her face now partly revealed through a veil of yellow hair, blue eyes full of baby tears, a mouth that trembled.

Even as she attempted a nervous twisting of her hair into decency, she caught the menacing look of the wrathful farmer fixed on Peter.

Peter, with an adventurous nonchalance, advanced a step to meet him.

They were facing each other on the narrow path, town wit and country wit.

Whilst all about was the trampled wheat.

"You're trespassing!" Adam told them.

The cool temper of the voice deceived all but Peter.

He had noticed the clenched fury of the hand that did not hold the lantern.

"Well — what about it?" asked the youth.

"Trespassers will be prosecuted," quoted Adam.

The cool temper became in itself a menace now.

He was speaking with the ease of one who has the law on his side, and will use its machinery to the utmost.

"Well, then — prosecute us," said Peter, cheekily.

But he had given a quick side-glance at the youth of the weak chin — then, at Becky, his face more easy as he caught her dark eye.

Becky had understood.

They were going to dodge out of this mess, somehow.

"Look at *that*," said Adam, flashing his lantern over the way they had come.

All the human feeling Uncle Nat had thought he lacked flashed from his eyes, throbbed in his voice.

"And for what?" he added, scornfully.

His contempt included the girls, now.

Becky stood it unmoved.

Her companion blushed.

"We were cutting off a mile of rough road," said Peter.

His voice had as much of explanation in it as was logical with his contempt for this clodhopper.

"You didn't seem in any particular hurry," retorted the farmer. "Name, please".

The two girls had slunk together.

Becky was whispering to Polly, advocating some policy.

With his eye on Peter, the farmer was conscious of this by-play. He kept his feet gripping the ground that blocked their flight.

"John Grimes — " began Peter, with a cunning semblance of giving in to a bad business.

"Won't come off," said Adam.

"If you don't get out of the way, I'll make you eat your earth," blazed Peter.

At that moment the nobility in him blazed up in full flame, over the attempt his clothes made at smartness, the hint of dissipation that would submerge him. It was the reckless courage that had discovered continents, and founded empires — the fighting spirit for which the town had no room. Peter ready for a scrap, was a different Peter from Peter the mud-lark, Peter the pierrot, Peter trying to dodge girls he had tired of.

"I wouldn't touch any of you town mongrels with a six-foot pole," said Adam.

The countryman's superior scorn of them was epigrammatic.

Whereupon Polly stepped forward and tried to talk nicely to Adam. To the little foolish attempts to talk him round, to make sheep's eyes at him, the farmer returned a smile that said he was woman-proof.

A gust of wind blew one of her blue ribbons in his eyes as she said they were sorry. He drew back, with so strong a look of contempt, that Polly shrunk.

"Your names," he said, rock-like.

Quite unexpectedly, Becky sprang forwards.

She pushed the big fair girl so violently that she was hurled upon Adam's great chest, a shrieking, scented, beribboned bundle of flapperdom, from which he strove to disentangle himself as from an asp. His hands got tangled in her hair, which had caught round his coat-buttons. Whilst the thought that the others were escaping made him ejaculate savage little words at her. His lantern dropped. He could hear the beat of her foolish heart.

"Becky! You cat! Oh — you cat!" she sobbed.

With a desperate movement she twitched away from him.

He heard the little, tearing sound made by the hair that had caught on his buttons.

Then he was after the youths.

Blind blows were rained amidst the wheat, then the townsters got free. He followed them, though out-distanced. His trembling of rage had been against him. He was not used to rage. It got into his head and bewildered his feet The laughter of Peter came up to him from the road.

They had trampled lawless paths through the middle of his field — and he had followed them — and they were gone.

Some vial snapped within him, and overspilled its bitterness, such revengeful bitterness as he had never known.

25

"You God-forsaken town devils," he called suddenly. "Get back to your town hell-holes. Why do you come here? Get back."

Then — he heard girlish sobbing, saw the ghostly gleam of a white dress.

The old Hebrew thirst for revenge was upon him.

Only — he did not want an eye for an eye, but twenty eyes for one.

He plunged through the wheat.

"Becky!" came sobbingly.

The girl had perceived him and was trying to run.

"Now — " he said, as he reached her, grasping her shoulder.

She made no answer, save terrified gasps.

The dark fear of her eyes shone through the gloom. She was biting her underlip in a childish attempt at restraint. It struck him that this time she was too scared to scream.

"I'm going to trespass," was his brief warning.

"Beck——" she began.

Then he was kissing her, in that raging passion of scorn and revenge against the tramplers of his temple, the heretics from the town. Each kiss was given as he would have dealt a man a blow — with the same steady desire to crush, to leave behind a scar. He was making the girl's vanity the scapegoat for the vandalism of her companions. Sacrilege for sacrilege.

Justice was satisfied at length.

"Now — get out o' my field," he said, thunderingly, and placing both his hands on her sob-shaken shoulders, thrust her out, till her feet were on the path, made her keep to it, then let her go, and watched her humiliated struggle up the round stone, over the stile.

Sex-proud tiller of the calm, silent earth he had grown to be like, he knew that she was on the verge of hysterics.

"Three steps down," he told her, with polite sarcasm.

She found her voice then.

It struggled up through tears, thin, feminine, with a thread of feminine viciousness.

"If there was only a man an' a monkey on th' earth," she told him, "an' you were th' man, I'd take the monkey".

She tried to laugh.

Her voice shook like Uncle Nat's fiddle-string, when he played "Annie Laurie".

"Get out o' my field," said the contemptuous, masculine bass.

"Wait till my grandmother, Betty Harker, comes to tell your dad — " she said with a childishness that made him smile.

Her voice was retreating.

Perhaps that gave it its forlorn sound.

The fact that it was Betty Harker's grand-daughter he had kissed, that the girl knew him, was staggering, but he had presence of mind to call a counter-threat.

"Wait till I see Betty Harker!"

Only silence answered.

She was gone.

He turned, found his lantern, re-lit it, and surveyed the damage to his field. His rage died away in impotent despair. He had found a clue to the names of the intruders. But — Betty Harker had lent his father twenty pounds last quarter towards paying off the mortgage.

Back again along the road, but he did not pass over the bridge and towards the barn-like kitchen lit by two candles, with Sary preparing supper in her dully patient way.

He went further along the road, took a wall-gap, and was soon climbing the slopes of a rush-singing, boggart-wild hill that was the doorstep to the moors. When he reached that dark expanse, the little pools were black save for the moon here and there, looking as if she were trying to drown herself, first in one, then in another, futilely. Ragged sheep passed like ghosts before him. The wind blew the moor-grasses erect, blew his hair erect, the dark shapes of a circle of hill rose round him as he still went up. Whilst the screams of the peewits fell down, down, down into an enchanted bowl of silence, — silence all the deeper for the thin, elfin-song of the rushes.

As he reached another hill it seemed to him that the wind gripped him, eager to help him up over the edge — into the silence, into the few stars. He went on and on, without stopping, until he reached a cold spring singing its way down through the bracken which made a little rusty accompaniment. It was Robin Hood's spring.

He plunged his bare head into the bubbling, silver coldness of it.

He was trying to wash from his mouth the touch of that soft, babyishly round cheek, the young, cold mouth, the whole shape of that face he had trespassed over. Whilst even as he did so one of Uncle Nat's sly hints of some weeks before insinuated itself into his reluctant, gibing mind. Uncle Nat had said that love had to tumble on some folk.

But by the time he had gone over Ashdale Pike and reached home again, he had entirely forgotten Polly Cherry.

The hotpot was quite dry.

Sary said this in her patient apologetic way as she scraped out the dish for him. He looked at his sister with a curious wonder as to whether she had ever had any of the hen-witted irresponsibility that made a girl run hazards such as Polly Cherry was running. For he had read the face of Peter.

Sary had a few grey hairs just over her temple.

"That'll do, Sary," he told her.

She looked at him, perceiving a human sympathy for her tiredness in his voice, this brother of hers whom she knew to think of nothing but clearing off the mortgage.

When he had gone to bed she roused her father.

He scrambled up, after much shaking, from the settle, blinking at the two candles.

Whilst he was getting his supper she looked at Adam's shoes. Ashdale Pike soil, she could tell it by the clay there. Something was the matter. Adam only went there after big things — such as missing to pay the mortgage.

Then she set to to clear Bob's coat away, and took up Adam's from the chair where he had flung it.

Something gleamed goldenly in the candlelight.

She looked at it fixedly.

"Look here!" she said to her father.

She pulled out several long hairs.

Benny stared at them dazedly.

Then he said, "What are we doin' burnin' four cannels, Sary?" His drunken surprise had died away into drunken apathy.

"He's ne'er made th' bran-mash," said Sary, suddenly.

Which startled her father for a moment.

Patiently Sary set to and covered up Adam's omission. Then she helped her father to bed, pushing him up, stair by stair, till he was safely in that bare, moon-silver room. Her thorough-going brother of the one passion was mixed up with some woman. That meant a splitting of his untirable energy. She wondered how it was going to affect the family fortunes as she made all ready for morning, and her heart shrunk from the contemplation of the splendidly superior creature Adam must have fallen in love with. Whilst at that very moment, on the same impulse that had made the yeoman plunge his head in the spring, Polly was allowing Peter to kiss her — in childish attempt to burn away the memory of those kisses that had stabbed her vanity. Womanlike, she had chosen not water, but fire. Whilst the woman Sary feared was this hen-witted girl, irrelevant, selfish enough to share Beck's chocolates, hide her own, and with no charm but that of a soft, blurred type of beauty that would make her at forty only a comfortable looking matron — this, a singing voice, and the very essence of youthful irresponsibility, were all the assets she had. There have been more immortal fascinators of wiser men than Adam Wild, with less obvious qualifications. And — who can read the heart of the most foolish girl who walks blind-folded on the tight-rope of life, laughing at all warnings that she may fall, and say what spells of magic, black or white, are hidden within it.

Chapter 3

Polly hears the news

Peter's watch had stopped and when he had struck a match to look at it he had not noticed that it was stopped. Polly was later home than ever she had been. She had come along dark, deserted streets to the serenade of cats. A drunken man had lurched after her once, so she had thought. He was really seeking for his lost pipe. Polly's fear where there was nothing to fear, her hardihood where there was everything to fear, was one of those inexplicable mysteries peculiar to flapperdom.

Her heart was yet beating in the panic caused by the semi-paralysed man hunting for his pipe.

She opened the door gently, crept into the passage, and hung up her coat to a loud whistling meant to convey utter innocence of the lateness of the hour. The thought of facing her Dad made her feel like a worm. But here she was, quite safe! What had they to worry about? As if she couldn't take care of herself! Peter had said she could. She got morally ready to face the music, and to enact that start of surprise as she saw the clock. As she stepped forwards into the darkness she saw that only a bar of red firelight shone under the middle door. It must be late. Dad must have taken Granny back to Cherrydale after her selling of pies in Narrowfields, his usual custom. She could dodge off to bed before he got back.

There would be her mother, of course——

But as Nan had let off the steam earlier in the day she would get off better than otherwise. Moreover, Nan would look on this disobedience as a bang in the eye for Cherry, and be pleased.

Polly pushed open the door.

She stared into an empty kitchen.

Her whistling fell off slackly — stopped dead.

She approached the supper table. Granny had been here. The cloth was on in her honour and the cup she always drank out of. Remnants of crumbs lay about. Polly tasted one. Granny's Saturday gift of pies. Then, she saw — a whole one, untouched on her Dad's plate, that his pot had had no tea in it.

She poked the fire into a blaze and looked at the clock. Her start of surprise was real enough. It wanted only twenty minutes to twelve.

It was borne in upon her that they had gone out to seek for her, that her Dad had refused to eat until she was in.

Then she saw Rag — inside at this hour!

Cherry always put the dog to bed religiously so soon as he came in on a Saturday night, to have Rag fresh for that Sunday morning parade.

It dawned on her that they must have gone to bed.

They had left that pie and pot for her.

They had left the door for her.

They were going to let her do as she liked.

"Hello, Rag!" she said, leaning down to pat Rag.

Her voice was wobbly.

The house was so forlorn.

After bracing up herself for a justification of being so late — this solemn deadness pressed upon her with weighty accusation — she drew out the baby chair she used to sit in, and squeezed herself down into it, before the fire. She was thinking of Becky, wondering how Becky would go on.

She could tell Becky they had left the door for her.

What a triumph!

"Hello, Rag," she said again, at this juncture.

Rag grunted and lolled out his tongue.

"Twenty-six and sixpence this week, Rag," she said, in a proud whisper. "An' — I *can* take care o' myself, can't I, Rag?"

She pulled the dog up on her knees.

He commenced gravely to lick her face.

Usually she defended herself against this procedure.

"Lick 'em off, Rag," she whispered approvingly. "Lick 'em off." Her face was screwed up in the painfully tolerating way that had angered Peter as he struck a match to look at her before kissing her to order.

Rag was unconscious of the martyrdom.

The rough red tongue went gravely over cheek, chin, forehead——

"That'll do, Rag," she said, decisively.

Which was just as she had said it to Peter at the same point.

Nobody here to scold; to pour her tea; to fasten the doors; to ask her where she had been and cause her to lie. The stunning new phase of freedom came to her with a cold desolation. She was being belittled to-night. Great things were happening to her, but in a topsy-turvy way. Two men had kissed her. The door had been left for her. And — why hadn't her father been her mother? Her old grievance came up again amidst the tumult and chaos of a day's memories that set up a milestone dividing her life from all the days gone by.

Rag whimpered as she put him off her knee.

She patted him as compensation, with that equivocal tenderness in little things, cruelty and lack of proportion in big ones, peculiar to the flapper.

Then, whilst she brooded upon the demoralisation of Adam Wild's kisses — rubbing her mouth to rub them off as a child would — she suddenly remembered that the little pink bow had come off her best hat and there wouldn't be time to put it on before going to Sunday School. The vital consequence of the matter thrust her childish fury against the sordid farmer out of mind.

Taking a candle she stole on tip-toe into the parlour. She entered it with a sharp consciousness of its dusty discomfort that always came upon her. When she had a parlour — all her own——!

Here, as she set the candlestick down on the littered round table with its faded cloth, she saw something that drove the pink bow out of her mind. Granny Harker's bonnet with its immemorial red geraniums glaring from the dusty blackness of it, stared her boldly in the face. She touched it as if it must be visionary. And, as she paused, it was borne in upon her that something was the matter with the house, something awful, something—— She walked out of the parlour, the candle-light on her blanched face. Granny Harker, who never would sleep away from home, was here.

"Mam!" she called up the stairs.

There was no answer.

"Dad!" she faltered.

The strangeness of the altogether strange night shook her girl's soul with terror.

She flew upstairs. On the top step the candle fell and guttered out.

"Mam! Granny!" she said, babyishly.

For Polly was only seven years old at that moment All her cocksureness, her adventuring with the fires of life, her premature attempts at womanhood were shed, leaving her a baby calling on those she loved in her light-hearted selfish way.

The stillness became full of bogies.

She rushed into a whitewashed room almost as light as day under the moonlight. The shadows of bird-cages were thrown upon the wall from an opposite one, for Cherry had once fancied canaries.

"Mam!" she said, shrilly.

A tousle-headed Nan, staring wildly, half rose from a tumbled bed.

"Oh — tha's come — bitch!" she said.

"Becky's watch stopped an'——" began Polly.

"Tell another, whilst thy mouth is warm," said Nan.

She spoke the words with mechanical use, but they did not bite.

She stared at the white figure as it seated itself on the bed.

She dropped the awful thunderbolt without a word of warning.

"Thy father's got his legs ta'en off," she said.

The little clock that half-dragged its wheels, then whirred palpitatingly, alone broke the silence.

Polly's face was staring incredulously into her mother's. Her voice came with a ghostly protest.

"Ooo!" she said, in a tongue-tied way. Then, "No. No".

"Ten shillings," wailed the shrew. "Ten shillings! That's all he can get in this world an' it mightn't be that much. Ay, a train went right ower him. They'd to take 'em off, right away."

Polly rocked herself.

Then she said, "It — it can't be true".

"It's true enough," sobbed her mother. "My God! Ten shillings. I shan't know which end on it to start on. What did I do it for? I never thought o' that——"

Her words conveyed nothing to the dazed girl, beyond the sordid priority of the monetary loss above all.

"Will he—— Did they say——Who——?"

She started three sentences without finishing one of them.

"They say he's a chance," said Nan. "That Breeze lad came to tell us." Then she returned to the economic plane.

Polly went downstairs.

The front door opened, shut, and Granny Harker came into the kitchen, bare-headed, just as she had been peering into the night for Polly.

She gave the fire a poke that splintered a big cob and lit up the kitchen — revealing Polly cowered down in the baby-chair, her hands covering her face.

"Oh, she's telled thee," observed the old Calvinist.

Polly nodded without uncovering her face.

"Ay. It's fine news to come hoam to — at this time!" observed Granny.

Through her fingers Polly saw the fat hand point at the clock.

Withal the roundest, slowest, easiest voice in the world, it had something merciless in it.

Polly rose from her crouching attitude.

Her face, drowned in tears she made no attempt to wipe away, looked half fearful resentment at Granny.

"It's soon enough to come hoam — here!" she said, though her voice trembled at her own wild courage. It seemed to her that the world was against her, cornering her, to-night.

Granny surveyed her with something tender struggling through the clouds on her brow — the tenderness she always fought against and would, to her dying day.

"Hasta ever tried to mak' it a nicer shop to come hoam to, lass?" she asked.

"Ooo! Leave me alone," said Polly.

She sat down again.

"Out o' the fryin' pan into th' fire tha'll jump, if tha doesn't mind," said Granny. Then she said, knowingly, "I did it mysel', so I know."

Whereupon Polly uncovered her eyes and looked at Granny with interest struggling through her misery.

Granny returned the look with a mild solicitude.

She set the kettle on to boil again, and plumped herself down in Nan's chair.

"What he'll do — without feet — the Lord only knows," she said, grimly, looking across at the easy chair. "Though she's my own lass. Well, what it is — is."

Polly went on crying.

"Eh, dry up, little cock-throstle!" said Granny, after a while. "Sitha! There's a sup o' tay, an' this pie. Come on. We mun go on eytin', or we'se make bad waur."

Whilst Polly ate, to her cheerful encouragements, she was mentally shaking her head. A giant down-fallen — a shrew no longer held in bondage — a seventeen-year-old lass who came home at half-past eleven, hawking a face with God's beauty and the devil's stamp of irresolution. What was coming?

"God help this house!" she exclaimed fervently, at length, in her slow, country accents. "An' — God help it."

As for Polly — she was fishing "sweethearts" out of her tea, according to the old irresistible impulse, and laying them out, one by one, in her saucer. She performed the rite with the minimum of interest, it is true. But her destiny, her wonderful destiny, tantalised her with curiosity — even in this awful moment, when it seemed to her that she could not be happy any more, never any more.

"Come here, I'll do thy hair, cock-throstle," said Granny.

So Polly sat in the old baby-chair, Granny's first present to her, and the old woman brushed out her hair.

And as she brushed, listening to the chirping of a cricket in the warm ashes, looking across now and then at Cherry's empty chair, Betty Harker came to the conclusion that Polly's feet needed to be set on a rock, and that they were such foolish feet they would never find the rock without help.

"Is that too tight?" she asked, plaiting the shower of gold into a cable.

"Just nice, Gran," said Polly.

She rose and flashed a moved, warm look at the old woman, through new tears.

Granny's handling of her hair had been balm on her sad heart — the little feather heart that might blow anywhere.

"Th' next time tha comes to see me," said Granny, "I'll introduce thee to a reight, grand lad".

Polly was silent.

The silence had varying qualities of surprise, suspicion, and — readiness for another scalp!

"Ooo, Gran!" pleaded Polly suddenly, "take me back hoam — to live with you again".

And Granny Harker found that Polly had not yet outgrown those two years lived with her, ten years ago, that the lass looked on that place with the cherry-tree over the door as — home; that there were depths in the lightsome creature.

"Tha could make this place a lot pleasanter, Polly Ann," she reminded her tenderly, using the little old name she had used to the seven-years-old-child.

"Ooo, Gran!" said Polly, tearfully. "You don't know. You don't know !"

"I've a bit of an idea what it's like," said Granny. "But — in this world, we can only try. An' as for my takin' other folks' childer, I haven't made sich grand wark o' my own it'd be justified. Besides — thy Dad needs thee."

Polly pulled her shoes off.

Granny's last argument had been unanswerable.

"Night, Gran," she said.

She knew better than to offer to kiss Granny.

No one had ever known the old Calvinist-democrat to submit to such tomfoolery. She said it was for folks with lots o' time on their hands.

"Neet, cock-throstle," said Granny genially.

It was her highest water-mark of sentiment, that quaint expression, in the old, slow voice. Beyond that she never went

By aid of a match Polly found the fallen candle, relit it and advanced into her mother's room. She set the candle down on a rush-bottomed chair with a big hole in it, and went downstairs.

She went up again with a pot of tea.

"Mam!" she said, standing by the bedside, "there's some tea here. It's sugared".

The shrew raised herself on her elbow.

Out of the exhaustion of revolving the ten shillings problem she eyed her daughter. She saw in this erratic thoughtfulness of the girl's a bidding for indulgence.

"Tha thinks tha'll get round me, now tha'rt not fleyed o' thy father any more," screamed Nan, suddenly, and hurled the contents of the pot. Polly stepped quickly back. But the liquor had gone through the thin sleeve.

She went downstairs.

Granny put salve on.

Polly's face revealed a hard, unyouthful cynicism.

She caught Granny's keen, grey eye.

She slid her young arms round the tubby, ungraceful, homely figure.

"Ooo! Granny," she said, with a hystericky laugh, "I'm too young. An' it's not in me. I don't care for aught but — dancin' an' lads, I don't. I can't help it. I didn't pick my pattern, did I? I were like to take after somebody, weren't I? An' — they're bad folk! I can feel 'em in me — pullin' at me, makin' me do things I don't want to do."

Granny stood erect with the big girl sobbing on her neck. She knew well enough whom the lass took most after, and her face grew more grim as she saw that vision of her prodigal daughter, of the guinea-gold hair.

"Tak' another cup o' tay up," she said, withstanding the temptation to kiss the girl. "As for lads — wait till tha sees that lad at Cherrydale."

But Polly went off, showing a disconsolate lack of interest, and without the second cup of tea. She was, as she said, too young to do gracious things without a return that elevated her in her own eyes.

As she nursed her smarting arm, sitting on the chair before the one thing in the house she had ever bought — a mirror — she soothed herself by a contemplation of her own face, viewing it from every point.

But as she heard Granny hobbling upstairs, with a long step and a short one, so it seemed, on account of her "gammy" leg (souvenir from Pa Harker, defunct), she hurriedly got off her things and jumped into bed.

Granny had taken up another cup of tea.

The shrew drank this one.

Nan's one cardinal virtue, filial respect, had been put into her by the buckle end of a strap in the days when Granny's tenderness had not come so near to the outside.

When Granny had undressed and struggled up on the bed, with much puffing for breath, Polly surprised her by saying, as the candle went out, "What's his name, Granny?" As Granny was sitting gloomily on what she thought must be the ruins of the Cherry castle, it took her some time to understand that Polly was alluding to the — rock.

"Oh — that lad," said Granny, after some thought "Little pouse, I thought tha were asleep."

Then she said, "What's th' good o' axin' that? It's nobody tha knows. Well, he's called Adam — like th' first man, an' his other name's Wild. I alius go to my dinner at th' Charity. Tha mun come to sing, an' we'll go up after. It's six months off yet, but — that'll be th' best chance, natural-like. Then her tone changed. "Eh, I wonder how yon poor lad is!" she said.

The human compassion in her voice for the son-in-law who retold her jokes, and whose jokes she carried about with her pies, was a contradiction to her iron theory of Pre-destination — and her iron worship of her close-cropped iron god, Cromwell. Whilst in her struggle against Destiny on behalf of Polly Cherry, it was characteristic that Granny's common-sense soul had chosen for the foolish feet a human rock. And the rock Granny had chosen was more human than Granny knew.

Chapter 4

The return of Cherry

It was Aunt Miriam, daughter to Obadiah Cherry, the porter's deceased godfather, who suggested, organised and stage-managed the gathering of the Cherry clan to welcome the broken one out of hospital. On account of the economic fight facing the porter, it was agreed that "everybody should bring their own" — making the feast a communal one. Aunt Miriam said it would cheer Cherry up if he saw they were "standing by him."

There had not been such a rally since the last family gathering, when Obie had died, leaving Uncle Silas, the oldest living branch of the Cherry tree, with the never-failing regret that he had refused to poor Obie the sum of five shillings.

Uncle Silas was the first arrival at the Cheer-up Party.

He wore the self-same coat in which he had been one of Obie's carriers. As he had enlarged considerably since then, he bore a comical resemblance to an almost bursting caterpillar, with the most knowing of pink faces, and the bluest of Cherry-blue eyes.

"Afternoon, Nan. Afternoon, Mir'am," he panted. The way from Cloughfold Farm to this house was long and weary, hard as the proverbial road of transgressors. He had undertaken it as a penance for not lending Obie that money, fifteen years ago.

He was fumbling to bring something out from a back pocket.

Polly had to help him out with it.

"Thear!" said Aunt Miriam.

She sat it down by the pyramid of pork pies Granny Harker had sent as her contribution.

The little gesture of the sanctimonious-looking Miriam gave the key-note to the whole gathering that was to come. She was fixing things up for the mighty one fallen. They were going to do their duties as Christians and stand by the one who had ever rebuffed all attempts at family consolation on account of his lack of worldly possessions, and his termagant of a wife.

"Ay, ay, this is a weary day," said Uncle Silas, sitting down. "There's allus summat for somebody."

He looked across at Nan, but the shrew did not reply. Her attempts at dressing for a mournful occasion had somehow contrived to bring out vast differences between herself and Miriam. The expression of her countenance might suggest that she was trying hard to look overwhelmed by greatness of the disaster that would face them in another hour, stripped of hospital wrappings — the broken thing coming back to the world of whole ones. Or it might only be that he was still struggling with the momentous question of how to deal with Cherry's ten shillings weekly.

"God works in a mysterious way," observed Aunt Miriam. "I don't think our family's been as grateful as it might ha' been. Maybe this has come —— "

"Nay, nay, lass," said Uncle Silas. "We'll not ha' that Accidents is accidents."

He took a consoling pinch of snuff.

"We'se ha' to do as weel as we can," he said, as valiantly and nobly as if they were his legs that were gone. "We mun look on th' breet side. An' after a' — he's alive. That's summat."

There was a short silence.

The optimism of Uncle Silas somehow or other had the effect of conjuring up all the tragedy of the big porter's fall.

"He'se done weel," said Aunt Miriam, striving against this. "If he could only think so. He'se got out a month afore they thought he would. Grand healin' flesh, they said, he had. An' — it'll be just as he makes it, how he surrenders hissel' to it"

Uncle Silas abruptly changed the topic.

Surrender was Aunt Miriam's pet subject — how you gained by losing — and won by giving up.

"Ay, ay," said Uncle Silas, returning to the healing. "Flesh heals soon enough. It's th' other that plays owd Nick. It's when yo' get a raw place where nobody can put sauve on. An' a man doesn't come down from six foot one — to half a man, as you might say, without a bonnie big bang inside him."

"That's where th' Lord will help him," said Aunt Miriam.

"Well, God helps him as helps hissel'," said Uncle Silas. "An' pity without relief is like mustard without beef. We shall see what we shall see." With which he rose from his chair, flecked his leggings with a tenderness that showed he appreciated the full value of legs, and went off with an air that said he had some trump card to play that would affect the destiny of his kinsman.

Polly showed him into the parlour and sat down with him on the couch — brightening its dinginess with her blue muslin dress — making, as Uncle Silas always said, "the only ornymint about the place." For some minutes they stared at a Siberian rabbit under a globe, a rabbit amidst barren snows, with dark, and sardonic glance of eye.

A smart patter of rain on the window-pane made the old man observe that it was fine growing weather. Polly made no answer.

"Coming to Cherrydale Fair?" he queried, with a droll look.

He regarded her proudly and with a certain surprise.

She had thinned a little during the six months. Her hair was up. When she turned her head it made a perfectly round ball of glory behind her head. Some of the cocksureness had faded from her look.

She had altered, with that subtle alteration which comes from the inside, and shines through the flesh. In repose her face had shadows of the discontent endured in this transition from girlhood to womanhood — this awkward, moody, dangerous age. There was something elusive in her personality.

"Coming to the fair and singing at the Charity," she answered.

In contradistinction to the lessening of the cocksureness in her look, her voice had an excess of it, as if some spiritual war was on within her.

Uncle Silas surveyed her again.

She bore the admiring pride of this old, old man, like a plant that thrives and spreads out under it.

"Ay. Tha'll do," said the old pig-breeder, his head on one side. "Tha'll pass in a crowd without much shovin'. 'My face is my fortune, sir, she said.' Well, sometimes 'tis and sometimes 'tisn't." Then he stopped, as about to say something else forgetfully.

He had remembered Granny's prodigal daughter, and that he had a message to convey from her to Granny.

Polly's face had quietened down out of the pleased vanity in which Uncle Silas was her mirror.

He stole a glance at her — when she was not looking, except at something beyond and behind the Siberian rabbit. The girl looked — worried.

Uncle Silas grew solicitous. He leaned forwards, until his look compelled Polly's. He had a mysterious air.

Polly's eyes were wide in surprise.

Uncle Silas made the most of this impression, did not speak out at once, plumped his two fat hands the firmer on his fat knees, and then spoke in a whisper that called for confidence.

"How has she bin wi' thee, lass?" he asked, jerking his thumb slowly towards the kitchen.

Polly's surprise changed into expressions that made it a study. It's final one, the one that remained on top, made Uncle Silas shift his position and feel that he had made a mistake.

"All right," said a hard little voice.

Two young cold eyes stared back at him.

Then Uncle Silas broke into an uneasy laugh.

"Naught wrong, lass," he said. "By th' Mass! I didn't know tha'd so much Cherry in thee. Well, — it'll happen serve thee weel. An' a little bit o' Cherry goes a long way."

Whilst in his own mind he was convinced that Nan had been leading this bonnie lass a regular devil's dance.

Then he saw a face at the window.

"Ted — by goff!" he said, excitedly.

A young man was smiling in at them, somewhat sheepishly. He wore a red tie with a bugle pin and had early snowdrops in his coat.

Polly went to open the door and take his cap.

Uncle Silas, through the crack of the parlour door, saw Ted looking at her.

"Grown, hasn't she?" he asked from within.

Ted nodded as he came in.

He stared again at the miracle of Polly.

Polly laughed.

Then Uncle Silas laughed.

And Ted laughed.

Ted's laugh had trombone qualities that made Uncle Silas hold up a fat forefinger to remind them there was tragedy in the house. And the checked, worried look came back to Polly's face. Tragedy on the door-posts! And she — only lived in the sunshine.

She went to open the door once more.

"Uncle Bob Rimmer," guessed Uncle Silas. "I can tell his foot. I've ne'er sin him since Obie——"

Whereupon he shook his head and sighed heavily.

"Well, how are we?" asked a little man with bowed legs and a shining head, and a short dab of a nose.

His voice matched his face.

He selected the easiest chair and dropped into it as by right divine.

"We're here," said Uncle Silas, solidly.

He looked it.

Uncle Bob took out a parcel and handed it to Polly, who took it into the kitchen.

"*Ham*," whispered Aunt Miriam.

Her expression was of pleased philanthropy.

She spread out the ham cheek by jowl with Uncle Silas' somewhat scranny pullet as if they were providing for Cherry for life.

After that the little front door was ever on the swing.

Within twenty minutes the parlour was packed in a way that justified Uncle Silas' remark that there was standing-room only. A couple of dogs, one belonging to Bill Henry Cherry, local preacher and packman, the other to a silent man addressed as "Jar-ge, lad," kept up an incessant rivalry of barking, whilst Martha, of Rainyharbour, also kept up her rivalry of chatter against that of the preacher-packman's cherry-lipped wife, who would, according to Uncle Silas, flirt with a stone-dead tom-cat. Beside the silent man with the glorious Irish setter under his chair sat a little, neat, white-haired, black-aproned old woman, who had brought her eternal crotchet with her. This was Dinah Cherry, youngest sister of Silas, and great-aunt to Will Cherry. Upon her cheek was a little bulbous growth, like a pink apple, into which morphia went twice every day of her life. She was telling Martha how it was that Martha couldn't get a lythe on her puddings. Ted, the organ-blower at Cherrydale old church, was telling how they caught a rabbit, he and Bob Wild, right in the wood that was a stone's-throw from the parson's garden.

Whereupon it was observed that Polly Cherry became very interested in the subject of rabbit-catching, until — the silent man gave a jerk of his finger towards the window he had never ceased to look through, steadily.

"Nay——" said Uncle Silas, eager to put off the facing of the broken thing.

The silent man nodded.

"It's here," he remarked.

Bill Henry Cherry cleared his throat as he always did, before giving out a text. But he was visibly moved.

As for Uncle Silas, he was bracing himself up by giving good advice to the others.

"Now then, yo' women," he sternly admonished the weaker sex. "No eye-water on this business."

"Ay," said Uncle Bob Rimmer, from the window, "it's it."

The ambulance van had stopped outside the house. A small crowd that had gathered waited to see what was to come forth from it. First of all came the man in a white jacket, then a stretcher, draped respectably, only Cherry's face showing. It was white, and wore a twisted smile. So much could be seen from the window before the crowd closed round — a gaping thing that was made of eyes, human eyes, all staring curiously, compassionately, morbidly, at this broken thing. The second man in the white jacket admonished the thing that hedged nearer, ever nearer, to see — to stare at the white face that was trying to smile.

"Polly!" called Uncle Silas, excitedly. "Open th' door."

But Polly had disappeared.

"Mir'am!" called Uncle Silas.

So it was Miriam, her sallow face set in a strained smile, who opened the door of the house Cherry had been swept out of six months ago, to return in this fashion.

As for Aunt Miriam, all the beautiful things she had meant to say jumbled themselves up in her head, and all she could think of was to warn the ambulance men, "Mind that mat" — for the mat had a big hole in it. There was something unanswerable in Cherry's face. Through its whiteness, and that strange, twisted smile, the pain-lines woven about mouth and brow, his eyes had the look of a stranger in a strange land, who cannot tell the things he knows.

As for the parlour — it might have been tenanted by a company of ghosts, listening to the march of the two men in white coats carrying this strange kinsman of theirs into the kitchen — this man they knew, yet did not know, this man who possibly had not yet found himself, for whom all was chaos, throb of flesh and throb of soul, this broken giant being jolted back to grapple with Life.

"This is — a day," said Uncle Silas, mopping his brow. His tone had a note of dejection very different from that he had used in the kitchen before he had seen Cherry.

"Well — " said Uncle Bill Henry, clearing his throat again. "What had we best do? Some of us had best go in!"

They listened again.

Cherry was evidently being seated in his chair. The casters squeaked.

"Easy there — easy does it," said the second ambulance man.

"Right-o," said Cherry.

His voice had lost some of its bigness, too, as if worn thin — flabby-muscled, despondent at this horrible nightmare that was proving itself every day a greater reality, and to which he would one day have to accustom himself.

"Some of us should go in," persisted Uncle Bill Henry, though he looked as if he thought the most sensible plan was to bolt.

"Tha'rt a talker," said Ted the organ-blower to the local preacher. But he only glared in answer.

"Let's all go," said Uncle Bob Rimmer. "We can't stop mutterin' an' mumblin' here a' day. An' there's naught to be fleyed on, as I see."

"Wait till them chaps has gone," said the silent man. The two men came down the passage.

The door closed behind them.

It was not possible to defer the trying moment any longer.

"I think," said the local preacher, in a whisper, "that this is a woman's job." But Aunt Miriam, who had also retreated to the parlour after the effort of opening the door for Cherry to pass in, shook her head.

It was then that Aunt Dinah said quietly, "Why — I'll go first." Her blue eyes were tearful, and the little pink apple on her cheek had gone pinker.

"Shoo allus had a pluck," said Uncle Silas, feebly.

So it was Aunt Dinah who walked into the kitchen where Cherry was sitting, waiting for them. He had somewhat of the jaunty air with which he had faced the world on that morning after giving Nan her thrashing. But here was no grim determination that had marked him then. His hands hung limply on the arms of his old chair.

The fairness of his complexion had become a bluey-whiteness, consequent on his loss of blood. The genial smile was a twisted thing — gone all awry, like life, like his vision that saw two Aunt Dinahs, both struggling to keep calm and say the most fitting word.

After a time Aunt Dinah found it.

"God's good, Will," she said in a trouble way. "He tempers the wind to the shorn lamb. He's good."

"Don't upset yourself, Aunt," said Cherry.

He spoke without that vitality that had characterised him — like a man under the spell of opium.

"But, He is good. I've proved it," said Aunt Dinah, as though she had been contradicted; she then burst into tears.

The others filed in past the chair on which she had dropped.

Cherry bore the steady downpour of advice, solicitude, sympathy and cheer-up philosophy without sense of resentment or appreciation. Only his blanched fingers tapped the arms of his chair — a restless tattoo, and he noticed that the old almanac with the crosses on the margin was gone, whilst in its place was a framed picture — "Wedded Love."

It was Aunt Miriam who brought Polly from an upper room where she had hidden herself, Polly, with a watery smile and trembling chin, who slid a cold little finger in her Dad's hand, and propped herself against his chair, struggling with herself.

"Ay, ay," said Uncle Silas.

Cherry looked at his daughter.

She had obviously suffered during his absence from the haphazard house. But it did not upset him in the least He felt absurdly callous.

"She's growin' up, Cherry," said Uncle Silas, admiringly.

The feminine portion of the onlookers, finding that Polly did not break down, after all, wiped away the sympathetic water that had filled their eyes.

"Ay. Some on us grows up, an' some grows down," said his sister Dinah, referring to her own loss of inches from a slight stoop.

It was felt to be a clumsy remark.

Cherry did not notice it.

The passivity of the great, broken man gave him a half-dead look, in contrast to those human beings around him, full of human sympathy.

But when Nan came into the kitchen he roused himself sufficiently to say, "Well, Missus?"

Nan had not been crying.

That cold, unemotional part of his mind which noted everything, guessed that she had kept out of the way so as to miss the display of family affection. It amused him in a grim way. After all, he would get no "sloppiness" from Nan. Nan was not eighty-eight parts water.

She did not answer that greeting of his, save by a glance that said she saw him, a curious, furtive look that he felt searched his weakness.

"If you like," said Uncle Silas, "we'll all go an' stand in th' coal-nook whilst you do all your clippin' an' cussin'. Why, it'll be like a second honeymoon." He winked knowingly.

"We can wait," said the dwindled voice of the weary man. "Can't we, Nan?"

Her glance said that she had gathered the irony of his meaning.

Cherry had kept his skeleton locked up very closely. His family only guessed that he and his did not "get on too well."

"Well, I suppose we'll have to make tea," said Aunt Miriam, and put on the cloth.

Cherry watched the cutting of great stacks of bread, with the feeling of sickness the sight of food always gave him, now.

"There'll be a pound o' butter there out o' that half-pound when tha's done, Mir'am," said Uncle Silas, to the butterer.

Martha of Rainybarhour was setting out cakes, and watching Polly critically, as a lazy young hussy.

When Aggie went past Martha for more plates they exchanged glances that told Cherry as plainly as if they had spoken, that they were telling each other, "Well, what can yo' expect, off a mother like that."

Nan was setting the cups in a leisurely way, with a something in her manner that plainly avowed Cherry's folk were no friends of hers.

The way in which Aunt Miriam looked at the kettle, to see how it was going on, gave her an affectation of great domestic virtues which Nan overlooked entirely.

"When's thy mother comin', Will?" asked Aunt Dinah.

It was a plucky query.

There had been trouble between Nan and Grandma Cherry. Dinah thought this was surely a time for letting by-gones be by-gones.

"She said she'd better not," said Aunt Miriam. "It'd upset her too much."

Which was a diplomatic way of putting the truth that Grandma Cherry did not know how she would be received in a house where she hadn't been for fourteen years.

"Oh, Mir'am, we'se ne'er eat all that," said Uncle Silas.

"Oh! You never know what yo' can do till yo' try," came a cheery voice from the passage.

"Betsy, as I'm a sinner," said Uncle Silas, as she came in. "I'll tell thee what — it's a long time sin' thee an' me sucked a toffee-stick together, isn't it?"

Granny looked plainer than ever from the fact that she was dressed in her best.

"Ay," she smiled. "We've washed our necks sin' then, haven't we, Silas? I'm not goin' to sit down, Nan. Hesta an apron? Hello, Will! Home again."

She flashed a look at the man in the corner. Her greeting "Home again" was as nonchalant as though he had been on holiday. Granny did not put all in the window that she had in the shop. Cherry knew that he ought to have appreciated her lack of demonstration. But he didn't. He didn't appreciate anything. There was a hard something within him that blocked him off from everything he had cared for and that cared for him. He was quite alone, in a world of jabbering foreigners, who tried their best to speak his tongue, to pass that hard barrier that had risen up between him and them.

"Come on, lass. Stir thysel'," Granny urged Polly, after having had a few inches of tape put on the apron-strings to make them meet.

The bustling scene mesmerised Cherry.

The kitchen did not keep still.

When he looked too long at Uncle Silas, Uncle Silas became lost in green snow. A crease of cloth made a burning bar of irritation across one of his tender stumps. He was as weak as a ten-year-old child, he, who had not known his strength. And these people — were come here to sympathise with him. To sympathise! Whilst he felt miserably that if they all dropped dead, it wouldn't matter to him. What a coarse, fat man Uncle Silas was! He liked money well enough to cut it with a knife and fork. Strange that he had never perceived it before. Uncle Bob Rimmer, too — he had once liked Uncle Bob Rimmer. He had no more intellect than a rabbit, and would have cracked jokes on his own mother's coffin. Martha, of Rainyharbour, what was she but a talking-machine to hang blouses on? Even Granny — Granny, once the apple of his eye, struck him as a rather egotistical old woman who put other folk in their places, but wouldn't be put anywhere herself.

"Well. Are we ready?" queried Granny, at length.

"Ay. I think we are," said Uncle Silas.

Uncle Silas was dying to eat.

Cherry knew he was.

"Now — who'll wheel him up to the table?" quoth Uncle Silas.

It was Ted the organ-blower who came forward and put his two hands on Cherry's chair back.

"Don't shake him more'n tha' can help, Ted," said Aunt Dinah.

The broken man gritted his teeth.

They were treating him openly like a broken doll.

"Mind th' edge of th' rug, Ted," said Martha, solicitously, looking naked sympathy at Cherry, a large brown teapot in her hand.

"Is that a'reight?" asked Ted, bashfully, of the rough man he had once gone ratting with.

"Ay," answered Cherry. He surveyed the table.

An unemotional rage had seized him — a rage of will and thought, rather than of feeling, or perhaps feeling was deep down, subconscious, buried under these mental attributes that had come to him as he was laid in the hospital, living a life of inaction. He had come to this! To be openly discussed as a broken article! His trembling hand took up a fork.

"Ay," said Granny, approvingly, "get summat down tha, lad."

"I've often noticed," remarked Granny, to no one in particular, "how we allus go on eytin'. It takes a lot to knock us off our meyt. Whatever comes or goes, we keep *that* up."

Cherry stole a side-glance down the length of the table.

Every one was eating with solid earnestness. Chins were wagging. Eyes were aslant in search of certain articles of food. The world went on eating, like a great, hungry beast, whilst — he sickened, yet pushed the stuff down.

An animal could creep in a hole.

A man could not.

Down at the far-end of the table Polly was being teased about dodging taking the last piece of bread on the plate, lest she be an old maid.

Some one was inquiring about Rag.

"Oh — it's at Sagg Farm," said Granny. "They say it's mendin', but I can't see it. I expect tha'll want it back, now, Will?"

"I'll give it three months," said Cherry, trying to rouse interest within himself, "an' if it hasn't straightened up then, I'll have it shot."

"Ooo!" said Polly.

Her face looked reproach on him, appearing from the round outline of Uncle Bob.

Quite suddenly it had come to the ex-porter that a dog that couldn't fight other dogs was in the same position as a man who couldn't fight other men.

The endless meal was over, at last.

Uncle Silas put his hand sideways across his throat and looked pathetically at Miriam, as a sign that he could eat no more.

'And — Cherry heard a remark that told him that they had brought their own food with them, to eat in his house, and that he also had been eating thereof. He tried to feel indignant, knew he ought to feel insulted, that on a day he would have risen up and ordered them out of the house for such a thing.

Now — he was wheeled away from the table, gritting his teeth at a double indignity, the place full of green snow, out of which he saw Nan, and Martha, and Aggie, both advising Ted, as chair-wheeler, to mind the rug.

"Tha wants to give him a tonic, Nan," said Granny.

Nan said nothing.

Whilst Cherry, in his chaotic state, thought that cocaine would have been more in his line.

The business of clearing away, washing-up, putting on the coloured cloth, was gone through.

It was Polly who reached down the phonograph horn, the phonograph, and operated, with Ted as her assistant, when the lamp was lit. Cheerful songs, with laughing choruses, each heralded by the "Edison Bell Record" — were chosen for him, and the circle around the fire applauded, and Cherry smiled, looking like a man pulled back by the lobes of his ears. There was a night of this to be gone through. This was human sympathy.

When they had tired of the phonograph, it was Aunt Miriam who got out a pile of hymn-books, handing them out. They had just started "Scatter Seeds of Kindness" — (Aunt Miriam had chosen this for Nan's especial benefit) — when the front door was flung violently open.

"I axed one or two of the Harkers to come in," explained Granny.

Thus did Cherry behold Aunt Miriam's conspiracy to turn this party into a Moody and Sankey debauch defeated — and beheld for the first time the astonishing spectacle of "Captain Brown" and his merry men, David and Joseph Harker, cousins.

Joe Harker was an expert on the jews' harp.

His cousin David sang in French — until Billy Breeze came in later, when he became astonishingly shy on learning that Billy "knew a bit o' French."

But it was "Captain Brown" who became the life of the little party. The way he could drink a man's health was a revelation. The way he could stand, back to the fire, a glass in his hand, filled to the brim, and pour forth the most emotional songs with the greatest gusto, without spilling a drop, was unique.

"Spill beer!" quoth the gallant "Captain." "Spill *beer!*"

He grew pale at the sacrilegious thought that any one could suppose him capable of such an act.

Who had brought the bottle of whisky no one ever knew. Let it suffice that it began to be passed round. When Joe struck up a hornpipe on the jews' harp it was Granny Harker who vowed she could jig a jig with Silas, and would, if it killed her.

Which she did.

Whilst the applauding circle had not the least idea that there was any danger of her dropping dead.

Cherry tried hard to be enthusiastic.

He could only feel "out of it" — an outsider. In his longing to get "home" he had never dreamed of this new self of his that would see in the house he had left, the folk he had left, a strange dwelling-place, and a new people, who had shifted their conception of him, who could not meet him on the level.

He beheld them get more affable, more warm-hearted, more tolerant to each others' failings, under the influence of the whisky, with a growing cynicism of coldness that made him as wretched as it could have made them, had they been aware of it. They only beheld a weakened man, with a heavy, drugged look. He beheld them as sages have beheld the folly of the world.

In their sympathy and the opening of their hearts they told him he should want for nothing. Aggie and Martha sunk their differences and cried over him together. Aunt Dinah assured him that never a night would pass but she should pray for him. Uncle Silas — Uncle Silas flirted with Aggie, whilst her local-preacher husband was debating the resurrection of the body with Uncle Bob Rimmer, until he discovered Uncle Silas and Aggie holding hands, when he became very white and vowed that if Uncle Silas had not been eighty, he'd have killed him.

Whereupon Uncle Silas went very red, said he was only in his seventy-ninth year, and could fight anything in this generation, which didn't know it was born. Moreover, he vowed that he would hold hands with Aggie again. Which he did. So that the local preacher ran at him; and was forced down into a chair; and given whisky; so that in the end he arose, vowed that he'd never had anything wrong against Uncle Silas, called him his best friend, offered to lend him money, and became a little more sober on Uncle Silas accepting the offer. As a Cheer-up Party it was very successful. People who had come somewhat dolefully, found that after all things might have been much worse. In the greatest of good hearts and spirits the company eventually went to find its individual hats, caps, bonnets, Polly holding the candle in the dingy parlour.

"Shut th' door," commanded Uncle Silas, in a whisper.

It was shut.

"Now," quoth Uncle Silas, trying at the same time to make up his mind if the hat in his hand was his own, "what are we goin' to do about it?"

Huddled together, in the shadowy room, Polly's candle-light just availed to reveal the expectancy chronicled on some of the faces, surprise on others, and here and there the sheen on an eye, the turn of a nose, as they looked towards Uncle Silas.

"What I say is," avowed Uncle Silas, one finger up, "we ought to do summat. There's about a dozen on us in a position to do it. I'm willin' to do my share."

The local preacher coughed.

Then he said, "Will he have it?"

Uncle Silas glanced fiercely at him.

"He can't have it if we don't offer it him," he said, in the same loud whisper.

Polly was looking uncomfortable and unhappy.

"A shilling-a-week'll hurt none of us," said Uncle Bob Rimmer.

"Hear, hear," said Ted.

"'Tis man's inhumanity to man makes countless thousands mourn," quoth Captain Brown.

Aunt Dinah was putting on her things, very carefully and noiselessly.

"Ted has his mother to keep," she said, in the same hushed way that all were now speaking.

"Now," beamed Uncle Silas, "that's understood."

Ted was protesting.

"Thee sit down!" said Aggie, and pushed him down on the couch and sat beside him.

Whereupon the local preacher hurriedly arrived at the decision that all there, excepting Ted, Aunt Dinah and Granny, should give one shilling per week to their unfortunate kinsman. As there were all in all ten persons (counting two absent ones) who could be expected to pay, some one was to go in and inform Cherry that ten shillings per week would come to him to augment the probable ten shillings compensation from the Company.

"Who'll tell him?"

Uncle Silas pointed at "Captain Brown."

So it was the Captain, in Uncle Silas' hat, who walked into the kitchen when Granny was saying goodnight to her son-in-law, and further advising a tonic, and telling Nan she must look well after him.

Captain Brown broached the subject in both prose and verse — with quotations from the Bible and Bobby Burns, and original interjections of his own. He talked five minutes before the man in the corner realised that this speech had some reference to himself, and that the others were standing with downcast eyes, and expectant faces.

They were offering him — *help*.

Slowly, the awful fact that they had dared offer him help, burst on him, surging through his brain, and the dull rage that had been passive became emotional, active.

Only the iron will kept back words that would have estranged him from them for ever.

"Not a blasted penny piece — " said Cherry.

His eyes looked at them like a thing's at bay, out of the dead greyness of his face. The force behind his voice was more than it could bear. The words fell on the air of the kitchen, a pathetic falsetto.

"Never refuse nowt but blows," said Uncle Silas, genially.

" 'Think gently o' your brither man
Still gentler, sister woman — ' "

said Captain Brown.

"Not a blasted penny piece," reiterated the man in the corner.

The sound of his voice, in its weak accent, was painful now. Granny winced under it. Polly trembled.

"Now, if tha'd rather not——" said the local preacher, who possibly looked a little relieved.

"When I'm short — I'll ax," said Cherry.

His look was a blighting thing.

Their protests became craven, though they knew they had meant it well.

They went out into the night

The door closed behind them.

The Cheer-up Party with its folk who ate their own stuff, and offered financial help, was over. Feminine sympathy, masculine fellowship, optimism, hymns, and bucolic joy, were on the other side of the door.

"Get ready for bed, Polly," said Cherry.

Polly got ready, took her candle, with a good-night to this new father she felt half in fear of.

In the other chair, facing his, was Nan, rocking herself.

"Doff my clothes," said Cherry, weakly.

The sickness he had felt at the tea-table came over him like a cold wave.

"Ay. When I've read this," said Nan.

He could see the yellow back of the novellette she had picked up. In the corner was the bed brought from upstairs, so that he would not need to be carried up and down. After the hospital cleanliness it looked almost dirty. The tick of the clock seemed to send the pendulum through his brain.

"I'm tired," he stated simply, after ten minutes, each one an age.

The dreams of what he would do when he got home, out of that hospital bed, were all gone now. He merely wanted to sleep. He waited, until Nan had finished the love-tale, knowing that this was done to tantalise him. For the once, he did not care to wage war. He had not the energy.

Nan ungraciously took off his coat, wheeled him up to the bed, then finished undressing him, turned down the bed clothes and half-lifted him in.

"An' if tha thinks tha can stop me doin' owt I tak' it into my head to do now, tha'rt mistaken," she said, undoing her stays.

Cherry looked at her wearily. '

Feet were gone.

So was laughter.

He would have only ten shillings a week.

To-night he was too tired to take up the gauntlet.

The shrew in bondage was a shrew at large.

Beyond him was a stone wall that limited all his vision.

He lay down before it, and slept, only to wake with his old dream of the iron beast of the glaring eyes coming down on him. Nan's snoring shook his frayed nerves. But at last he slept again, with the degenerate wish, which he felt ashamed of as he wished it, that he might never awaken.

It was ten o'clock in the morning when he awoke. Nan was just moving about in the redness of the kitchen, the blind yet undrawn. Upon a chair before the fire were the clothes he had left at Billy's, on that morning when he was six foot one. Billy had brought them in, now he was home. The long legs of the trousers dangled over the chair. He looked at them in a numbed, thoughtless way whilst Nan made breakfast. Then he said, "When am I to get up?"

He could not get up now without her aid. She dressed him in the way that said she wished him further. Polly was coming downstairs, yawning. It was Polly who set him a bowl of water to wash his hands and face, and pushed him up to the table. As she did so, he caught sight of Nan's look. It was jealous to a degree. Polly's hands pushing his chair to the table gave him the acute misery he had first felt when being wheeled on a stretcher in the hospital. He sat and tried to eat the burnt bacon, to drink the smoked tea. The battle of life in the haphazard house had begun. He was taking his tonic. It was bitter.

On this day he scarcely spoke a word.

He gazed into the fire in the thought-numbed way of the wretched.

Whilst from the yard next door came the whistling of collier Jack, whose wife was yet scolding. He was brushing his shoes to go out. At least — he could get away.

Chapter 5

Cherry comes to a decision

Three weeks of utter dependence, of rising late to do nothing where he had used to rise early to take part in a world of action, of sitting jammed between a wash-boiler and a drab wall, to the destructive criticism of Nan's voice, had further degenerated Cherry. He had discovered that three weeks in a man's life can be an eternity. He dimly felt that he was being hounded down to depths of hopelessness and helplessness such as he had never dreamed life could hold for him. Will Cherry, a man who could break sugar-string on his arm-muscle, sing sea songs, and double his wages by tips. The physical effort of these three weeks had been bad. The mental effect was worse. Such remnants of hope that had clung to him were riven away. Cherry was a practical man. Apart from dogs, he did not theorise. The only books in the house were three in number: "Grace Darling" was a school prize of Polly's; "The Book of Fate and Two Thousand Dreams" was Nan's; the Bible was a present from Grandma Cherry and was sadly disfigured by having once been flung on the fire by Nan because Cherry remarked that his kipper was a little overdone.

In these three books Cherry found no lasting interest, a dissatisfaction in not having been educated was part of the substratum of his dark thoughts, after divers attempts to concentrate on any one of these books.

But, for the most part, he was conscious of making no definite charge against Fate. It was impossible to be definite in the presence of Nan's voice and in this topsy-turvy house.

For three weeks there had been no cyclone.

The street was beginning to feel disappointed.

Every morning and night he had the crowning humiliation of being dressed and undressed by Nan. There were times when it took all his effort to contain himself, as she twitched at his buttons. Moreover — he was conscious that all was not going well with those stumps of his that were now all he could call legs.

Strange twitchings of the nerves would wake him in his sleep. But the days were the worst to bear — the long deserts of naked light, over which sounded Nan's voice, nag, nag, nag, like a jarring clock that had been wound up by some demon away back before creation, and would not stop till the crack of doom, but go on, clank-clank, till a man could not hear any other sound for it, till it pulverised his brain and broke his mighty heart.

It had been washing day.

From ten to four the Cherry castle had been dirty clothes, wet clothes, clothes on the rack overhead, clothes dripping moisture on him from above, clothes rooked round his chair, clothes being folded by Nan, who anathematised him as a lazy hound because he smoked as he sat.

Irony of laughter had been in his heart all day. With the physical weakness, and its ensuing degeneracy of will there had awakened a corrosive cynicism, which perhaps, had he known it, kept him from going mad.

Now — the domestic earthquake around his chair, was over for another week. Next week, he would be there again. And the week after that. And always. Till he got used to it — this rotting, this weakness, this living apart from the movement of the universe.

He was thinking this as he watched Polly dressing up for choir-practice. Nan was washing herself at the sink. Her best clothes were airing inside the fender. Nan would not die deliberately. There was no hope that way. She was now going for a night out, Tanner Fold way.

Whilst she got ready Cherry tried to solve the question that asked why a woman like Nan could buy a picture like "Wedded Love" and hang it up to look down on scenes such as would happen in that kitchen. For Cherry could not deceive himself. Another cyclone was imminent. Nan was unchanged. And — there was no manner of appeal to such a woman. Had there been — the silent appeal of his broken strength, his vanished lightheartedness, would have been eloquent. She was the Stone Age — that thrust the weak children out to perish, that left the sick and aged to die, that had to be wooed by a club. There was no appeal. Had there been, Cherry would have died before making it — to a woman.

He sat watching her put her black hair into a chignon.

Polly was almost ready, flitting here and there between the smoky lamp, humming little snatches of melody, ready for the practice. Polly had tried to tone herself down, in sympathy with her Dad's affliction. Polly could not Billy had teased Polly that the natural history definition of a "flapper" meant "a young duck." It was true. But the "young duck" once or twice had made Cherry something "nourishing," though the first time it was burnt, the second time salt to brininess. After which erratic movements towards helping her father's destiny, Polly's conscience was momentarily appeased.

"I'll be back soon," said Polly, music-folio in hand, and her hat on in the artful tilt that Becky could never accomplish.

"Tooraloo, Polly," said Cherry.

Nan became vigorous in her attempts to get off, when the door closed behind Polly. She stuck green pins in the big, black chignon, laced herself up into an amazing circumference, buttoned her boots with a hairpin, and finished dressing at top speed. Then she stood, in her hat with its great feathers, and the coat that was gaudily green, in the light of the smoky lamp.

"I'm goin' to have a bit of life, I am," announced the Amazon.

"Drop a cob on," said Cherry, referring to the dying fire.

He asked it in the command he had used ever since his first discovery that some women, like some dogs, only obey the command, and won't meet a man on the level.

"Ax God to drop a cob on," she laughed contemptuously.

He was silent.

"What is there for supper?" he inquired.

It struck him sometimes as peculiar how they stuck to the old formulas of common speech, when their relationship had changed so. There he was, asking what there was for supper — when he couldn't get it.

"Oh — a wind-pudding'll do thee good once in a while," said Nan.

She said the words with an intonation that reminded him acutely of his economic downfall. A fire of rage went through him — but comet-like, died out in that negative weakness that would not admit of strong emotions, yet Half-dead men cannot retaliate like lions.

"I'll leave the door for thee," he said, trying sarcasm.

Even his wit had deserted him. It was a thing that belonged to his vitality, it seemed.

"Tha can suit thysel'," she said, gaily. "My name's in the rent-book."

Even as she flung a taunting glance at him, before going down the passage, he recalled that the rent collector had asked him about something or other "being all right," a week ago, and that he had disinterestedly nodded, without understanding.

Nan had disenfranchised him.

He was no longer a citizen.

His lack of interest had been taken advantage of by Nan. She was legally boss of the castle, as she was spiritually its rein-holder.

"Nan!"

He called the word after her, with six-foot-one imperiousness.

The banging of the street door was his answer.

He had fallen another step.

Sitting in his corner, hearing the feet of men and women pass his door, the ignoring of his lot made him feel that he must hurl himself against his four walls. He struggled against this last humiliation he had sustained. But human nature had reached its limit of endurance.

Will Cherry wept — like a little child, with the heart of a man.

She had stolen his vote.

He wiped his eyes on the red and white spotted handkerchief he used to take his breakfast in, to eat in the porter's room. Columbus! It was bad enough to pawn a broken man's watch, his clothes and his phonograph; but — to pinch his vote! What would come next?

When it was over, he looked around the little kitchen as if to assure himself that none had seen his weakness. Moses and Daniel were sublimely unconscious of this human display. But he felt a greater depression on account of having given way to it. A woman had made him "bawl."

He sat regarding the cinder-choked hearth.

By virtue of his past supremacy he had kept Nan sufficiently in order to have the house "half-way decent." *Now!* He looked around him.

His depression grew.

The sense that he was going down, down, that Polly and he were drifting slumwards, Tanner Foldwards, with Nan at the helm, became a painful obsession. When dirt increased, on the top of the disturbances, they would be told to quit. Gradually they would drift down into little street, after little street, each slummier, until Tanner Fold got them, and Nan was in her right environment.

In his weakened state the picture became a nightmare.

He had fallen into a half-stupor of sleep and weakness, when a knocking on the kitchen door startled him.

"Eh — I said I'd come if it kept fine," said a comical voice. A comical figure of a woman followed it, staring round-eyed as she advanced into the lighted kitchen. She was stubby, blue-eyed, middle-aged, and wore a straw hat that had once been a man's holiday hat, a man's jacket, and short skirt. She carried a huge, brown portmanteau, dilapidated enough to have been Noah's. It almost dragged her to the earth.

Cherry started at this apparition.

She stared back at him.

Then — she burst out laughing.

"Well," she said, "if I haven't gone an' gotten into th' wrong house. I wanted the house where there's twins."

She laughed again.

Cherry smiled.

She stirred the sense of humour he had thought was dead.

Then she plunged into a long apology, and explanation, and autobiography, all interspersed by the little bursts of merry laughter.

"Eh — them's two nice picters," she said, suddenly, and set the brown portmanteau down, whilst she walked up to inspect them more closely, rough hands on her hips.

"I had an uncle were an hartist," she confided. "Ay, he could paint owt. But he took to drink. They often do. Poor things!" She laughed the comical laugh. She appeared short-sighted and walked to poke her snub nose into the pictures. Then she said backing, "Well, I'll have to go, mister." She took up the brown bag, which flew open, and let out a scrubbing brush.

With a burst of comical laughter she picked it up and thrust it inside the bag, shutting it, and saying to the brush, "Thee keep thy nose in there."

She had seen Cherry staring at the contents of the bag.

"I'm a cleaner," she said, cheerfully. "An' I'm not ashamed on it. Eh, if it weren't for us, some o' them top nobs wouldn't be able to sleep in beds. Poor things!" She laughed the funny, contradictory laugh.

"How much to clean this hole up?" quoth Cherry.

Jane, the charwoman, looked around, screwed up her eyes as if to gauge the extent of the dirt and said apologetically, "Do you think you'd be hurt at a tanner?"

"I don't sweat folk," said Cherry.

"Now — I never *do* sweat," Jane told him. "That's why I've rheumatics. Eh — aren't yo' married, mister?"

She was kneeling down by the brown bag, taking out the sack apron, blue spar, bottles of brass polish, packets of dry soap, and cloths of all textures and colours.

"She's out," said Cherry.

She looked up at the legless man from her kneeling position, shook out a cloth and said, "Oh," glancing round the place again. She had sized up the situation, and looked simple sympathy.

She pushed Cherry's chair into the corner near the bed, whilst she commenced an onslaught on the floor with the broom.

As the dust rose she sang, just as Cherry had used to sing about his work. There was a lightheartedness oozed from her personality that affected even him. Her old skirt flapped in and out of the dust-heaps she made, her blue eyes shone through the dust-mist, the blouse that was obviously a gift and fitted her skimpily, had its sleeves rolled up over arms reddened by much contact with water, and on each wrist was a grimy "bracelet" left from the last clean-up she had been at. The man's hat on her head was tossed aslant and wobbled as she sang:

> "I'm Burlington Bertie,
> I rise at ten-thirty,
> And Buckingham Palace I view;
> I stand in the yard,
> When they're changing the guard,
> An' the King shouts across,
>   'Tooraloo.'

The Prince of Wales' brother,
Along with another,
Pats me on the back an' says
'Come an' see Mother!'
I'm Bert.
I haven't a shirt!
If they ax me to dine I say 'No.'
'I've just had a banana,
With Lady Di-ana,' —
I'm Burlington Bertie,
From — Bow."

The broom was now going with such a good swing to the tune, and she was so happy that Cherry forgot his woes for a moment, and at the end of the song put in a short "bow-bow" that just rounded it off.

Which pleased Jane no end.

She began to ask Cherry questions about his legs. Perhaps the moment had come when the restrained agony of his heart was ready to burst forth. Jane became a safety-valve. Whilst, as she listened, and shook her head, she would twirl a cloth round the brass rod over the fire-place, or brush at the kettle, her head on one side to catch sight of any dirt lurking, her eyes looking frank, childish sympathy, of a very fine order, whilst her mouth let out little ejaculations like "Oh." "Well, if ever." "Eh, to be sure." Her work never ceasing, nor her sympathy of listening.

Then, when he had finished, she astonished Cherry by observing, one hand on her hip and the other holding a blacking-brush:

"They've spoiled a pair, that's what they've done," she avowed, cheerfully.

He stared at her.

"I mean," quoth Jane, "if your wife had got mine, they'd have bin a good-matched pair, an' I don't believe we should have had a wrong word."

She made the awful observation quite simply, staring genially at the man in the corner.

"We" meant Cherry and herself.

Even as he wondered whether or not he should blush she laughed, and he decided he needn't.

"Is he a bad 'un?" queried Cherry.

Herein Jane showed the first signs of discreetness.

"Ay," she nodded, "but — he's mine."

Whereupon she shut up, and commenced to sing the chorus of "Burlington Bertie" whilst she dusted, dusting Cherry's chair, with him sitting in it as unconcernedly as though he had been made of wood.

"Ay," she murmured, on putting the rug down straight to the mark of the now whitening hearth-stone, "God knows why we get mixed up as we do. But we do. But there's a lot o' things we can't make out in this world. Now, some foak says everything has a purpose. Now, what good are cockroaches? Will somebody tell me that?" She picked up a cloth and shook it disgustedly.

When the hearthstone was quite snowy and dry she sat down the fender, glittering with her polish and elbow-grease. In ten minutes all was finished. Cherry took out a small tin box from his pocket and took from it one shilling.

"Nay," said Jane, struggling into her man's jacket "I *wo-ant.*"

But after ten minutes of argument they decided to split the difference. She gave him three pennies from her pocket, as change.

"Eh, I might ha' clean't lamp-glass," she said. Then, "But I've gotten th' offices to do, yet. An' — he's as jealous as a bull." She picked up the big bag, staggered towards the door and said, with almost masculine gallantry, "Well, keep your pecker up, mister. We mun live in hope, if we die in despair. An' — shall I come again?"

Cherry hesitated.

To invite her again might be courting disaster. But the comfort of the extra cleanliness was too tempting.

"Ay. Come next week, at the same time," he said.

Humming "Burlington Bertie" she went down the dark passage, almost falling over the ragged mat, her cheerful laughter coming back to him. Then the door closed.

Polly came in half an hour later.

"Go an' ax Billy Breeze to come in and bring his draughts and his 'Encyclopediae Letters Co' — " said Cherry.

Polly laid down her music and went off.

Billy was not home, but Grandma Breeze would tell him when he came.

Polly made supper, covering the hole in the cloth with the sugar-bowl and the dirtiest places with the plates.

Then she heaved a great sigh and put on an apron.

It was as she was putting on the pan with the fat to make chips that she saw the house had been cleaned up.

"There are angels hovering round," warbled the man in the corner.

Jane, the charwoman, with her light heart and light pocket, and the bad husband, and the great query as to what purpose cockroaches served in creation, had worked on Cherry like a tonic.

Polly could not get the mystery out of him.

So she made the chips, whilst she dreamed as she heard them sizzle in the hot fat, of a dream-farm, with dream-servants, and Adam Wild, whom she would twist around her little finger, whilst she wore silk stockings and ate raspberry jam every day. She made up her mind most firmly that she must wash the blue muslin dress, to-morrow, against the Spring Fair and the Charity. Only three weeks — then she and Becky would adventure in Cherrydale.

Billy dropped in just as the chips were ready, a huge volume under his arm, which, on Cherry's advice, they left until after supper.

Billy wheeled his friend up to the table.

Cherry minded it less than he had ever yet done. But whether or not it was because he could accept favours from Billy, or because of the tonic Charwoman Jane's personality had been, he was not sure.

To Billy this Polly-made supper was ambrosia.

Cherry found the chips rattier fat-sodden, the tea weak, and the bread and butter too inclined to break into crumbs. But he only observed that she was doing well.

It was after Billy and Cherry had argued half an hour on a certain point in the Workman's Compensation Act, as set forth in the "Encyclopaedia Britannica," whilst Polly stitched flowers into a new hat, that the sound of a woman's voice came down the street

To Cherry there was only one voice like that in the world.

It was Nan's.

Moreover, it was drunk.

"Bed, Polly," commanded Cherry.

He was again the man to fear.

Billy took "bob-wires" with the "Encyclopaedia," back exit.

Nan came in with a loud backward fling of the front door.

"Come in, Lizzie," she shouted, at the top of that awful voice. "We are as God made us. An' them as doesn't like us can lump us. We're as good as they make 'em, without paint. Come on. Don't be shy. Take my arm an' call me 'Willy!'" With which remark she staggered in, followed by the woman addressed as Lizzie.

Lizzie resembled a weasel, being red and small of eye, furtive of look, and long-bodied. On her cheek was a patch of brown court plaster.

Nan's chignon was fallen down her back.

The feathers in both women's hats were lank and spiritless. It was raining.

They screeched like a couple of hyenas.

Cherry's rage blurred his vision.

Nan, frying-pan in hand, came up to him and gave him a slobbery kiss. Nan had got drunk to show him how she could please herself what she did with herself.

"That's him," she said to Lizzie, who looked a little sleepy, as she sat by the fire. "He gave seven-and-six for me. I got him for nowt, an' a ring chucked in. An' he thinks he's my boss."

They screeched again.

But after a while, Nan began to cook something in the frying-pan. She still retained her hat, though her green coat was on the floor.

Cherry looked across at the woman Nan had brought home.

Then——"Clear that woman out o' this house," he commanded with his six-foot-one authority.

The end of his apathetic toleration was come. His voice was twisted into that weak falsetto that had sounded when the family offered him a shilling a week each.

Moreover, he saw the two women as four.

That weakness of sight, consequent on the loss of blood, was on him.

He wanted to murder Nan.

But — she did not take up the offence at his command that Lizzie go.

She laughed as at a chained eagle.

His heart began to thump great sledge-hammer throbs of rage. Chaotic pictures of her banging his mother's head against the door-stones, fourteen years ago, of the little coffins that had held baby bodies that would have been men now, *had she cared enough*, came up in and crazed his brain. The kitchen was full of queer snowflakes, varying in size from three-penny pieces to half a crown. All the emotion that had been kept under, which he had thought was gone, rose like a lion now. The indignities he had endured these past weeks — loomed up like mountains.

Then he watched them cut sausage and sheeps' brains, saw them as through a dark glass of enchantment, eating, laughing and screaming — until the woman next door knocked on the wall for order, which made them worse. Lizzie, having fed, fell asleep. Cherry was nursing his wrath.

Nan began to go over the history of their married life. Soon she was a shrieking monstrosity. But it was a reference to his mother that brought Cherry's murder-rage to a head.

"Hell-cat!" he hurled at her.

His uttermost rage emitted only a strangled whisper.

She laughed.

What happened next he did not know — what connecting link led up to the realisation that he and Nan were in conflict, that the cyclone had burst and that she was fighting with him as though he were yet six foot, without mercy. Her thumb and fore-finger hooked themselves in his cheek, via his lip, so that only a low murmur of his rage could be heard, half-articulate. With one hand he held on to the chair. With the other he defended himself and lashed out at the Stone Age woman. He had a dim sense that Lizzie roused from sleep and came towards them, and self-preservation told him to look out for any movement towards his eyes. His strength was evidently more than Nan expected. He got her down by the throat once — her head on the arm of his chair. But Polly's shriek made him lose nerve and lose his grip. He never got the advantage again. Lizzie, Polly, Nan and Cherry were all mixed up, and Cherry looked up, through blood, in a dazed way, to find a policeman within his kitchen and see the note-book. They had disturbed the peace once too often. And his skeleton was out of the cupboard. As for Nan — dishevelled and half sobered, she was asking the policeman if a woman couldn't have a few words with her own husband, in her own house, in a free country.

Polly had apparently gone to the door and cried murder, and the policeman had entered.

To which the man of law merely answered that anything she said might be used against her.

When she burst into a passion of tears and sank on a chair.

Lizzie had slunk away.

The policeman went out.

Polly locked the door after him, on the faces of a small crowd.

The cyclone was over.

Polly bathed her father's face.

Then she went to bed.

Nan crawled upon the bed in the kitchen and was soon snoring. Had he desired to lie down beside the shrew, he could not do so. She had merely forgotten him. Moreover, he felt that he could not have trusted himself not to strangle her had he been near. The patter of the rain came to him as he sat in the chair by the dying fire. The lamp-glass smoked more deeply and the oil stank. Finally, the light died out. In the darkness he sat, through the long, cold hours, unconscious of the cold or the darkness. He was thinking. He was reminding himself that a man with brains needn't be beaten by the Stone Age. He could kill Nan, of course. But that would not be mastering her. So far, even with feet, he had only kept her under. Things were very bad. Before him, like an inspiration, was the face of Jane, the cleaner, as she said cheerfully, "We mun live in 'ope, if we die in despair." He took it as his watchword, sitting in the dark and cold, and thinking more deeply on Nan's moral and spiritual make-up than ever he had thought in his life, walking round and round it and finishing up with the platitude that after all, she was a woman and there should be some way of winning her round. Beside this great feat, even the economic fight looming ahead of him became insignificant. For after all, if he could scarcely live with Nan, he was sure he couldn't live at all without her. He was a one-woman man, just as some men are one-dog men.

Chapter 6

Living it down

Nan did not come too near Cherry's chair during the next day. Her attitude was like that Rag had once shown, on being cuffed for eating a chicken. In Nan's case, however, it was fore-fear instead of aft-fear. That Cherry would "have it in for her," she did not doubt for a moment.

It was as she swept the hearthstone that she noticed its unusual whiteness.

"There are angels hovering round," hummed the man in the chair, and let out further hints, with odd smackings of the lips and winking of the eyes to say what a gem of beauty this feminine visitant of his had been.

Apparently, the ruse had not succeeded. Everything was conjecture.

He was trying to get at Nan by jealousy. She must have a weak spot somewhere. He was trying to find it. But beyond a look of utter contempt, Nan gave no signs that she resented another woman's invasion into her domestic circle.

Cherry felt despondent at the result of his art. He went wearily back to the bashful appeal of Paul to the Macedonians, asking them to give a good collection. Cherry discovered that he liked Paul, his reasoning, his pride in always following his trade of tent-making whilst he continued as an agitator — his magnificent endurance, and cool defiance of prison, lash and doom.

"If we'd had a son we'd have called him Paul," he observed once to Nan.

She started at the confidence.

Their eyes met in a mutual memory of all those little sons, buried one after the other.

Then — hers hardened.

"Every man as is born should be strangled at birth," avowed the Amazon.

For, to Nan, every man born was the inveterate invader into a woman's liberty.

It was a cry worthy of those early Amazons of which the woman-hater is the masculine reflex.

Cherry grinned at the idea of a man-less world. But the brief flash of his old humour faded on Nan answering a knock at the door, to return, followed by a parson — one of those men with feminine voices, and look of super-humility that comes from a sojourn in this wicked world.

Aunt Miriam had sent him.

Cherry anathematised Aunt Miriam as he endeavoured to talk to Mr. Watts. Because he was "downed," weakened, these vultures were after his soul, on the false pretence of giving him sympathy. He sat answering Mr. Watts in "Ayes" and "Noes," and as the parson went out Cherry, felt that cut off as he was, the fibre of his manhood was yet of sterner stuff than that of Mr. Watts. There was the atmosphere of tea-party and mothers' meetings about Mr. Watts.

Noon brought a bundle of literature from the Brand from the Burning Publishing House.

This also, Cherry set down as Aunt Miriam's work. But it was the letter from the Company which engrossed him most. His hands shook as he tore open the envelope. It was brief and business-like, in very clear typewriting that left no doubt of the Company's intention to award him ten shillings per week — reckoning his earnings at the porter's pound they had paid him weekly for five-and-twenty years. According to the Workmen's Compensation Act, they were giving him half of his earnings.

He looked down on the paper, with knitted brow.

Nan was standing, trying not to look concerned.

Cherry told her the contents of the letter.

"When our Polly's gone," she said, "we shall ha' clean teeth."

Cherry blushed.

His body tinged with shame at the idea that before Polly "went" they could feed on her. He had peculiar notions about parents feeding on their children.

"Tha'll ha' to give the dog up," yapped Nan, triumphantly.

For a whole year and a half she had agitated for the removal of Rag. Persistence was one of her savage virtues. In this economic catastrophe that would press heavily on herself, too, she could yet triumph in the near accomplishment of a victory for the removal of the rickety dog.

Cherry stared at her.

He was realising the Titan she was.

He rendered her unwilling admiration.

What a soldier she would have made!

But — she was quite a misfit here.

That evening, as he sat smoking, the sticky Salvation labels bearing the words, "The Meek Shall Inherit the Land," and "Prepare to Meet thy God," which had been stuck upon the jamb-stones, in irony of spirits, by Cherry, he thought out his letter to the Company.

He was making a bid for the whole of his porter's earnings, and justifying it on the grounds that his reading of the word "earnings" included also the tips by which he had doubled his meagre wage. Billy Breeze came in to play a game of draughts, and posted the letter on going out after supper. Billy had suggested that Cherry instead of rotting in the corner, by the wash-boiler, should have a machine made specially for him, similar to one used by a legless man he had seen at Cloughford. In this Cherry acquiesced, saying he would "see Bill right" if he'd order the machine.

Thus started the great battle in the heart of William Cherry — the battle against the sense that ever ridiculed his broken body.

Owing to Billy's assiduous efforts, the machine came in the middle of the following week. For two days Cherry made no attempt to go out on the thing. The wash-boiler assumed havenish qualities he had never seen in it before. It was on a wet morning, two hours before noon, that Grandma Breeze saw him coming laboriously up the flagstones. He had a chalky hue of countenance that alarmed her, and his attempt to smile in the old way hurt her so much that her eyes were full of tears when he reached her.

"Do you think you're fit to be out?" she queried.

Cherry smiled the twisted smile.

"In the pink," said the dwindled voice.

After he had gone she sat down in the yellow-stoned kitchen, and had what Grandad Breeze defined as "a good bawl."

Cherry proceeded on his way through the town.

Heavy mist clogged the air of the streets as he passed through them. He had the strange, almost uncanny feeling that he was in a foreign land, so changed and painful was his journey through the old town. The market-clock was lit up, owing to the murk. It was like a great, leering face laughing at him. He met a few people he had known, and they shed more sympathy on him. He tried to believe that he did not hate them, as they gave their narratives on their personal feelings on hearing of his accident. They were people of Narrowfields, genuine, well-meaning, warm-hearted people. Yet — he hated them. He zig-zagged along on the flagstones, like a man in a bad dream. Women peeped at him, sometimes, through the misted windows. They were sorry for him. Some men would have enjoyed it. He hadn't been built for a cripple. Now, if he had been made like that chap in the next bed to him when in hospital — the chap who didn't want to go home because he was tucked up six times a day by a pretty nurse, and fed and washed like a big baby — how much easier it would have been!

He had all the hard temper of the man facing possible ridicule for the first time.

Every eye that rested on him seemed to prick him like red-hot needles.

He passed outside the police-station.

Some hazy idea of seeing the Inspector about the episode with Nan had been in his head all morning! But, this irritant new sense of self-consciousness unmanned his resolve. He trundled back to the haven by the wash-boiler.

The exhaustion of his journey, physical and mental, was upon him as he rapped at the door.

Nan came and opened it.

She helped him ungraciously up the step with a "Oh! back already" sort of face.

For a moment he wished she had been of the soft sort. Then — with a swift revulsion of feeling he began to think that he was becoming feminine, in his crippled state.

Mechanically he ate his dinner.

But he could not read afterwards, when Nan had pushed him into the corner.

He lay back with closed eyes.

On one occasion, opening them suddenly, from a brief sleep, he encountered the steady gaze of Nan. There was in that flash of a look he caught, triumph, mixed with something he could not fathom.

Whilst the old apathy of weakness — reaction from his first endeavours to grapple with life, that had become a giant all at once, was back upon him, rain set in. In the dead of the night it was always raining. In the morning the dull sound of rain gurgling by the street kerbs came to him. Mist hung on the walls of the stone-yard opposite, and the mallets of the workers in the sheds, stamp, stamp, became to the man sitting motionless in the corner, curiously like the sound of stone men, on stone feet, marching with stony boots forwards, on a great stone road that was — the world. It was a curious fancy. He recognised it as such himself, but he was not sufficiently analytical to trace in his fancy the stirrings of his mind, under the apathy of physical weakness, making a symbolic picture out of those common sounds made by the stone-workers, a picture wherein he was typifying the yet subconscious determination to march on, spite of all obstacles, to some new place in the world, to conquer all things, by sheer will, courage, and "sticking it"

Nan went to Tanner Fold some little time afterwards. Cherry had sent a postcard to the little charwoman, asking her to come in if she saw a chalk mark on the window-sill. As soon as Nan had gone, Cherry got Polly to chalk the window-sill, before she went out to the practice. But she had to be let into the secret. How she giggled. Polly was very busy these days. She was making herself a new dress out of pink zephyr, and a new hat for the Charity, whilst singing-lessons and lads alternately took up most of her nights. The reluctant spell Adam Wild had put upon her was almost vanished, though she looked forwards very much to the Cherrydale Tide that was approaching. She would sit down in the drab, dirty kitchen, sewing away at the pink dress on the old box of a sewing-machine that Cherry called a "crushing-engine" from its din, singing bits of Grand Opera and dreaming flapperish dreams. For her life in the hap-hazard house had never yet been an integral part. On this night, before she went to the practice, she made Cherry a cup of Oxo.

"A1, Polly," Cherry commented, as she took the cup from him.

"Dad!" she said, as she stood quite ready for the practice.

"Humph!" said Cherry.

Polly blushed.

"Do you think I don't care?" she asked, looking at him very straight.

In the sheen of the lamplight her eye took a resemblance to Aunt Dinah's when Aunt Dinah was young.

Cherry looked up, smiling — almost his old smile.

"Well, I do," she avowed, suddenly, passionately.

She had come up to his chair, put her arms round his neck, and was kissing him, whilst something wet touched his cheek.

She was gone, leaving him with an impression of still waters under the froth of this flapper exterior, and with a feeling of surprise, not altogether unmixed with fear. She was the child of that line of Harkers who at times cared too little, at times too much. She had the warmth of heart that belonged to the Cherries. What a combination!

Whilst he pondered it, Jane arrived, with the brown bag — and — a black eye, which she apologetically half-blamed herself for. Tim had done it. But she had been to blame for not covering it up from the air.

Cherry watched her in the same old cloud of dust, a ministering angel of the queerest order. The black eye gave him an odd feeling of revulsion — became an offence, crying out against the light of the twentieth century that could yoke iron to steam. Whilst as she poured out the story of her struggling life, its persistence of endurance, of passive courage that would make all fiction fall before its fact, his indignation made him feel quite sick, until he remembered — that the way of brute force had been his way of dealing with Nan. He stared at the black eye until it made him feel quite sick. He sat in thought after Jane had gone.

Polly came in before her mother.

Nan had not got drunk this time.

If she noticed the change in the kitchen she did not show it — or get wild. Cherry's heart sank. She was not jealous. It was like being against a stone wall, to which one could find no entry, a door to which there was no key.

Every morning for another week she got him up with the same attitude of resenting the job, and every night she lifted him into bed, whilst he gritted his teeth at being lifted by any one — most of all, Nan. There was no danger of the cyclone for another week. Nan was studying election literature. Nan took after Pa Harker in her political views. Nan would vote Blue. She was a great upholder of the Royal Family.

To Cherry it seemed that the grey days were all alike — excepting that washing-day was a little worse than the others. He would say to Nan, sometimes, looking at the clock, "It's like to be after that time."

But it was not.

He discovered that Greenwich time is not the way to reckon time at all, in the matter of living. He struggled painfully to read a little, but his attention wandered. There were so many things to conquer. Nan — and the Company — and, last but not least, himself, the dejected, hating, sensitive, morbid, inward-driven self that was as much of a stranger to him as though some other man's soul had crept into his broken body — with only this exception — that there was the load of bitter memories brought from that past life of his, six-foot-one-life, manly and glorious, to this — wherein he wandered round and round, in a maze of thought, wondering how to get over difficulties that were so simple, when one had — feet.

The days went by without his being the least bit aware that in an infinitesimal degree, he was adapting himself slowly and painfully to his changed conditions — that this agony was killing itself, as do all agonies.

Least of all did he realise that the sight of Jane's blackened flesh was changing his whole philosophy of life. It took another week before that revulsion of feeling he had felt took definite shape in a weak resolve not to hit Nan again.

Chapter 7

Adam Wild

Spring in Cherrydale!

Which is as though one would say, "Spring! in heaven."

Blackbird flutes busy in the silver coldness of mornings that come "at seven"; larks rising from grey fields sparkling under the sunrise with a million beads of dew — larks rising for their brief glory, dropping defeated, rising again for a few seconds longer. Lambs dancing and worrying without end at the teats of their mothers, who can scarce crop the short, sweet grass for them; brooks tumbling head over heels through vivid sluices in the hills; a light breaking out on the face of those little hills, where the young green blades relentlessly elbow the old grey blades, crying out for room, yet more room, eager to come up and breathe the air. The bareness of the country breaks into a few friendly trees at Cherrydale, so that the carrier, standing up on his cart as he drives lazily along under them, is forced to "duck" a little, and even then gets a baptism of cold moisture dropped upon him from those dew-drooping beeches. Cherry blossom in the orchards, blobbed with the same cold moisture, shakes brilliant, pendulous tears into the emerald of the grass below, with the swinging up and down of a speckled thrush, singing, singing, without the slightest idea of why he sings, only knowing that he must. Green fire in the bushes. Blue pools in the sky. Never had Spring danced so suddenly with her sun-lantern upon the little grey village.

Every day brought crowds of birds back.

The April sun felt like May's.

A pair of martins were half way through the building of a home, against the very hinges of Susan Thorpe's bedroom lattice. She did not dare to open it for fear of their ruin. Which her mother said was nonsense, that windows had to be cleaned. But Jabez, sparse of words, backed up his tender-hearted daughter.

Mrs. Thorpe was spring-cleaning. She generally started with Susan's bedroom, and ended with the stones round the family grave, getting them decent against the Charity. There was the same bustle going on in every one of the houses in the village, the farms on the hillsides. Was it not Cherrydale Tide? In some mysterious way there was a link between the Tide that brought fat ladies and lion-tamers and the cleaning of those little houses.

Jabez Thorpe had been out two hours, early as it was, stopping wall-gaps, repairing fences, and shouting at Ned Thom, his labourer, who was slow of understanding. The two men sat now at the long table Susan scrubbed with fine sand every week. They were engaged on the serious work of dispatching pink ham, white and golden eggs, and sippets of bread toasted in the fat, whilst between the mouthfuls they mumbled out a discussion of whether or not a cow should have her dew-lap pierced for a cold.

Susan was kneading snowy dough in a brown dish set on a wooden stool by the shining fireside. Suddenly, the cur on the hearthrug started up, growling uncertainly.

"Who's that?" came Mrs. Thorpe's voice from the scullery, where she was green-washing.

"It'll be Wild," mumbled Jabez. "Saw him reading a pink bill in Betty Harker's window. He said he were bringing thee some mushrooms he'd gotten. For me — they're a bit strong, horse-mushrooms."

Susan stared.

Her father's tone was nettlesome.

"Well, I makes a practice o' refusin' nowt but blows," came Mrs; Thorpe's voice.

The tone of it told Jabez not to be a fool — at least to be as little of a fool as he could.

For as the dawn had crept up he had told his wife that if Wild started coming there again he should want to know what he meant, and should tell him he wasn't going to have his lass upset by any man, or he'd take it out of his skin. Which only proves that Jabez had walked cow-byres so long that he had got into a very simple way of looking at things.

When Adam stepped into the cleanly prosperity of the Thorpes' farm-kitchen he felt a peculiar atmosphere so soon as he set his foot over the brass threshold.

He nodded a nod that included every one in the kitchen, and sat down on the wooden bench under the deep-silled window where Susan's blue and white hyacinths were coming up.

"Tha'rt nearly a stranger, Adam," said Mrs. Thorpe, coming in from the scullery, the red of her cheeks, the green of the greenwash, Jabez's orange muffler on her head to save her hair, giving her a variegated appearance.

"Nay — " expostulated Adam.

Susan went on kneading, after that one look of welcome in which her cheeks had grown less pale.

Adam took from his pocket a bag of mushrooms, whose fresh scent strove with that of hot coffee on the hob.

"By! But they're grand uns," commented Jabez.

His tone, however, lacked some warmth Adam had always been accustomed to.

"Get a dish for 'em, Susan," said Mrs. Thorpe, giving him a look. Susan at once ceased kneading, pulled wisps of dough from her fingers, rosy with the task. Adam watched her with meditative pleasure, her quiet movements, the readiness to smile, the trim figure in its June-blue bodice, the sleeves rolled up to the elbow.

After toppling the mushrooms into the dish she went back to her kneading. But he caught her look on his face, once — a look of pleasure, shy pleasure that he had come again. Whilst her loyalty, her industry, her cheerful content, shone out in contrast against that town-girl whose memoried face yet disturbed him.

There was silence for a little while, after Mrs. Thorpe's thanks.

"Heard from Uncle Nat?" queried Adam, shifting his foot.

"We're getting his room ready," said Mrs. Thorpe.

Another silence fell.

"How's them bits o' bacon o' thine going on?" asked Jabez, obeying a prompting look of his wife's as she helped him to more pink ham.

"Six of 'em are about at the last gasp," said Adam without emphasis. But the muscles of his neck twitched.

"They are — Hanover!" ejaculated Jabez, altering his first thought, on Susan's behalf.

He looked at Adam, his expression losing that cold something he had first greeted him with. Six fine bits o' bacon dying two weeks before ready for market. That touched the vials of his sympathy.

"Tha turns luck back, Wild," he said at length, gloomily, and attacked his ham.

"Seems so," agreed Adam, smilingly.

Jabez looked at him with the admiration of a man who has only known prosperity. Whatever Wild felt he never whined. He worked.

"Well——" said Mrs. Thorpe, sorrowfully.

"Fever," said Adam, shortly. "Going to report."

"Make him a cup o' coffee, Susan," urged Susan's mother. Her motherliness enfolded Adam.

"I've only just had my breakfast, aunt," he said. He always called Mrs. Thorpe "aunt" when the memory of how she had held his mother up to meet death crossed his mind.

Susan slashed the dough across smartly with her knife, covered it with a cloth white as new-fallen snow, and set it gently on top of the steel-topped fender.

She was ideal.

He acknowledged it to himself much as he noted the points of a beast before buying it. But, distraught as he was with the approaching loss of the pigs, he wondered if she would ever be quite so fat as her mother.

"Don't trouble, Susan," said Adam, as she set the kettle on the rackan-hook.

"It's singing," she told him, pleasantly.

It was.

"I'll go along wi' thee an' have a look at 'em, lad," said Jabez.

Adam nodded acceptance of his company.

Whilst Adam wondered if Jabez had been a little riled on account of his not getting a sitting of eggs from him this year, as Susan brewed the coffee in a fat, brown jug, he sounded him on the subject. No, Jabez had not cared about that.

"How's that little cauf?" queried Jabez.

"She's a grand little calf," said Adam.

"She is that" said Jabez.

The gawky man lit up in a wonderful way.

Adam nodded.

"Believe me or believe me not," said Mrs. Thorpe, "Jabe came home fair ill as he hadn't bought that cauf hissel'".

Jabez nodded to say she wasn't far out of it.

"A bonnie thing," he said, with almost poetic feeling. "A rare bonnie, livesome little beast. Didn't I say so?"

The Thorpes had this comical way of asking for each other's backing on most unimportant points, whilst they ganged their ain gait on the big ones.

"Tha did, Jabe," assented Mrs. Thorpe. "Ay, he did, Adam."

Adam nodded to show that he did not doubt their united testimony.

A burst of sun filled the kitchen, showing up its super-cleanliness.

Adam laughed.

"He needn't wish he'd bought her," he said.

Susan Thorpe looked across at the young man with swift-leaping sympathy at worse trouble up at Sagg Farm.

Then, as she saw Adam looking at her intently, she coloured and became over-busy with her loaf-tins, her little hand bobbing in and out of them with the greasy cloth at a great rate.

"Tha doesn't mean to say th' cauf is deein' an' a' ?" said Jabez, incredulously. He had to get out of his chair and stand up in the fullness of his feelings.

"Right as rain," said Adam, slowly, "for all Bob an' I can see, but — she's droppin' her cud in the bush. We opened her mouth, as far as we could, but——"

"Tryin' to look in a cow's mouth," said Jabez, dryly, "is like trying to see what a woman has in her mind."

"Anybody 'd think to hear thee talk——" began Mrs. Thorpe, indignantly.

"Nay, lass," said her spouse. "Adam knows me."

He winked at the young man.

Then both the Thorpes stood gazing at the tower of ill-luck who had likewise risen from his seat.

"Droppin' her cud, is she?" queried Jabez, out of his brown study.

"It's enough to make anybody believe in witch-craft," said his spouse.

"Just harken these women!" gruntled Jabez.

"Say what tha likes, Jabe," she persisted. "There may be such things. I remember my grandmother being loused, an' a cleaner woman never lived. But she shut 'em wi' a boilin' o' pig's blood an' earth fro' a churchyard for I remember her stirrin' it round wi' th' porrich stick——"

"A damned queer thing," said Jabez, "this droppin' her cud. It beats me. Well, I'll just get my coyt on."

He went off, leaving Mrs. Thorpe still describing to Adam the lousing of her grandmother's sheets.

Then Ned the labourer ambled off with a side-wink that might mean anything or nothing.

Mrs. Thorpe suddenly discovered that at the snail-gallop speed she was working she wouldn't have got through her cleaning by next Tide, never speak of this.

"The coffee's ready now, Adam," said Susan.

She was poking the fire up as she spoke.

The rosy light on her country fairness strengthened that likeness Adam had noticed in her to a daisy. She was a pink daisy, now.

They were alone together, netted somehow in the quiet brightness of the kitchen.

He remembered that he had come to ask her to go with him to Cherrydale Tide — almost, but not quite a proposal; anyway, a prudent proposal that left an easy way out for either party. Things were coming to a crisis at Sagg Farm. The yellow-faced man was shouting out for the quarter's interest on the mortgage. After all, Susan was not a Gorgon, but one of the bonniest lasses in the village.

"I've sugared it, Adam," she said of the coffee.

Over the edge of his pot his eyes met Susan's.

They were scanning him with a look of that shy pleasure that had greeted his long absence from their house.

He did not question any longer Uncle Nat's having spoken the whole truth when he told of Susan Thorpe being over head and ears in love with him. The tender picture of her praying for his wheat, came into his memory.

Susan's last loaf-tin was greased and set on the oven-top. She seemed at a loss for something to do, and inadvertently stepped upon the dog.

He decided to plunge — even as his right hand scrumpled into a hard ball, inside his pocket, that pink bill whereon was set down, "large as life," as Granny Harker had said, the letters of the name of the only girl who had ever made him act like a born idiot.

"Soprano: Miss Cherry of Narrowfields."

He was scrumpling it all up and knew it, as he looked at Susan and finally said, "Would you like to go to the Tide, Susan?"

For a moment, in the shock of the surprise, he began to think Uncle Nat had been wrong, after all. Susan's eyes looked aghast at what was next-door to a proposal, then she blushed crimson, and said hesitatingly, "I — don't — know. I——" The eyes turned on him suddenly sparkled in a way he had not thought Susan's eyes could sparkle. For one little flash they looked like another pair of girl's eyes, on account of that sparkly quiver.

"Sarah and Bob are goin'," said Adam.

For as Susan had hesitated he had thought of that paper at home from the yellow-faced man — the date coming nearer, nearer, with every dawn.

Then indeed Susan's eyes lit up with that sparkle that makes the eyes of all girls look curiously alike.

She drew a quick breath of delight

"Oh — yes, I should love it," she said.

She was red and white, and that unquiet look in her eyes made her a little unsusanish.

He set it down to the excitement of being going to the Tide, with — himself. And — he hoped Bob would not mind going along with them, since that took the edge off Susan's shyness.

"You should see Bob bring 'Punch' out when he swings the big hammer," he said, trying to put her at her ease. She was going. She had promised. He mentally snapped his fingers at the yellow-faced man.

"Mr. Wild looks strong," said Susan, in a low voice.

If Adam had not been so jubilant on having got one across the yellow-faced man he would have heard, perhaps, the uncertain, almost tremulous way in which Susan said the name of the brother who never crossed the Thorpe doorstep — or any other doorstep for that matter, save that big house of the moors, swept clean by the wet winds.

"Strong as an ox," said Adam.

Silence fell again, through which, slightly embarrassed, he felt her studying his face again. She was both shy and not shy. He couldn't quite weigh Susan up.

"Well — we'll wait for you by Betty Harker's. No later than seven, Saturday," he said, finishing up his coffee.

He straightened his shoulders in the peculiar way the Wilds had — as if shaking off any tendency to lean long before it made itself felt. Susan noticed again the shadowy likeness to the boy with whom she had once tended sheep on Whitemoor, the boy who had grown into a moor-mad man who could see nothing but dogs, hares, grouse, and who merely said as he met her in the lanes, "Hello, Susan," and passed on, quite forgetful of that time when she promised to marry him, a maiden of eight, answering a man of ten, and — one of the ewes got drowned under their dreamy guard, and Bob was afraid of his father, and they buried it under the red moor soil, and said they had never seen it, so that it was always a great mystery.

He caught the full glance of her eyes as he settled down from that shaking of himself.

Whatever doubts he had had that Uncle Nat was mistaken he had none now. Whilst he could not dream that Susan was seeing herself and Bob, sitting on a stone wall, promising never, never to tell what became of the old ewe, and solemnly wetting their first fingers with their tongues, and drawing them across their throats, saying weirdly, "Is that wet? Is it dry?" according to the most solemn covenant of the northern child.

"Ready, Adam," said Jabez from the doorway, as though he had been waiting an hour.

All through this embarrassed conversation which had endeavoured to be quite natural, they had been able to hear Jabez shouting at Ned across the space of a field, and calling him different names for fool.

"O — " said Adam, meeting Jabez's eye, "I've been asking Susan to go along wi' me to the Tide, and she wonders if you and her mother object."

"An' with Sarah — and — Mr. Wild," said Susan.

Her efforts not to blush were unavailing.

"Oh, that's it, is it?" said her parent.

His old grin had come back.

The barrier between him and Wild was quite gone.

And — Adam tumbled.

Jabez was thinking that perhaps the lad had allowed himself to get sensitive about his ill-luck, that that was the reason he had shunned the farm for some time. Had he known that this was what was driving Adam towards Susan——! Susan Thorpe was the apple of the gawky man's eye.

"No-a," he said, standing with his back to the fire, "I've no objections. Lass, what says ta?"

Whereupon Mrs. Thorpe came in.

"Can you spare Susan a night off to go to the Tide with me and Bob and Sarah?" asked Adam.

He felt that he had almost committed himself, now.

But he was still relieved to think that Bob going left him a creep hole if — if he could save Sagg Farm some other way.

"Lad," said Mrs. Thorpe, laying her hand on his shoulder. "We can allus do without that as we can't get, in this world."

There the matter ended.

"Come on, lad," said Jabez impatiently, after ten minutes, wherein Mrs. Thorpe had returned to the lousing of her grandmother's sheets, and the visit to the wiseman, "let's be goin'. These women! They'd talk till the cows came up."

They passed out into the fresh joy of a spring morning. Between the first field and that hill whereon stood Sagg Farm, they heard half a dozen larks sing. They likewise passed never a wall or fence but had a pink bill advertising the Charity upon it. This, they agreed, was Granny Harker's trumpeting of the *début* of her grand-daughter. At the police-station with its creeper greening over the porch-door, they reported the indisposition of the pigs, and the constable said he would send the "Board" along.

Jabez stayed quite a time at Sagg Farm, for so busy a man. His opinion on the pigs coincided with Adam's. Adam, aided by Thorpe, made a strenuous endeavour to examine the calf's mouth. All to no purpose.

"I should tow on wi' her a bit, Wild," advised Jabez, regarding the animal mournfully. Its evolution from a plump, frisky thing into this sad, thin animal was enough to clinch Mrs. Thorpe's saying that it might be witchcraft. They tracked her wanderings that morning by the cud she had dropped.

When Jabez had gone, Adam set to work, cleaning out and whitening shippens, barns, hen-cotes, in a very determination to beat Destiny at her own game, by work. At intervals he broke off, to go and survey the pigs mournfully, and fret at the tardiness of the "Board" in coming to inspect them.

At dinner-time he went inside the house, where Sarah was "thrang" spring-cleaning. Old Wild was out drinking. He always went at it like a madman as the anniversary of his wife's death approached.

His empty chair waited him in vain, at table.

Bob came in whistling, a young hare held head downwards and Rag trying to reach it, to his amusement and Rag's quivering excitement. It might have weighed three-quarters of a pound. Bob flung it on the table as his share in the morning's work. He had gone out early, leaving the milking to Sarah.

The joy of life inspired by the rolling glory of Whitemoor breathed out of the young man. He had silver catkins in his coat, which he flung off to the whistled tune of "John Peel," sitting down to eat the great dinner Sarah had made.

Sarah looked from one brother to the other in her quiet, troubled way. Bob didn't do right. But he was six years younger than Adam and unlike Adam he had not upon him "the weight of seven kingdoms." Sagg Farm would be Adam's legally, when old Wild died, as it was his virtually, by right of work. Alike in form and feature, there was that unlikeness about the brothers which weaves dissimilarity into faces cast in the same mould. Adam took after the mother who would not lie down to meet death — but must be held up.

He said nothing verbally. But the cloud on his brow was at length perceived by Bob.

"What's th' good of worrying?" he asked, boyishly. "Next year at this time somebody else will be trying to find out if the water supply is wrong here, Adam. Sagg Farm is as good as gone. After all, it's a sort of cowardice to go on fighting when the waves are over you. A sport will give in — and laugh."

Adam answered nothing.

His eyes had darkened in his grim, young face.

But after a time, in which he had fought down his impatience at this inertia, he remarked shortly, "There's that bull wants ringing."

They went out together.

Whatever their differences they always went out like this, good friends at heart.

Sarah set in to get the pictures up, the varnishing of the old chairs done. She had barely started when her father came in. He collapsed upon the settle; sank into slumber — and Sarah went through his pockets. He had let fall strange hints lately.

All that she found was what looked like washing-soda, crystals, wrapped in paper. After smelling them she tossed them in the fire. Suspiciously watchful as she was she would have been horrified had she known they were poison crystals.

From outside came the roaring of the bull, being "rung."

When Bob started to work he could work with any man.

All day they expected the Board of Agriculture.

It came after sundown, in the form of a young man in goloshes and kid gloves. The pigs were dead by this time. Adam had carried them out on the hill-side, ready for investigations. The young man, taking off his kid-gloves, had them cut open from throat to stomach. He tested their hearts, and the bags that enfolded them, and Adam surprised him by knowing almost as much as he did.

Almost!

Not quite.

"It is a great pity you did not think to bleed them," said the young man, "for they would then have been quite fit for food. It was not fever, but an epidemic that taints the blood".

Adam smiled ironically.

When he went into the house he found his father drinking whiskey again, in the barn-like kitchen where the lamp and the flickering candles only served to blacken the shadows and the corners.

"We'll ha' to bury 'em, Bob," said Adam, practically.

Bob went readily enough.

The sun was going down post haste behind the hill.

They had just buried the third when old Wild came out. He cried over the little pigs, stated that it ought to be him, not the pigs, they were burying, protested against their being buried without ritual, and, half a noggin bottle of raw whisky in hand, began to sing (he had been a soldier in his youth) :

"We buried him darkly at dead o' th' night,
    The sods with our bay-o-nets turnin',
By the te-de-de moonbeam's glimmering light;
    And the lantern dimly burnin'."

Which sent Bob into hearty laughter.

But — Adam was too much disturbed by the loss of the pigs, and about the calf he had given twenty pounds for only a month ago, dropping its cud. He went in to read over the typewritten letter from the man whose fingers were closing round — Adam's soul — Sagg Farm, his *grande passion*. Many a man has a more ignoble one than this grand passion of Adam's. But it might be truthfully written of the young farmer that his worship of the place where his forbears had lived and toiled so long was becoming a mote in his eye. It was deadening his conscience to all else but ancestor-worship — perverting all the tenderness the average human being has in him to give out to human beings into tenderness towards what, after all, was only stone, mortar, and black beams, and the soil of one particular hillside.

So far had his mania seized him, so dammed had become his human tenderness towards others of his kind, that he could not perceive any other reason for Susan's acceptance of his invitation to the Fair than love for himself. That there was any meanness in marrying her for that pot of brass that would save Sagg Farm did not occur to him any more than it occurs to a savage to worship more than one god. In short, Adam was well on the road to one form of savagery when Polly Cherry came into his ken. His moloch was Sagg Farm. Sarah killing herself under his eyes, without his seeing it, his bitter thoughts of his joy-loving brother, his colossal condemnation of his father — all tending to isolate him from his kind, whilst he worshipped every cobble in the old farm-yard, every beast that cropped the pastures, every cloud that piled snowily against that green hill, in that lonely, feline love of place that has built up finished things for generations to enjoy. Flesh and blood had come to combat that spell of stick and stone — flesh and blood of the lightest-hearted flapper whoever looked sideways from under her hat. That he cremated the pink bill he had ruined whilst he asked Susan to go to the Fair, only shows how far the spell was working, even as he went forwards with his project of marrying Susan.

He went that night to play Ludo with the Thorpes.

Uncle Nat had arrived — and Susan was knitting him a new pair of socks. Mrs. Thorpe took a hen-pie out of the oven for supper.

He got back to Sagg Farm quite late.

As he went up the hillside he noticed that resemblance it always took in the darkness — to a great head, with two eyes of flame and a mouth filled with fire, too. He carried with him the memory of something altered in Susan from his seeing her earlier in the day, a new shyness, coupled with something almost vivacious, for her. Her laughter was a pleasant thing. Whilst from the others at the farm — from Uncle Nat, down to Ned the labourer, there had been a knowing sympathy.

Late as it was he went into the barn with a lantern, where they had left out one of the pigs. It was characteristic of the man that he turned even his financial loss into a mental gain. He was studying anatomy whilst the others slept — whilst the village slept. Sarah was asleep, still waiting to pour out his tea for him, when he went in. He looked at her sleeping countenance. It worried him, subconsciously. He shook her gently.

"I'm — not asleep, Adam," protested the woman prematurely bent through struggling along with him, to save Sagg Farm, sleeping six hours, toiling like a man — almost looking like a man, save for her soft eyes. Her kinship to the blurred beauty of Polly Cherry flashed across his mind again. The rough redness of her hands annoyed him, accusingly. Did she need to let her hands get like that?

"Go to bed, Sarah," he said, as she sat up, blinking at the clock. "I'll pour my tea out."

She stared.

He spoke as he might have done to a tired child.

"I am — a bit tired," she acknowledged.

Whilst she looked at him in undisguised wonder.

She was taking her candle to go upstairs when the ceiling shook above them.

"Father's fallen out of bed," she said.

Adam went leisurely upstairs.

He came down a few minutes later, and went to the peg that held his cap. Bob was coming downstairs, too, and entered the kitchen as Adam turned round on the mat and said to Sarah, "Fetching a doctor. Old man's tried to poison himself. Don't touch him — or we'll get into trouble."

The door closed behind him.

Bob, white as death, observed to Sarah, "Anyhow, it'll be diluted with lots of whisky. Maybe that'll save him."

Sarah nodded.

The slow tears of a repressed nature stood in her eyes, drying before they could fall.

"If the old man could have had a fresh start — where mother hadn't died," said Bob, "I don't think he'd have gone to pieces like this. It's been torture to the poor old chap to live on here. *Seven years.*"

"Our Adam hasn't bin there — yet," she said, in extenuation. She referred to the ways in which the sons of men love the daughters of Eve.

"It'd do him good," said Bob, who hadn't been there either, for that matter.

They went up to look at their father, careful not to touch him. Sarah sat and rocked herself on the edge of the bed, making never a sound. Weak as water — yet more human, more worthy of love, than the Adam who had said irritably: "We might get into trouble."

"I'm — g-goin' d-down!" said the tender-hearted Bob. He was crying.

Chapter 8

Cherry Tide

"Well! What hesta left thy father doin'?" —asked Granny, who had been waiting for the two girls in the doorway of her shop-cottage.

Polly met Granny's cheery gaze for a moment or two before answering.

Then she said, as she took off the hat specially manufactured to catch Adam Wild's soul, "Oh — we left him peeling potatoes."

Granny stared, looking startled for a moment. The idea of Cherry descending to the task of peeling potatoes gave her a shock similar to that a good Royalist might feel on viewing a king washing his own shirt. Then, on second thoughts, she realised that this was possibly part of Cherry's diplomacy.

"Nay, come in, lass," she said to Becky.

So Becky came in.

The clean, small kitchen where no one could tell exactly where the kitchen ended and the shop began, changed subtly, with their entry. The cuckoo-clock striking made them start, then giggle!

"An' how is them limb-narves of his?" queried Granny, returning to the topic of her son-in-law. Then she said sharply, "What art doin', Polly?"

Polly blushed.

She had been slyly using a face-leaflet.

"I think soa," said Granny, as she put the thing away. "Tha'rt nice enough without powder."

Becky sat with downcast eyes, looking, Granny decided as if she couldn't say "peas". Granny did not care a lot for Becky.

"The doctor thinks he'll have to have an operation," said Polly, patting her hair. Then she put a bunch straight. "When there's a bed empty," she added.

"Oh — ay!" said Granny.

She looked across quite fiercely at John Bunyan, who, with his companion picture John Milton, was blissfully unconcerned.

"Well," said the old Calvinist "What is, is, I suppose."

She commenced to make her stew, in the back-kitchen. Polly and Becky explored the house, the garden, and finally went out into the lanes, to see what kind of flowers — and lads — Cherrydale grew. Incidentally they found black snails and threw them over their shoulders, for luck. Then they wandered back again. Granny gave them macaroons to fill their mouths, and a love-tale each to fill their minds.

It was whilst Granny was yet busy filling the white-lined dishes that a step sounded on the cobbles just outside the door.

"Polly," called Granny. "Just serve 'em, wilta?"

Polly reluctantly laid down "Parted in the Church Porch."

Her inquiring eyes stared full into the Airedale-brown ones of Adam Wild.

Becky looking up from her book, recognised him, and got behind it again.

Polly was very pink.

It seemed to her that her face and neck were stuck all over with kisses, made visible to this young man, who was also a little embarrassed. He seemed to have forgotten what he had come in for.

"Gotten stuck, Polly?" called Granny, breaking the awful spell.

Polly's giggle said that she had.

Granny came out, wiping her fat, dimpled hands on a snowy huckaback, and saying "Thi father's reight. Tha couldn't feight thy way out of a sugar-bag, lass."

Then, her good-humoured glance saw whom the customer was.

"Oh — it's Adam," she said. "This is my grand-daughter — Adam, Miss Cherry. Now what's ta think about her?"

She looked at Polly with eyes that said she was the finest lass in the universe, which was somewhat comical after the remark she had made about her a moment ago.

Adam smiled prudently.

What did he think of her?

He hardly knew what he thought — except that her bare neck offended his Puritan instincts. In the broad light of day she outshone that vision that had haunted him of how she looked under the rays of his lantern, the wheat waving behind her. One portion of his brain was standing her beside Susan Thorpe and saying that she was like a half-gaudy petunia beside a daisy, and the other part was listening to Granny asking him if it would not be better if Polly had a bit of a practice before Sunday. He nodded indefinitely. The face skin of him tingled with the sense-memory of his trespass over the girl's face. He had the intensest desire to escape.

Polly went and sat down beside "Parted in the Church Porch."

Adam ordered the tobacco old Wild usually called in for.

"Well — how is thy father?" asked Granny, with sympathy.

Adam frowned slightly.

"Pulling round," he answered.

He did not look over-glad.

"An' how did that cauf go on?" asked Granny.

Jabez Thorpe had been telling her of the beast.

"She had got a nail driven into her under-jaw," said Adam. "They found it — at the slaughter-house, when her head was off."

"Well, tha has some luck!" commented Granny.

Then she said, "I'm fain thy father's pullin' round."

Adam did not second this.

Despite her admiration of Cromwell's iron sincerity in theory, Granny nowadays found it somewhat harsh. Having a heart that may stop at any minute makes one look kindlier on life and people — sometimes.'

Granny changed the subject.

She noticed a holiday look about his attire.

"Going to a weddin'?" she queried, with a wink.

Adam pocketed the tobacco.

"Nay," he said awkwardly. "Only taking Miss Thorpe to the Tide."

Granny saw her great plan of matchmaking, for once in her life shattered. It had seemed to her Adam would have sense enough for two. She had wanted him for Polly.

But all she said was, "Tha might do waur nor hang thy hat up there, Adam. Susan'll have a pot o' brass when she's one-an'-twenty."

The young man reddened.

"Bob goin', too?" queried Granny.

Failing Adam, the younger brother mightn't be a bad match.

Adam had resented Granny's speech, though he said no word. Granny saw it all whilst fixing the weights that had fallen down. Truth pricked, she thought, with genial malice.

Adam merely replied to the query regarding his brother going to the Tide.

"If he gets back," said Adam. "He's over the Gouds with Ted."

"That's thy cousin Ted, Polly," said Granny to Polly.

Polly tossed them a disinterested look from behind "Parted in the Church Porch."

Adam's mind was obsessed with the soft roundness of her cheeks — that peculiar indefiniteness of feature which made it look as though it had been moulded into vivacious beauty, then had a hand laid on that blurred and made it indescribable — all save the eyes, and the round chin with its deep dimple and the beautiful singer's throat. These stuck out in the memory. The rest could not be classified.

"H'm, yes," murmured Polly, politely, and retreated once more behind her story.

"Good afternoon," said Adam.

Becky's book was shaking.

Adam could scarcely have got out of earshot when she went off like a bottle of fizz, and Polly, after a futile attempt to withstand the desire, joined her. Their giggles worried Granny, who tried to find out why they laughed. But all that they would give as the reason was that Becky had christened Adam — "John Willy, from heaven."

Granny smiled.

"If somebody'd make a right fool o' Adam Wild, he'd be a decent body after," she said. "But I doubt he's backed the wrong horse, for that. Susan Thorpe would make a fool o' nobody. Two wise folk weddin' — there's no sense in it. An' Adam's head had that big bump o' self esteem when he were only a bairn, it could ha' been used for a hat peg." With which she went back to the stew-dishes.

As she brought them out and set them on the table, she informed the two girls benevolently that she was going to take them to the Tide. Becky turned green with disappointment. Polly's eyes filled with water. Going to the Tide — with an old woman! Alas! Seventeen looked on the world turned to dust and ashes.

Out of a silence that made her ask them if they'd lost their tongues, Polly inquired casually if Adam Wild was a rich man. All farmers in novelettes were rich.

"He'll be the richest man in these parts, one day, if he can only see for lookin'," was Granny's epigram.

Polly interpreted it literally.

Seventeen and seventy, with a heart that dots and carries one, esteem riches differently.

When Susan Thorpe came in shopping that afternoon Polly studied her points, cold-bloodedly. She was just the kind of girl Adam ought to marry. But Polly had an experience of boy-lore that Susan had not.

"Does she sing?" asked Polly, of Granny, later.

When answered in the negative Polly's spirits rose.

At seven o'clock Granny was sold out, lock, stock, and barrel, as she phrased it. It was ever thus at Cherrydale Tide. She stacked up the fire, donned her bonnet wherein the flaming geranium stood symbolic of her democratic leanings, and brought down her goose-head umbrella. The two flappers had been dressing an hour. Polly had donned the blue muslin in very irony of soul. She had likewise let her hair down and put it in a thick plait — to show that she was a baby, she had whispered to Becky. She did not look far from it either, as she said it.

Granny went out to put up the shop shutters.

Sunset glamour filled the one-streeted village, with the stream flowing through it.

Susan Thorpe was coming along. The sun-glory was on her face. It was an unusually animated look.

"Have you — seen Mr. Wild about?" she asked Granny.

She asked for Adam whilst she was thinking of Bob.

"Down thear — by that cherry-tree," nodded Granny.

Adam had been waiting five minutes and had finally gone out of reach of that girlish laughter from within Granny's shop. It stopped him thinking.

Granny peered sideways as she put up her second shutter. She could just see the cherry bloom, and Adam dark against it.

Susan started back as she saw there were no other people — other than this determined-looking farmer.

"Where are the others?" she asked.

She felt faint.

"When Bob gets on the moors," laughed Adam, "he forgets time. We can be walking on."

Susan was not convinced.

Moreover — Cherrydale would talk.

She stared hesitatingly at the cherry tree.

Adam argued Cherrydale gossips down. He had an idea for a moment that this was the right time to propose to Susan — and that the cherry bloom wasn't a bad setting. But he was so sure of Susan — the moment went by. His determination overbeat the gentle Susan. They went towards the Tide — the many lights casting that glow in the sky, feeble rival of the sunset If Adam Wild had not been so determined to make himself not only marry Susan, but love her, so obstinate on self-conquest, so iron-firm to save Sagg Farm, at any cost, and incidentally, himself from Polly Cherry, thus making this girl's heart the buffer between two unwanted disasters, he would have realised that this white silence of Susan's was a very different thing from that blushing shyness of modesty, or even of fear of gossips.

Absorbed in thinking out a letter that would keep off the yellow-faced man, soothe him down, with Susan trailing along by him in dumb misery, these two wholly estimable young people went towards the folly of Cherrydale Tide.

Four miles of dew-drenched, dew-scented country, blackbird thrilled — and they scarcely spoke a word. And so much may a man's wish be father to the thought that Adam took this as a good augury of their being suited to each other.

During this walk Bob was out ranging on the Clouds, getting into alternate fits of rage and admiration, according to the behaviour of his dog, Ted the organ-blower describing a place where rabbits asked to be caught almost, whilst ever at their heels louped Rag, the pedigree dog. He breathed hard but manfully, walking on his "wrists" as Polly termed his forepaws. Moreover, he wore the leggings. His eyes shone doggy love of Bob. His tongue loppled out redly. He imitated the antics of the dog who was ranging — quite unmoved by the laughter of Bob and Ted at the sight.

After a hard run of fifteen minutes, Bob's lurcher caught a baby hare. Rag seized and ate it, skin and all, in a space of time short of miraculous.

Then — the hunter in him satiated for a time, Bob looked back over the way they had come. *The Clouds.* The moor merited its name at this hour.

He saw the light in the sky and gasped, suddenly, with the horror of a pleasure-seeker who had almost forgotten a treat in store. "Cherrydale Tide! Let's hop it, Ted."

They "hopped it," Ted keeping his eye skinned for the gamekeeper, all about them the darkness of the moors — that cloudy soberness, save where the moor-pools filled with the gold of sunset and the vapours of the sky leaned a rosy cheek against the dark earth. The curlew's on-the-wing cry seemed to float out of infinity.

Bob was utterly, gloriously happy, with a happiness Adam's struggle could not invade, nor his father's weak folly, nor Sarah's worriting lest he be caught poaching. Whilst even at that moment, there was fluttering to the Tide a "petticoat" destined to invade the peace of that debonair mind. Never again, never again, it was written, should his eye look on the Clouds with quite the same free anchorite's feelings roused in mind and heart.

Henceforth, the moor would speak to him with a new note — that was after all only the echo from his own soul.

Ted went to Sagg Farm whilst Bob "dressed up" for the Fair, if pulling off a silk muffler, putting on a front and tie can be described as "dressing." Old Wild was laid on the settle. Sarah had just come in from putting the hens up. She had an old overcoat of Adam's on. Sarah always made Ted feel sorry. Femininity had died in Sarah — under that task of working to save Sagg Farm, at Adam's relentless pace. She looked so like a man that it was not wonderful that Adam forgot she was a woman. She walked like a cow.

She went nowhere beyond the farm and its fields — unless it was on a "sticking" expedition, after a windy night. She rarely spoke — unless spoken to, about work. She was that tragic thing — a farm drudge, doing two people's tasks, and in addition, responsive to Adam's care, Bob's moods, her father's weaknesses. She was a woman under those masculine things she wore, troubled about many things, and, as all the village said, faced with the workhouse if ever Adam married, and his wife did not "take to her."

"Going to th' Tide, Sarah?" queried Ted, with that awe of her on him.

Sarah laughed.

It was tired laughter, untinged, however, by bitterness.

"I think," she said, "I've got past that sort o' thing." Ted counted her up on his fingers. She was twenty-eight — just a year older than himself. She looked fifty.

Ted went out, thoughtful, as he always felt after a visit to Sagg Farm.

"Couldn't your Adam find a farm wi' less work an' better pasturings to it?" he queried.

"Lots," said Bob.

"Then why——?"

"Adam'll stop by Sagg Farm till it drops on top of him," asserted Bob glumly. He met Ted's eye.

"Because," he answered it, "it's Sagg Farm, and he's named after the first chap took it on. It's a fancy. The iller it does the closer he sticks to it — like some fools of women sticks by ill husbands."

They went down the glimmering hillside, over the wishing-bridge, along the road, through the now deserted village. At the end of their second mile they came upon Granny and her charges. Granny was "winded." She sat under a hedge. The girls had bidden her "rest" — but were thinking unutterable things.

"Why — it's my cousin Polly!" ejaculated Ted.

Whereupon Granny got up, took his arm, and left Bob to Polly and Becky. They walked one on each side of him, according to town etiquette. Ted pitied the shunner of petticoats, going gawkily along between the two girls. A queer Bob this, compared with that one who sang "Drake's Drum," roaring it out above the blowing of the moor-wind, to the accompaniment of the whitened rushes, the shaggy bents, the whirr of moorfowls' wings.

He was still mum at the end of the third mile.

Whereupon Polly made some remark Ted could not overhear. But he saw Bob look at her with less of instinctive distrust of petticoats. Bob began to talk dogs to her, a distinctive mark of favour.

And Ted set his fair cousin down as being as fause as a rat — nay, fause as the fausest rat that had ever holed.

But all Polly's fauseness was only softly-smiling interest, and the upward glance that, when properly accomplished, makes the mere male realise himself as a very wonderful being.

When they reached the first street lamp, and Bob saw the face of this girl to whom for half a mile he had been talking — worms — and areca — he collapsed, mentally.

His ear tips grew scarlet.

They went on towards that pandemonium of sound made by six roundabouts playing six different tunes, interjected by sirens shrieking, drums beating, roaring of lions — and above all this, the laughter and talk of half the people from half a score villages round, and an exodus from Narrowfields.

It was the Tide.

Into it, trembling for her bunion and her purse, they piloted Granny Harker. Cherry had asked her by note of hand by Polly, to keep her eye on the girls. She wondered what that Narrowfields doctor would think of her living a quiet life if she wished to live, as she struggled in that Tide of laughing, joking, swearing, horse-playing merry human beings, who had temporarily turned into irresponsible children. Callow youths tickled Granny under the chin with ticklers on wire, and asked her if she'd brought her goloshes. Red-faced men with hoarse voices hawked the aigrette-like ticklers. A fat man staring about him in bewilderment as to how he should get out of the Tide now he had got in it, trod on Granny's bunion — and she asked him to look where he was going — to the laughter of all about them. It was at this moment that a young man touched Polly on the elbow. "Oh — hello, Peter," she said nonchalantly. Peter attached himself to the party. It was the Tide where "more and the merrier" is watchword. But Bob looked suspiciously at him, nevertheless.

Bob made the bell ring every time in the shooting gallery. Bob hitting pasteboard rabbits that hopped aggravatingly slow, then flew aggravatingly fast as the shot went, Bob winning a cake-stand for Granny in the deceitful tub-throwing game — and paying three times as much to get it as it was worth, Bob trying to resist the call of the girl in the green blouse, "Once through the mouth and you get your money back," became a figure round which the gaping crowd gathered. He was so light-heartedly earnest at a Fair. It became a matter of life and death to him that he knocked down the pipes in the grinning, open-mouthed cardboard face. Yet he was laughing all the time. Whilst into his pocket ever went his hand, and he had quite forgotten that he was spending part of the egg-money belonging to Sagg Farm. But when he brought out Punch, and was patted on the back by the old chap with the machine that registered the force behind a man's hammer blow, when the old man said, "My lad, that's the first time Punch has come out *this* Tide" — Polly hung on to Bob's arm, to let the admiring young women standing around know that this muscular fellow was a great friend of hers. Whereupon the young women measured Polly, and looked at each other as much as to say they wondered what he could see in her. But then, when they got into the lion-show, and the beery-looking man with the imitation tiger skin over his shoulder, standing on a stool and looking over the heads of the crowd, made his sublime speech before going in to the lions, Polly let go of Bob's arm — and Bob felt lost, abandoned, the sun gone out. It was in vain that he told Polly all this was flap-doodle, that this speech was made every time, that the lions were as harmless as cats brought up in a Dolly Varden hat.

"Think of the courage, patience, perseverance, which it has required to subdue these noble creatures of the jungle," wound up the beery-faced man.

Granny didn't think they ought to be allowed to go into lions' dens, though, truth to tell, she would have been very disappointed had anyone stopped Lorenzo from going in. Polly closed her eyes and said she dared not look, but could not help opening them as Lorenzo worked up the lion, whilst Bob wondered that an old woman so plain as Granny could have a grand-daughter so beautiful.

"He's to do that to make 'em look wild," he assured Polly. "Tame! Tame as shrewmice."

Whizz-bang.

Lorenzo just got out as the lion's paws came crashing against the door.

"I wonder what we should do if one got out," grinned Ted. "Rummy Tide it'd be!" Which made Polly turn pale, and Bob assure her that lions never did get out of cages.

Peter, left to talk to Becky and Ted, caught Polly's eye once. She grew quiet under it. Peter was putting in a claim.

As for Granny, she had summed Peter up as a young man who wore gold hoops on his fingers. Never, in Granny's long life had she known any young man who wore gold hoops on his fingers do any young woman any good. They left the lion-show, just in time for the circus. It was a struggle to get up the steps through that crowd.

"I wonder how much a week *he* gets for makin' a fool of hissel'," quoth Granny, of the clown.

The lady in the blue tights and spangles began to beat a drum then, and drowned everything. Bob paid for the party — more egg-money! They stumbled down into the circus, smelling of sawdust and paraffin torches, horses and guinea-pigs. Polly sat on a long box next to a red-faced man who looked half-seas over, according to Granny, who liked to talk as if she had been in the Mercantile Marine. Once Polly wondered what there was in the box. "Guinea-pigs, no doubt," said Bob, and sat down on the other side of her. It was a true old-time circus. First came the lady in the blue tights, leaping on the white pony's back, waving a ribbon, cheered by the crowd, the villain with the rose cracking his whip to make it throw her. Which made Granny wish it would kick him. Then came the boy in ruby velvet, whom Granny liked to believe was the son of the lady in the tights, as he would be a bit of comfort to her, poor thing, having to jump about like that for a living.

The young man in the ruby velvet said he would place on his forehead, his knees, his throat, his feet, a glass of wine, without touching it with his hands, and afterwards drink it. Which he eventually did — really very clever. Though one astute countrywoman said it was amazing he was not drunk, seeing he was doing this all day, if it was wine.

"Ooo, Becky," murmured Polly, as he rose with a great and noble air. The youth in the ruby velvet made a collection for himself, which was vaguely explained by the villain with the rose. But nobody minded. Was it not the Tide? Polly was in such a flutter when he came to her that she gave him half a crown instead of a penny. But even that was forgotten as the thinking pony, shining like brown satin, trimmed with pink paper roses, and looking exceedingly knowing, was led into the ring.

It is quite true that the pony told the time of day.

He also told the time it was by a gentleman's watch — that was a quarter slow. His white foot struck the minutes, when the villain with the rose told him to, and then the hour.

"Well, if ever I saw——!" laughed Granny, leaning forwards, and giving a bald-headed man in front of her a crack on the head with her cake-stand. Whereupon the bald-headed man's wife made remarks about some people having been brought up in a wood. Whereupon Granny gently rubbed the bald-headed man's head — and said folks with soft heads shouldn't come to the Tide, and there might have been a free fight ensue, but for the pony coming round at this moment.

"Find me the gentleman who would rather drink a pint of beer than go to church," said the villain with the rose, darkly.

There was then great consternation amongst the young men who were total abstainers, lest the pony make a mistake, and their sweethearts believe the pony. Grins, and complacency amongst the men who valued a pint of beer, and didn't mind being selected. Round and round, in a great hush, went the pony. He stopped once before a young man with a white face and eyeglasses. Protests from the young man with the glasses — hysterical giggles from the women round him, then — the pony went on, and the young man breathed again. But at last the pony stopped. He stopped in front of the red-faced man seated beside Polly.

"Is it the gentleman on the back row," said the villain. Pony shook his head decidedly.

"Is it the gentleman sitting on the box?" quoth he.

Pony ponders gravely, then nods fiercely, three times.

"That's right," guffawed the man next to Polly Cherry.

"Well, if ever I——!" laughed Granny again, but managed to keep the cake-stand off the bald-headed man this time.

How the pony selected Polly as the young lady who was deeply in love, to her indignation, need not take long to tell. How the party went out, after discovering that Polly had been sitting on a box of serpents, on which she would sit down no more, though the serpents were then round the neck of the villain, and how Bob went into a show that had nothing to show but a freak pig and two distorting mirrors, also need not take long. Though, by telling the crowd outside what a rare show it was, and getting them in, to take others in as a Cherrydale Tide joke, set the drunken show-man on his feet again. Whilst the noise grew louder; lights burnt brighter;

more and more people surged up; and the young folk went on the switch-backs, flip-flaps, or rocking horses, in the swing boats, only Granny would not "have a packet" as she said folk were "put together so queerly." But after they had topsy-turvied, she went in with them to see the lady with the leopard spots, who apologised for not being able to show further than the waist. How Polly got into a peep-show, after great argument with the show-man, who said she had her hair down and they might be prosecuted, until Polly solved the problem by pushing her hair under her hat, remains to be told, and how she said to Bob, after they came out, "All that fuss! Just to look at people pulling their stockings up." Which made Bob laugh, and realise a soul of exquisite innocence, cunning as she thought herself. But Granny had not liked the demeanour of Peter in the show of the leopard-spotted lady.

Granny began to speak of going home.

Her heart was dotting and carrying one.

Her bunion had been jumped on four times — and she had begun to realise Tides were not good places to which to bring bunions.

They reached the "Mayflower" — that big boat that was visible all over the Tide, going up and down, with its shrieking load of girls, taken in by lads who mocked their shrieks, and truth to tell, got them in so that they had a good excuse for putting their arms round their waists.

"Going up here?" asked Bob.

"Polly! It'll topple thee out," said Granny.

But Polly went, when the boat stopped, up the shaky scaffold-like steps, Bob holding her safely, the others coming behind. Into the "Mayflower" these pilgrim souls of youth stepped, adventuring as those graver souls of long ago adventured. Up the steps. Still they came, whilst a couple of grinning beefy-faced giants waiting to pull the ropes thick as polonies, called in stentorian voices: "This way for sailing."

Peter sat in the stem, with Ted.

Bob, Becky, and Polly, were at the bow.

The middle of the boat soon filled.

There was only room for two at the bow.

Polly was just quivering, thinking they were moving when Becky whispered, "Oh — John Willy from heaven."

Adam Wild gravely piloted Susan Thorpe towards the only seat. He found himself between her and a girl in blue muslin — and a large hat that touched his face.

"Why, Addy!" called Bob, in surprise.

Adam at the Tide with Susan Thorpe was an earthquake to Bob.

Susan Thorpe's eyes were like bits of dark velvet in a tired, white face.

"Sit down!" yelled the rope-pullers from below. "No standing up."

Much pulling by the two panting men below, then — the "Mayflower" began to go, got a soul into her. The fun commenced. Polly's was the first shriek that rang out. At the sound of it Adam recognised the girl in blue muslin. A shriek like that in a murder-scene would have made an actress her fortune.

"Hold fast to the irons," he told Susan Thorpe.

She linked her arms around the protecting rails behind her.

The occupants of the boat saw the Tide become a multi-coloured mass — swimming lights. A chorus of shrieks rang out now, as she went up and down, to the cat-calls of young men, the mimicry of those rope-pullers below, whom the girls thought were now talking a personal spite in sending her higher, yet higher.

Polly's laughter, Polly's shrieks rose above the others. Paler and paler went Susan Thorpe as she clung to the unsympathetic irons. Cherrydale Tide was almost upside down now. People standing below said it shouldn't be allowed. The great irons that poised the boat creaked. Those in the bow looked down on those in the stem, those in the stem then looked down in the bow.

"Ooo! Ooo!" cried Polly Cherry, growing too terrified to shriek, yet still enjoying it — in a terror of delight going to perdition, yet——

Then — down she came, down, down into the uttermost gulfs, and — Polly had seized blindly on to the arm of Adam Wild, her face buried in his coat to shut out the awful sight of the Tide below them. Her muslin sleeves flapped against his face. He sat stiffly upright so as not to have the touch of her hair in his eyes. Whilst the sirens of beauty and of song called to him, as they have called to man from immemorial ages.

On the other side of him industry, modesty, wisdom clung more tightly to the rails, her face twisted into a brave smile, her lips twitching, and Peter, looking down on Polly from his end of the boat, saw a flushed face lift itself from Adam's chest, recognised the farmer as lights from a roundabout streamed momentarily over his face.

Giddily they came down to where Granny was waiting.

There was a great introduction.

"Safe on terra-cotta," laughed Granny. "By! Anybody as goes in there ought to be insured."

Then they set out back to Cherrydale: Adam and Bob, Ted, Polly, Becky, Susan and Granny — all but Peter, who was training it home.

Through the silver splendour of the spring night they walked back to Cherrydale — the blare of bronze roundabouts' trumpets fading away under the cold, tiny voices of brooks, whispering of grasses, silences singing between, save when they spoke of all they had seen.

"Ay. It's a bonnie neet. One more an' one less," said Granny meditatively.

"It'll be too late for Polly to practise," she said later, but Adam said it wasn't too late for him.

Susan Thorpe would not go up to Sagg Farm.

Adam took her to her own farm-gate.

Bob, Becky, and Polly were gone up to Sagg Farm.

"Enjoyed thyself, Susan?" asked Jabez, as she sat down.

She had been rubbing her cheeks with her hands all the way across the fields, to give them colour before going in for her parents' inspection.

"First rate," she said briskly. "But, I'm tir't. I'll go to bed." She fled before that colour, brought by the rubbing of her hands, had faded.

Whilst round the yellow-keyed harmonium in Sagg Farm kitchen a quartet of young voices rolled the "Hallelujah Chorus" down into the silence of the night. Then Polly sang her pieces for the morrow. And as she sang, she became again the tender priestess of song, joyful song, untouched by the sordidness of the drab kitchen at Narrowfields, caring nothing for lads, scent bottles, and cheap trinkets. She was youth, singing, with its face turned towards the sun. But even so had sung all the Harkers, but one — whether they sang in choirs or pubs.

Whilst the organist's heart followed that fresh voice as a bird follows the fowler's cry —

"Youth and Song and Beauty!
A trinity of gifts, surely."

But — not gifts that would make her a helpmeet for a poor farmer.

Rag went delirious on Polly meeting him again, by light of a lantern upheld by Bob near the kennel. Polly was touched, too, but giggled at sight of the leggings Rag slept in.

Adam let Bob take the girls to Granny's cottage.

After Bob's return Adam found one of her white gloves — violet-perfumed.

He kept it until he saw her make eyes at the tenor and the bass at the Charity, next day.

Then, as Bob said he was going down that way he asked him to call at Granny's and give it to her, once of the girls having left it. Bob accepted the ambassadorship. But when Granny asked Adam, later, if they'd seen aught of a white glove at Sagg Farm, as Polly had lost one, he prudently said "No." Bob had kept it.

The siren had left it — as her challenge.

Bob had taken it up.

Polly went back to Narrowfields in high spirits, satisfied with her work. Adam and Bob had words about the egg-money. Susan Thorpe was sent by her mother to get a recipe from Sarah. Sarah was gathering eggs. Adam was gone for provender to town. Bob asked Susan the best way to catch a girl — confessing that he knew more about rabbits. She looked so demure, such a little Quakeress that Bob said, "Give me some tips." She smiled and he thought she looked somewhat delicate in the morning light. Before she left she was well on the way to being his mother-confessor. He was to tell her the progress he made, and she would advise tactics. When Adam came back from town Bob was working industriously at a fence, capless, singing gayly:

> "Oh, take when you can,
> The word of a man,
> But in love — the advice
> Of a la-dy!
> Fal-da-la-a; fal de-la-a;
> In love — the advice of la-dee."

Chapter 9

Cherry loses his case

Polly went back to Narrowfields in high spirits. Had she not left behind her a challenge in that scented glove? She had likewise left a copy of "Whisper, and I shall Hear," on the Sagg Farm harmonium, the said copy having her address in the left-hand corner.

She arrived home on the edge of dark. Involuntarily, as she entered the little street, she listened for her mother's voice, shouting anathema at her Dad, the street, and the world in general. But all was calm. Either the storm was over, or had not burst.

The odour of hotpot met her as she opened the door.

The drab kitchen had on it an additional gloom, arising from a cracked lamp glass, and a consequently lower light The economic struggle that had always existed in this house was of so naked a character now, that, skeleton like, it grinned and rattled.

Cherry was trying to read, by the firelight.

His strained intentness of expression faded somewhat as he perceived Polly.

He winked to show that he observed her, and laid down his book on the wash-boiler.

His winks had become "stagey" things now, hard to believe in.

"Well, how's Granny Grunsticks?" he asked, trying to be sociable.

Polly was just opening her lips when Nan bounced out of the little scullery.

"Oh, tha'rt back again, arta, bitch?" she asked. "Hunger brings th' crows to the nest."

Polly took off her hat.

Her countenance spoke a great reaction from a childish delight in having had a good time, to a hopeless protest against having returned to a bad one. Her way of setting her headgear on a blue ornament her Dad had won at a Tide long ago showed the easiness with which she sank under pressure of this negative atmosphere.

Nan dashed back into the kitchen, on some pretext or other.

Cherry mustered a smile.

It was sometimes hard to go on taking Nan as a joke. She was such an interminable joke.

Then, he saw Polly suddenly recover her equilibrium.

She got out plates, proceeding to warm them.

"Where hesta learnt *that*?" quoth Cherry.

He never saw any one kneel on the fender and warm plates without remembering his care-free life before he had met Nan — at the Tide. His little mother had used to kneel so.

He felt a spur of interest in Polly's following of the great cardinal point in all good cooks. Sometimes he found himself getting interested in things. But his interest was of a flickering, evanescent nature. Before Polly could answer, he no longer cared to hear the answer.

"Oh — I saw some one do it, at Cherrydale," said the girl.

As she spoke she had the vivid memory of Sarah, like a tired mummy, kneeling on the fender of the great, sanded kitchen — and a companion picture of Adam, handsome in dark blue coat, looking across at her visioned self, like a man stock-taking.

It was Polly who set her hands to wheel her Dad's chair to the supper table. But Nan came up at that moment, gave her a thrust that almost hurled her over, and took control of the chair herself.

Polly gave a faint giggle.

The man in the chair looked dazed — wonder at what was happening. Then he sank back under the cloud-cap of physical and spiritual dejection.

In the old days he had liked his meals. They made strength — to go on working. Now — he sat drumming whitened fingers on the table, waiting for his portion. But he strove to cheer Polly up, after Nan's left-handed greeting.

"How's Champion Ragus Divibus Rattibus, offspring of Champion Crompton Orang?" he asked.

It was the first direct inquiry he had made about his once great passion.

Forthwith, Polly gave a spirited account of Rag, the kennel, Rag's having been cured of worrying cock chickens by having one hung around his neck for a week, of his leathern leggings, made by the village cobbler, giving him the look of a dog turned commercial traveller. Cherry smiled. He half felt he'd like to see Rag in those leggings. But Polly was compelled to say that she didn't see that he walked much better, amending this, however, by the statement that he was jumping up most of the time, so perhaps she couldn't see improvements.

"We're liable for licence," said Cherry.

He stared down at his steaming hot-pot.

"I think we've enough on here, without dogs," yapped Nan.

The common sense remark, that in any other would have been a simple reminder of the economic pressure, became an insult from Nan.

Cherry's burden of dependence crushed him, like a concrete thing. He went on eating, perfunctorily, but the savour had gone out of his food.

He pushed the half-empty plate away, listlessly staring at the picture of "Wedded Love" on the wall, the ideal, the strength of the man supporting the weakness of the woman. Nan had never been weak. But he had provided for her. He had nothing to share with her, now — and they were both of them living on Polly. He sat staring at the picture, painted by some well-fed artist — and quite suddenly, it melted away, and beyond it he saw a world of jungle law, where old age vampired on the young, the young on old age, people feeding on one another as it were, not just the rich on the poor, but the poor being made to feed on each other — children, even, watching one another's mouthfuls enviously, young *cannibals*! For Cherry, scarred by great hurt on great hurt, was now a mass of quivering sensations, morbidly quick perceptions, where he had been a robust giant, without time for deep thought, or even for deep feeling. Cherry, in his own words, was "off his trolley."

"Aren't ta eatin' that?" queried Nan.

He felt sick.

"No," he said.

He felt yet more sick.

The scraping of her spoon on his plate went through him.

Then, he had one of the quick revulsions of feeling common to him. He became conscious that the fibre of his manhood was going. He was feminising. Did all cripples feminise? Better to brutalise, he thought savagely as he was wheeled to his corner.

Polly, after clearing the table, unpacked the generous parcel Granny had sent with her. To her Dad she handed a colouring pipe and a quarter of a pound of plug tobacco. There were a pound of Cherrydale sausages for Nan and "Parted in the Church Porch." For Polly there were six bottles of scent, that Granny had found she could not sell.

Whilst Cherry stuffed the pipe with the tobacco, Nan was watching him.

She could not discover whether his "singing low" of this week-end was submission, or diplomacy. Cherry looked up, and caught her glance. It reminded him of the admixture of triumph and suspicion a cat shows towards a half-killed thing.

He winked the comic-tragic wink in response to it.

For quite a long time there was silence in the kitchen, broke only by the fluttering of the pages of Nan's novelette, and the puff-puff of Cherry's pipe. He had been in tobacco-starved misery all the week-end. Perhaps the pipe cheered him, for he again took up Southey's "Life of Nelson" which Billy had said was man's meat.

"What's that tha's gotten, Polly?" asked Cherry.

Polly had given a little excited exclamation.

She flushed.

"I bought a 'Raphael's Almanac,'" she confessed, haltingly, "to see if you'd won your case, Dad. Listen! It says, "A good day for seeking favours, dealing with superiors, women, and the Law".

Cherry looked at the irresponsible one.

"One woman's enough for me," he said.

Polly giggled.

Nan looked at him suspiciously, as one pondering his sincerity.

"For *Law*, Dad!" said Polly.

Then she said, "I'll brush your clothes."

On the morrow was Cherry's great ordeal in the Borough Court.

"Thee mind thy own clothes, bitch," said Nan.

Which astonished Cherry a little.

But before he could do more than wonder, Billy Breeze knocked, and followed his knock, cap in hand, and his usual amiable bashfulness in his eye as he saw that Polly was in.

"Well, how are we?" he asked, in the excess of vigour he always used now, so as not to appear down-hearted.

Cherry understood Billy.

"In the pink," he said.

Billy sat down in the chair near the sewing-machine of the battered box.

"Ready for morning?" he asked, lamely.

Billy had his cap between his knees, like a little lad; he was studying the floor critically. The Union had selected him as the fit and proper person to ask William Cherry if his case failed on the morrow, whether the Union should fight the thing for him in a higher Court. The Union had been astounded to hear that it was possible that "earnings" might be inclusive of tips, according to English Law, and that every man hurt, therefore, might totalise his earnings as inclusive of such, and claim double damages. It was worth a fight, if Cherry's case could create a precedent.

At last, Billy burst out with it.

Billy had no more tact than a guinea-pig, and was as transparent as glass.

"If we don't pull it off this time, Cherry, old man," he said, blushing, "better luck next time."

Then, he unburdened himself of the task laid upon him.

Cherry stared across at him, with a little of the look he had turned on Uncle Silas.

Billy suddenly got an inspiration.

"Cherry," he said, earnestly. "A man should sometimes look on himself impersonally. This is a fight for the next man."

There was a long silence.

Billy realised it as Cherry's assent He had spiked the proud man's guns.

A great relief was on him as he went out He had struck a blow for his mates' well-being, and still possessed his friendship.

Nan hung Cherry's clothes over a chair.

Cherry had almost beggared himself in paying for them, out of pawn, for this occasion of the morrow.

Polly carried a candle, and her new hat carefully upstairs.

"Good luck, Dad," she called down, midway.

"Tooraloo, Polly," he said.

The colouring pipe and Polly's return had made him feel more of a man, somehow. In these devitalised days little things made such a difference.

Nan was already undressing herself.

The way she ripped at her stay-laces made a sharp whipping sound in the stillness of the kitchen.

"If it's only ten shillings a week thee gets," she threatened, "I shall take a child to nurse."

Cherry made no remark.

He got dog-tired at this hour.

He waited, in sick, demoralised fatigue, until Nan pushed his chair to the bedside. Then she took off his coat with the impatient gestures usual to her.

"Tha'd be in a poor way without me," she said, unloosing his collar.

It was the triumph of the Amazon over the mere male.

She had got him under, now, and didn't mean to let him forget it.

His blue eyes looked at her.

The dim light of the broken-glassed lamp was over them both — the woman taunting, the man's face giving no index to whatever he felt.

Then a contemptuous nobility flashed lightning in that blue eye — an indescribable look of triumph even in debasement, before which Nan's sloe-dark eye dropped its lid. It was the look of one physically bondsman to a lesser man, who was mean even in triumph.

It flashed for only a few seconds.

She gave his collar a peevish toss across the house.

Then — pushing his chair to the bed she watched his pitiful scramble from chair to bed, hearing the gusty panting of fatigue — finally, when she had let him know his full weakness, she gave him late, reluctant aid that threw him, dog-tired, into the bed. She pulled the clothes over him with a veiled triumph — as though she coffined him alive, till she chose to aid him again.

His blue eye regarded her fixedly from the shadows of the red curtains that screened the corner off in the daytime.

It had the same half-tortured, half-contemptuous look.

"I wouldn't have done it by thee, Nan," he said, like one stating a dry fact.

The low quiet tone was calm as a lecturer's on mathematics.

Cherry was training his will as he used to train his muscles.

Nan turned the lamp down.

"Jesus wept!" came her voice out of the darkness.

There was a defiant tone in the old phrase — burning, amazonish, but under it was a faint sound of something like fear.

There was a manhood in this broken hulk which she could not degrade.

That old under-current of reason which she had ever hated was rising to combat her undisciplined emotionalism. It was the cold quality that divides the savage from the civilised. As she laid herself down by the side of the physically broken one, who was still struggling with those windy gusts of exhausted breath, she felt an almost superstitious sense of a fetter which she could not see — the awe of a strength she could not classify, the feeling that she was dwarfed and made petty — by this man now almost as helpless as a child. It was the haunting awe of fear wrung from the Stone Age, and rendered to an age that dissects life and death, measures the star-spaces, and fathoms the sea.

Cherry was changing Nan's fear of him — from a physical to a mental fear.

When the exhausted man was sunk into deep sleep, Nan tossed about. She could dimly perceive Cherry's countenance — weary, sleeping, with the worn look of suffering, mental and physical.

She stared at it until it began to assume oddities of expressions — agonising, awful, now fiendish, now glorious. She knew it was the effect of the curtained gloom, and the way her mind had cowed for a second only, before his. Yet she shivered. Then, turning her gaze away resolutely, she made herself sleep.

When she awoke she found Cherry awake.

He watched her dress, light the fire, and saw Polly come down, drink her hot tea, and hurry off, in a panic because the whistle was blowing.

Nan dressed Cherry at seven o'clock that morning.

It was, he thought, a diplomatic move on her part, an augury of some grain of faith that he would win the day. His degree of economic power was also domestic power.

He read Southey's "Life of Nelson," after breakfast until time to get ready — the vision of the delicately-bodied lad with the titan soul inside it, ever before his eyes, making those sensations his own, whilst sometimes the vision of ice floes came to his sight, the crackle of ice, and always he saw the struggle of the mighty will.

"Tha'll ha' to be shapin'," yapped Nan.

She set him the dish of water on a stool.

He came back to the drab kitchen, in the morning light — its ugliness, signs of poverty, and lack of anyone caring for it.

"Towel, Nan," he said.

Whilst there was no humility in the tone — a sudden sorrow had sprung up in him, for this mate of his, companion of this hand-to-mouth struggle. For a moment he saw Nan as he had never seen her before, a captive thing like himself. His tone conveyed a note of comradeship almost. For a moment his personal limitations had broken down. He was wishing that he possessed things to give to Nan seeing that her life in this drab kitchen had been a cramped one — remembering wincingly all the occasions he could have taken her out with him — and did not.

She dressed him with a little more care this morning. There was no tenderness for him in it, though. She was turning him out decent — to fight for that pound a week.

Then she put him on his tricycle, Cherry helping himself as much as possible.

He trundled down the passage.

The step gave him that jerk he always feared. He went with difficulty up the incline of the street. Several women were watching him from the little door-ways, skimpy women in drab clothes, with brooms in their hands.

He turned his head once, to look back at the woman in the doorway — his own particular bit of poverty-limited womanhood.

"Tooraloo, Nan," he called, on an impulse.

He saw her start at his publicly affectionate greeting.

She jerked her head, and went indoors.

Billy was looking down the street towards him.

At the end of the second street it started to drizzle with rain. They were quite wet when they reached the Borough Court. A policeman, in the little ante-room, informed Cherry that his was the first case. Billy walked and Cherry was carried through the doorway into the echoing, oak-floored little Court, with its high windows.

The confused mental picture Cherry always had of that ordeal, with the magistrate's clear voice succeeding his own mumbled words, of Billy chipping in when he shouldn't have done, and being called to order, of the burning thought that they were being treated like children, of the humiliation of being carried up into full sight of the Court, so that they could hear him better, and of his voice almost failing him entirely, remained a thing to shudder at the memory of, to the end of his days.

The consciousness at last, of being in the presence of a machine — trundling, without feeling, over human destinies, came to him crushingly. The climax came when the magistrate gave the verdict, in the dispassionate voice of the Law.

"That the findings of this Court, on this case, are, that the meaning of said Act was that the word 'earnings' be interpreted as said wages paid to an employee, and not, as plaintiff asserts, including the tips that come to him by way of his work, and as marks of favour."

Cherry had lost.

The option, however, of taking the case to a higher Court, was still his.

He breathed a deep breath as he got outside.

Rain was still falling.

The tricycle wobbled a little under his nerveless guidance.

It seemed to him that every one who looked at him knew of his defeat.

The nearer he got home the more he dreaded Nan's face — when she heard.

Billy walked by him in silent misery.

"Shall I come in with thee?" asked Billy.

Cherry shook his head.

He went down the street alone, rapping on the door to be taken in.

Nan gave one glance at his face.

Then she came out — and lifted the front wheel over the step.

"The dog-licence has come," were her first words.

Cherry heaved a deep sigh.

For once, he did not feel the demoralisation usual to him when Nan lifted him upon his chair by the wash-boiler.

He had been under the wheels of a great machine. All else was a pin-prick.

Menson came down that evening, representing the Company. He spread out thirty bright half-sovereigns on the little table with its smoky lamp of the cracked glass, tempting them with the back pay of the last half-year.

Cherry looked at it indecisively.

Then he said, "I can claim that, if the Higher Court says I'm wrong."

"Thou silly devil!" yapped Nan, when he'd gone. "Why didn't ta take it?"

Cherry pulled at the colouring pipe.

"Because — I'm going to have as much as I can get," he said, with a certain dogged fervour. Afterwards, he wondered if he mightn't as well have given in with a good grace. It was perhaps another half-year's uncertainty — another half-year of the humiliation of *living on Polly*.

That night, wet as it was, he trundled out into the rain.

He went along, until he reached his favourite house of call.

Four hours passed, in which the company in the kitchen became merrier and merrier, Cherry amongst them. His moroseness was gone. He sang, shouted and laughed with the best, with still an atom of himself, a miserable, cold-blooded atom that he could not make drunk — that was still sober, despite all his efforts, when he trundled out into the dark, rainy night, towards home, with the fire out, as that sober atom in him knew it would be.

Billy Breeze, who had learnt from Nan that he was out, saw something whizz down the semi-gloom of the street. It was Cherry. The flickering lamp-light fell on him for a second. How he kept his seat became a miracle. Then he stopped, three doors past his own place and began to rap feebly at what he took to be the gate of his castle.

Billy went to the rescue.

Nan and he got Cherry inside.

He was placed on his chair, staring before him into a dead fire, like a man struggling with a weighty problem.

"B — Billy," he stuttered, after a pause in which he evidently found it a little difficult to say just what he wanted to say. "W — what I w — want to know is — 'Where's — hic — G — God ?' "

"Shut thy daft face," Nan told him.

She pulled off his coat. As she did so the button-hole Polly had got for her father, fell on the floor — faded as his hopes.

Then, in full sight of Billy, after she had got Cherry on the bed, she went through the pockets of the tragically short trousers.

Cherry was still lost in drunken ponderings on the whereabouts of the God of the Universe.

"What's this?" quoth Nan.

She held out a scrap of green paper for Billy's inspection.

"He's been buying a lottery ticket of somebody," explained Billy, and turning the ticket over explained that it was only a quarter ticket, and about the great wheel at Hamburg that went round and round, making a fortune for some one when it stopped. They were mostly frauds, such things, he said.

Nan gave the shadowy figure behind the half drawn curtains a withering look.

"If he'd been sober," she said, with a deeper insight into human nature than Billy could have supposed her capable of, "he wouldn't have risked a penny piece. Their lot was all born in chapel-vestries" — which unique utterance regarding the line of Cherries, closed the conversation, for Nan, taking charge of the solitary shilling in her man's pocket, and the scrap of green paper, turned her back rudely on Billy.

He left the melancholy little house where Polly's beauty was like a taper-gleam in an abyss of gloom.

Some day, when his pal's economic position was secure, Billy was going to ask Polly to marry him.

The next few weeks drifted by without event, save that Polly received a letter and the music-copy back, from Bob Wild. Cherry was midway through Southey's Life of the splendid Horatio, and spent a few hours out of doors, each day. For the rest, he sat in the ingle-nook, planning now one way of escape from economic dependence, now another — abandoning each by turn.

The squall had several times appeared on the horizon — but had not broken.

One evening, as Cherry rapped and was taken in, after a run on the road that ran to Cherrydale, under the stars, he found a white-faced Nan.

All that he could get out of her at first was that she'd seen a "sign" — meaning, a sign of death. The knocker had lifted up, three times, falling on the door like thunder. No one had been there.

Cherry did not tell her of the small boys he had seen at the game.

"Summat's goin' to happen," she told him.

Cherry laughed.

He was feeling physically stronger.

The mighty courage that had stuck to Nan, but been almost killed, on awaking on that never to be forgotten day in hospital, to find himself, without legs, was reviving, stirring itself, becoming a vital thing. Nan lifted him on the chair in the corner, and promptly prepared his supper.

"When are we goin' to have our next row?" he asked, meditatively. "I'm missin' 'em, Nan. I don't feel at home, like."

"Tha can ha' one now," she snapped, "if tha wants."

The squall swooped near.

Then — Cherry saw that she was still thinking of the mystic knocks. And — quite suddenly — her superstition, as her jealousy, became part of the chain by which he would keep his male-rights.

"Is that kid comin' in the morning?" he asked.

Nan nodded.

'We can't live on air, an' lie on the floor," she said, moodily.

He stared across the supper table at her.

Again, that big softness for the little shrew, the softness that he had thought quite dead, stirred in him, that compassion for the struggle to make ends meet going on in this little house. There was a hole in her blouse — a dowdy blouse. Daudling about the streets aimlessly, on his wheels, he had seen well-dressed women, and drawn bitter contrasts. Nan and he had never known they were born.

Nan found that compassionate look in her mate's eyes more than she could stand. Its spell was something to fear.

"If tha looks at me like that, I'll throw summat at thee," she said fiercely.

Cherry's hand went slowly into his pocket.

"I saw some ear-rings in a shop to-day," he said, "would just ha' suited thee, Nan."

"Ay," she remarked, caustically, "when tha's no brass tha can see 'em."

He brought something out of soft paper.

Nan stared — in unbelief of her senses.

He was holding up a pair of pearl ear-rings, with green glass drops.

Then — she had snatched them from him, and had them in her ears and had the damp-spotted mirror out in a flash.

Nan was a woman — withal a hooligan.

Cherry was using missionary wiles.

But she gave him plainly to understand, in her subsequent manner, that though she accepted them, she abated no whit of her power. After a while, she wondered where he had got the money.

"Borrowed it," quoth Cherry, nonchalantly.

He gave her evidence.

Then — she gave him a grudging look of admiration. He had "gone into debt" to buy her ear-rings. She hadn't thought he had it in him.

Next morning Cherry was awakened by the crying of a child, to the chorus of clogs going past the door.

Peeping through the bed-curtains, he saw the child's mother, in factory shawl with a big bundle, and anxiety lest little Rob should keep on crying, when she had gone.

Nan held the struggling child — a little lad of just over two years, with a head kinked over with red-gold curls, two frightened eyes like a young pup's, and the rest was dishevelled blanket and red shawl.

"An' I've brought his milk — " said Rob's mother. "See, Rob. The lady'll be his mammy to-day. Eh — do you think he'll cry long, missus?"

"Not he," said Nan, decisively.

"An' his little britches is here — an' his waistcoat, an——"

"Mammy, mammy!" shrieked little Rob.

The woman paused, distracted between his appeal and the sound of the whistle screaming at her. "Late, late, late!"

"Eh — but we're lite to work, aren't we?" said Rob's mother, apologetically, to no one in particular.

"Mammy — !" shrieked the little lad.

Then——

Rob's mother looked at the woman whom she had been told by some one wanted a child to nurse.

"You'll not hit him, will you, missus?" she asked pleadingly. "I've never hit him in his life."

Cherry saw Nan look back at the mother who was scarcely older than Polly.

"Jesus wept!" she said, with emphasis. "What do you take me for?"

But she had winced.

There was a great outcry when the door closed, for "Mammy." There were two terrible hours in which little Rob would not be comforted. 'I want my mammy' was the one reply to all they could say. He was so tired out that he slept at breakfast-time whilst Nan and Cherry breakfasted.

'Where's this from?" quoth Cherry, as he opened a green envelope.

Nan watched him open it.

He stared at it like a man in a dream.

"It's my name," he said, at length. —— "But — I've bought no ticket in the Great Hamburg Lottery. They say I've won."

"Tha has, when tha were drunk," said Nan,

They stared at each other.

Then, "How much?" asked Nan.

"Two thousand marks," he said.

"Is that pounds?" asked Nan.

"I don't know," he said.

Billy Breeze had lent him a dictionary.

Nan reached it.

"We're worth one hundred quid," he said, dazedly. Then, querulously, "Nan, why did ta pawn my phono'? We should have bin able to set the 'Hallelujah Chorus' on, now".

At the end of the week the street was amazed to see great things going on in that front parlour of the Cherries — to hear men knocking, all day, shelves being fixed, great box-like partitions being made in the room, and finally a board being fixed under the window, then brass rods, on which hung curtains. All was made clear when a sign appeared over the door, on which was painted the following inscription:

W. & A. Cherry,
Fent Dealers.

Cherry had made the shrew his partner. He was trying new tactics, breaking down the barriers of antagonism by trying to introduce co-partnership. He didn't believe in it industrially. But he did in the domestic realm.

The exchange was synonymous with the change of the name in the rent book. Cherry was once more a citizen, with a vote. Nan had half-reluctantly sold a vote for partnership in the shop.

The street was skeptical about the business.

But when Cherry went forth on his wheels, with a box in front of him containing his wares, it began to believe a little. There was something in the countenance of the once ruddy giant that told he was out to try. Struggling with his limitations was his will — bigger than his body now.

"If only he'd had a decent wife," Nan heard on the other side the baize curtains, one morning, "a help-meet, as you might say, I daresay he'd have done very well. But she's so — heathenish — as you might say. They'll never make it pay."

Nan withdrew.

She was a fighter by nature.

Previously, she had fought Cherry.

It was still only a dubious truce that existed between them. But she was now concentrated on her hatred of the little street. She was determined to make it eat its words. Their shop should be a success. When Cherry came back, tired, and a little dejected from a morning of poor results, he was surprised to see in the window a square card, on which was written in Nan's giant pot-hookish writing:

"Shirts and working aprons made to order."

She only yapped at him in response to his query as to why she had done this.

"Tha'll ha' to give th' little lad up, now," he said.

"Nowt at t' sort," she said.

And a light leaped out at him from her eyes.

It was the first flash of motherhood he had seen in Nan. He could only reconcile the change in her towards children to the slow change that comes to human beings, in the space of fourteen years. Little Rob called her "Mammy Cherry" and had all that innocent fondness for her an animal gives to the hand that feeds it. Cherry sometimes thought that if the lads had lived, she would have been like a lioness with her cubs. But the great inconsistency was, she had let them die, without realising it. More and more the ex-porter was wonder-filled at the anomalies of human nature, his own in particular. He was still only a shadow of the man he had been — but, he was getting used to it, and — they had not had a row for five weeks. He had the date in his breast pocket-book. He wondered, sometimes, if the sight of those crosses on the almanac had not sometimes enraged Nan into outbursts.

Polly regarded the shop as a child does a new toy.

And a great advertisement appeared in the *Narrowfield Herald*.

Cherry was doing the thing "*large.*"

The door bell began to tinkle quite frequently.

Meanwhile, the N. U. R. put the proposal before its members that Cherry's case be taken up.

Meanwhile, through the law's delays, Cherry trundled about his business. He had not much faith in law, now.

As for Nan, she snapped and sewed on the sewing machine that made a noise like a crushing-engine, sewed and snapped — often wondering as to the meaning of the three knocks that had fallen on the door that night One day she went down into Tanner Fold. She came back early — shaken, and white.

The "three knocks" according to Nan, had been given by the departing soul of the repentant Lizzie, who had died, after a drinking fit. Whether she took it as a warning or not, Cherry could not tell. But she kept a civil tongue, and a big fire, that evening, and made a potato-pie for supper. Whilst his mind realised that when the storm did break, long delayed as it had been, it would be one of the fiercest they had known.

Meanwhile — he was having a rest.

His colouring pipe was tinted a golden brown now. Little Rob called him "Daddy Cherry". Rag had caught his first rat, and was reported in glowing colours, Polly had got a quarter of a column's critique in the *Herald* on her rendering of "I know that my Redeemer Liveth," and — the shop was steadily making headway.

Cherry's misery was now of an intermittent character. His life was being reconstructed — slowly, painfully. There were odd moments when he found himself forgetting his infirmity. But they were only moments. He was conquering himself no more quickly than he was conquering Nan. Somewhere, when he was quite, quite old, he sometimes thought, he would come to a quiet, twilight place, where he would regret nothing. For Cherry did a lot of thinking, now. There was quite a little woof of thoughts running through his days and his evenings. They all tended one way, to a greater sense of being indivisible with the rest of the world, and towards a greater tolerance to Nan, a firmer resolve, when the storm did burst, NOT TO HIT HER.

Chapter 10

Nan disappears

Cherry's mother had not crossed the threshold of her son's house since that unfortunate day when she had ventured over it on hearing that little Ted, the fifth infant that had progressed towards heaven via infant's diarrhoea, was almost at the journey's end. It was fourteen years ago, this very month, since she had opened the door, proceeded into the kitchen with a smile, spoken a few gentle words — and found something spring on her, push her out of the house, with her hair down her back.

Her only connection with the house of the unlucky number since then, was the frail link of sending Polly a birthday card. Never once had she omitted that. She had apparently only just realised that Polly was growing up, having this last time changed the card with bird, flower, or child nursing an animal in its lap, for — a book, namely, Doctor Kirton's "Happy Homes and How to Make Them," of which Polly deemed only the chapter on "Courtship" as worthy of giggling interest.

On a certain sunny day in summer, Cherry went on his wheels to see his mother, and — to be cried over. He found her greatly changed.

For the first time he heard her give instructions as to where and how she should be buried, allotting her blue willow dinner service to Polly, along with her gold ear-rings. Cherry returned through the streets with a desolate feeling upon him. His repressed emotions resolved themselves into a determined vow to bridge over the quarrel between Nan and his mother, or die in the attempt.

Cherry had progressed during the past weeks.

He was becoming an adept in the game of bluff, even of self-bluff. With life turned to ashes and the journey up a steep road "winding him," he assured people that he was in the pink, and more than that — lived up to it If he collapsed, he collapsed when no one saw him.

Every evening, dog-tired, he came home to the grind of the everlasting sewing-machine, and Southey's Life set itself to the rhythm of that steady grind.

The outward expression of this struggle he had begun showed itself only in faint horizontal lines above the bridge of the nose.

Through it all, he coloured the pipe Granny had given him. It was now a golden tint.

Nan had said she could do with some one to "clean."

Cherry suggested Jane, the sand-hawker's wife.

In some peculiar way he looked on the time he had first seen Jane, as the waking of his real desire to grip Life again. Jane, apologising for Tim's giving her the black eye, had made Cherry blush, though he knew that on every single occasion when he had struck Nan, she had asked for it.

Nan was a little jealous of Jane.

Jane was very free of speech.

"Life's a funny thing," Jane had said on one occasion, leaning on the handle of her brush. "Look at him an' me, now 1 Wasn't we just cut out for each other. But God didn't see it."

Her earnestness, and Nan's look, made comic opera for the man sat in the corner.

He had got back, by the persistent game of self-bluff, a half-baked humour and courage that helped him through these rough days of transit.

There was upon him, each day, a new wonder, when Nan did not have an outburst. But he did not deceive himself. Nan was only holding herself in.

Beside using his brains to placate Nan, it cost him quite a penny in trash jewellery and blouses. He was as conscious of having to use strategic cunning as a statesman walking on the brink of a revolution.

Sometimes, he believed there was an almost imperceptible change in Nan since the night of the three knocks, which she had since found out coincided with the night of Lizzie's repentant passing-on. Nan had always been superstitious. Moreover, she was reading the tracts which the hounder of his immortal soul was still sending to Cherry. She read them chiefly for lack of something else to read. Cherry took a glance at them once. Then, he did not wonder at the link between Nan and the tracts. They were written for crude souls — humourless souls, capable of believing in and making hells. The local colouring was melodramatic. The soul-queries were pointed. The positivism was like a load of bricks.

Business had brought out in Nan some qualities that surprised him.

"You don't know a chap till you live with him, an' then it's too late," was one of Granny's sayings. "An' you don't know a woman when you do."

Cherry believed it as he saw the furious vigour with which Nan ran the sewing-machine.

She would work hours at a stretch, without food — when another woman would have fainted.

She might have discovered a North Pole by her single virtue of savage persistency. But she was built all wrong for a little house, the mothering of a foolish girl, and — the coddling of a broken man.

Sometimes, in his most devitalised moments, Cherry wondered if anything could ever happen that would make Nan "coddle" him. The idea would make him smile.

He was pondering now on whether to acquaint Nan with his being about to invite his mother to Sunday tea. He could not think clearly, on this evening. He was too tired, he, who had never been used to "that tired feeling" — who had laughed at newspaper advertisements showing people with tragic faces and those word printed under.

Polly had joined a Cookery Class. She had bought a real cook's apron and had it on at this moment, with a real cook's expression. Nan was finishing her bit of hemming at the machine. Plates were warming. The house had a drowsy, good-night look creeping upon it.

When, into its peace, came little Rob, and Rob's mother.

The look on her face as she came forwards into the light told that something unusual had happened.

"Oh——" said Nan in surprise, getting up from the machine. Then, "Had you forgotten his little sleeping-shawl? It's there, aired"?

"Nay, I've another at home for him," said Rob's mother.

Her voice trembled.

Little Rob ran from his mother to Nan.

"Well, you see, Mrs. Cherry——" began the woman in the shawl, hesitatingly.

"You can say what you have to say without 'Missus'," remarked Nan. "I don't need a title."

The postman had once informed Nan that "missus" was a title. She never forgot to throw it out in irony, at Cherry.

"Well——" said the abashed little mother again.

Nan lost control.

She set her hands on her hips.

"How many wells make a river?" she asked.

She was preparing herself for something now, a suspicion that was coming to her, with insulting force. Cherry and Polly both felt it, too.

"Well," said Rob's mother again, "it's a long way to carry him. I'm fleyed on him takin' cowd. An' a woman 'as lives by me, she says——"

The look on Nan's face stopped her further utterance.

A dead silence fell on the kitchen.

"Jesus wept!" said the shrew, in a way Cherry had never heard her say it before. "Tha'rt takin' him away!"

Then she re-iterated, fiercely, "Takin' him away from me!"

Rob stared at his foster-mother.

Then from her to his own parent.

He began to blub.

Nan picked the child up roughly.

The colour had left even her lips.

As Rob's mother said afterwards, you could see she was a "bad un" for she went white. Red anger was the sign of wholesome anger that would stop short of murder, in Narrowfields.

Beside the round rosiness of the child's face Nan's looked now corpse-like, save for the two live coals of her black eyes.

She held the golden-headed lad a little way off from her, with a look of an inquisitioner on her face.

"Has Mammy Cherry ever done aught wrong to *thee*?" she queried, with a strange emphasis.

Little Rob could not understand it at all.

He blubbed louder than ever.

"My God!" said Nan, shrilly. "I've treated that child better nor if he'd bin my own. May I drop dead just here where I stand if that's not true."

She stood Amazon-like, waiting for Providence to strike her, then when it did not — she turned upon Rob's mother a look under which women made of sterner stuff would have quailed. Rob's mother lost her head entirely under it. She began to cry. Whilst out of the tears came divers excuses, each one contradicting the last.

It was at this moment that Cherry chipped in.

He took out the colouring pipe and laid it on the boiler, then spoke with the male's deliberation.

"Nan, if she wants to take him away — let her," he said, quietly. "There's no law against it. But she doesn't need to lie about it. We shan't eat her."

Then — Rob's mother broke into open confession.

"Somebody" had told her that Nan would thump the child. She had been so uneasy she could scarcely mind her work. So she had come to take him away.

Nan set the boy down on his feet.

She turned, and without a word began to gather up his toys — the doll she had made from shirt-clippings, the woolly baa-lamb drawing a yellow cart, the counting beads Cherry had bought. She wrapped these up in the sleeping-shawl, parcelled all up, and — the door closed behind little Rob, leaving in the house a big, lonely hole that had not been there before.

The remarkable feature in the whole thing was that Nan set up no defence.

For two whole days she went about in the same utter silence with which she had heard why little Rob was being taken away. If it was pride that smouldered in the depths of her eyes, it was a Lucifer-like pride unlike that of ordinary womanhood. As she did her doorstep she looked up and down the little street with a look that made any woman meeting it go in suddenly — excepting an old Irishwoman, who "stared her out." She took down the card that said she made shirts and working aprons. Those she had not finished, she left unfinished, and told folk they would not get, without any explanation.

Nan was on strike.

On the third night she went off, without saying where she was going. Tanner Fold, Cherry guessed. But her return did not coincide with the time the Tanner Fold journey would take. The look she had gone out with was intensified. Her silence, however, had broken. She yapped out staccato replies to Cherry. But she did not begin to sew again, as partner in the "business."

On the next night she went off again, at the same time. As she put on her hat before the glass, Cherry said, mildly, "Look here, Nan. I'm not a jealous man. But if I catch any other chap fool enough to go round with them feather's o' thine——" He broke off there, and began to whistle "Good-bye, don't sigh, you'll be an angel by and by."

Nan gave him a queer look.

"Tha needn't be jealous o' him I go out wi'," she said. And went off sharp.

Cherry looked at Polly.

She was sitting on the end of the fender reading "Lancashire Cookery Book," and cooking things gloriously in her imagination.

Nan came in again at the identical time she had previously returned. To the tick, Cherry summed it up.

He was puzzled.

She had not been drinking.

Nan had finished drinking as soon as she begun, after that one glorious headache, after her round with Lizzie. Nan didn't believe in hurting herself.'

It had been pouring with rain.

Yet — the feathers were not out of curl.

But he said nothing.

"Where's our Polly?" she asked.

A faint astonishment fell on Cherry. "Our Polly" was tame, indeed, for the shrew.

Nan appeared to catch it in the glance of his eye.

"Just run out for a breather," he told her.

"Th' bitch is allus out," she said in something like her usual tones.

Cherry had sent Polly out with the momentous letter asking Grandma Cherry to tea on Sunday.

By now it would have dropped into the box.

He almost wished he had not sent it.

But this was too much like dallying as he had dallied fourteen years, letting that old trouble harden until now it would need a pickaxe to break into it and demolish it.

Cherry went about his business and came home at his usual times. He had experienced these silences of Nan's for longer than he cared to count. But there was something different in this one, something he could not classify.

"If tha wants another kid to noss," he said once, "I can get thee one at a place I call at."

Her face expressed scarlet rage at the idea.

She expressed the fact that she wanted no kid, with language that made Cherry realise his mistake, without altering his deduction.

Then the same silence fell again.

On the Friday Nan set to and cleaned with unusual vim. On Saturday night she was out once more, coming in with the same sort of look, coupled with a deep dejection. Cherry himself was feeling bad. Those nerves in his left stump of a leg were giving him jip. Polly had received another letter: from Bob Wild and was busy writing one back.

"This street," said Nan, whilst making supper, "wants wiping off the face o' th' earth."

From which sentence Cherry came to the conclusion that his first deduction had been a right one. Nan looked on herself as having been robbed of the child she had nursed, by the street. She was as wild as a she-bear robbed of its cub.

On the Sunday morning a soft rapping at the door.

Polly went.

"Why, it's little Rob," she called.

"Mammy Cherry," called Rob's voice, "Wob's got some new pip-pips on. White pip-pips."

"What have I to do?" called Polly, helplessly. Then, "He's coming in. Ooo!"

Rob walked in sedately, hands in his pockets, his eyes proudly on the white slippers.

"Hello!" he said, peeping in on them at the door-way of the kitchen. He nodded his curly head. Then he strutted in.

"Wob's got white bitches," he observed, standing by Nan's chair.

He looked like a new sort of angel with a Dan Leno seriousness that was irresistible.

His blue eyes gazed up in puzzled wonder at Mammy Cherry.

She did not look at him.

"Wob's got white bitches," he repeated, looking up at her. She did not look down at him.

"New w-white b-bitches!" he said, his lip beginning to wobble, and putting his hands in his pocket once more, he advanced to the hearthstone, turned his back to the fire, and mimicked "man," all the time looking to see Mammy Cherry look back at him.

Nan did not look at him.

Quite suddenly, he burst into tears, and ran and clutched her apron.

"Run home," said Nan suddenly, looking down at him "Run home. I'm not fit to be trusted, I'm not."

Rob's crying stopped. He had caught a word that reminded him of something. He put his hands in his pockets again, returned to the hearthstone, and observed with the man-like attitude of back to the fire, "Not fit to tust."

He repeated what he had overheard in connection with Nan like a parrot, and with blue eyes fixed on Nan. Perhaps, he thought, that would make Mammy Cherry laugh.

"Put him outside," said Nan, to Polly.

Polly took the child.

Struggling and kicking he was carried out. On the threshold she gave him a tiny kiss and — a big chocolate drop from her pocket. Then — gently, and almost with tears, she closed the door. Rob sat down on the doorstep. At intervals they heard his voice come up the passage, sometimes dolefully, sometimes hopefully.

"Wob wants to come in——"

"New white bitches——"

"Oppey door, Mammy Cherry——"

"Wob'll punch th' door——"

"Oppey door, Daddy Cherry——" (this as a last resource).

"Wob wants to come in——"

Then there was a long silence.

After which — the door gave that noise which doors give in response to a kick. It was Rob's last word. Cherry looked across at Nan.

"Little devil!" she said, and burst out laughing. She had spoken the words as affectionately as other women used "darling" or "pet."

And for a moment, meeting Cherry's eye, she was startled, for fear she had given herself away.

To cover her tracks she was yapping all morning.

Apparently, she was quite normal, and there was no sign of the squall coming down, as they sat at the tea-table. Cherry was waiting for his mother's knock. It came at length. So tremulous and feeble was the sound of it that Nan might well be suspicious that it was Rob come back again. Polly went.

Cherry felt sick.

Suppose Nan burst out again whilst his mother was here.

He was really in a funk.

Suppose Nan started where they had left off fourteen years ago! He would have to sit there and——

114

"Ooo!" came Polly's astonished voice. Then, "Come in, Grandma."

Nan looked at Cherry.

He did not look at her.

But he felt her look and all it boded.

There was a little pause.

"I'll come in if I'm welcome," said the gentle voice outside, with dignity.

Cherry mastered his chaotic fears.

"Welcome as flowers in May, mother," he called.

He tried to make his voice hearty, but wondered how it really did sound to cool outsiders. Then he realised humorously, that nobody here was cool.

Grandma Cherry came in.

In her little bonnet trimmed with lavender velvet, a yet dark curl shaking on each side her gentle face, where the roses were beginning to fade, her hand clutching almost convulsively the umbrella she always rolled up to the most refined attenuation, she might have touched any heart. She took the chair nearest the door.

"Pull your things off and sit up to the table, Grandma," said Polly.

Polly knew she was under penalty for this, but could not help it.

For a moment Cherry saw in Polly a boldness of courage he had not guessed she had.

Grandma Cherry looked like a little girl in size, compared with Polly.

Nan spoke never a word.

She sat staring down at her plate.

Even when Grandma Cherry was given a place at table, she did not speak or look. The little kitchen felt full of ghosts — ghosts, that brought sick children crying in their arms, and stirred up three different sorts of griefs in three different sorts of hearts.

Grandma Cherry ate as an old woman who never forgets that she had seen gentlemen's service might eat near a caged lioness, with only a row of uncertain bars between.

Grandma had not got the reception she had expected from her son's letter. But since she was here, with that pluck that had almost reached the degree of a martyr's in Aunt Dinah Cherry, and was quite well-developed in Grandma also, Cherry's mother decided that before she left that house Nan should have the piece of her mind which she would have got that morning fourteen years ago, had the door not been slammed before she could get her utterance.

Cherry, Polly and Grandma kept up a little running stream of conversation during tea, and after.

Grandma said she did not intend to stay long.

She began to put on her things.

Then, she stood in the centre of the drab kitchen, futilely trying to tie her bonnet-strings.

"Nan," she remarked to the woman who had still not spoken to her, "why did you do what you did to me that morning?"

It was part of Grandma's pride that she would not allude to her head having been banged against the door-cheeks of her own son's "own house".

Nan stared across at Grandma.

Then she rose out of her chair, as if a sitting position was untenable with the attitude of her mind.

"Because," said the shrew, speaking with a new, yet terrible restraint, "you said I might well ha' church-yard luck, for I put my childer into the grave."

The charge came forth with a new meaning to Cherry, since he had witnessed her mood since Rob went away.

She had cared for the children.

She had also — allowed them to die.

She was like a woman who liked plants but couldn't rear them, because short of something that would enable her to understand their needs.

"That," said Grandma, again trying to tie her bonnet-string, "is a lie."

The two eyed each other.

"You said it to them who said it to me," said Nan.

Grandma Cherry looked across at her daughter-in-law.

"All that I had to say to you," she said, in a way that carried its own conviction, "I said to your face. That morning, when you did as you did, I came to help you, as I'd have wanted any one to help my own lass. You had worked on the pit-top, and you were only young. I came to give you the benefit of my experience. I had buried two myself — the same way, before I had him," pointing to Cherry. "I was married young. So I came to help you. And I also came to say," she continued, "that I was sorry for having kept a bit aloof. I had brought myself to the idea of his having married you. *I had seen I was wrong.* I had seen it as an old woman sees things, who has not long before she goes to her long home, and knows that 'All is vanity.' And I had come to tell you, Nan. Whatever anyone told you I had said — that's the truth and the other was a lie." She managed to tie the strings through once, then said shakily, "*And you did as you did.*"

Polly went to her aid and tied the bunches under her chin. Polly's eyes were full of tears, too.

Nan's were staring across at Grandma, vainly trying to convey that she knew she had been in the right.

The woman who had made the mischief was dead, had been dead ten years. Nan was wild enough, had she known her resting place, to have ripped her out of the grave, and strewn her bones over Narrowfield streets. But she kept up that cover of knowing she had been in the right She had not the nobility that is swift to acknowledge and is sorry it has made a mistake.

In this strained silence of brazen assumption of contempt in Nan, that contempt which she knew belonged rightly to Grandma Cherry, the old woman put on her gloves and again seized the refined umbrella.

"Annie," said Grandma Cherry (and very funny "Annie" sounded as a name for the shrew) "if you're willing to let by-gones be by-gones, I am." Poor Grandma Cherry, she thought she used diplomacy by speaking as a defaulter too.

Her little gloved hand was shaking like a leaf as she held it towards Nan.

The shrew's face was a study.

Grandma Cherry had not only forgiven having her head banged on the door-stones, she was — picking up where she had left off fourteen years ago. She was wanting to be friends.

Whiter and whiter went Nan's face.

Then — her voice came rough with passion after Grandma's gentle voice. So rough and agitated was it that the tone was exactly as though some one invisible was trying to strangle her.

"I'd sooner," said Nan, "spit in your eye."

Thus did Nan find it hardest of all to forgive Grandma Cherry for being innocent of that she had nursed against her for fourteen years.

"Very well, Nan," said Grandma.

Polly closed the door after her, very gently, when she was quite at the top of the street. It seemed like closing the door on a pathetic, little human-faced saint in a home-made bonnet with lavender-velvet bows.

Cherry sat with the mixed feelings of a man who isn't quite sure whether he has made a mess of it or pioneered the way to something better, at least. Grandma had robbed Nan of the illusion she had been nursing fourteen years. But whether parting with a grievance made things better or worse Cherry could not tell. Women were beyond his computations. They always did the thing you least reckoned on.

Polly was undecided whether or not to go to church.

When three-quarters of an hour had passed, and Nan showed signs of making an attack on Cherry, the reflection that she had half-promised Peter to walk with him after church, and the fact that she had on her new dress, swayed her decisively.

She left her parents sitting one on each side the hearth, in the way that Cherry sometimes sarcastically referred to as the Darby and Joan style.

Polly had a glorious triumph that night.

The minister introduced her to a man who had come ten miles to hear her sing, and who said warmly that to hear her sing as she did, did him more good than all the sermons in the world. He hoped she would have a wonderful future.

What was more to Polly, she had a wonderful walk, with a wonderful moon in a blue velvet sky, and Peter telling her how beautiful she was — whilst all the time, if he had only known, she was trying to believe that he was Adam Wild. Becky walked in front with the youth of the receding chin.

Polly tripped lightly down the street after nine o'clock, glad to hear as she entered it, nothing but the strains of a wheezy harmonium playing "Lead Kindly Light" All was serene, as her Dad had used to say in the old days, when he was six foot one, and cracked jokes, and stood about, with his hand on his heart, and one arm outstretched, singing to Nan, "I don't know why I love you, but I do," winding up with some kind of dance which he said was "the serpentine" but which looked more like a bear's.

One or two women were standing in the little door-ways. She thought they looked at her with the sort of interest usually bestowed on her, after "the street had been up." It quickened her pace. She almost ran down to their own door.

Entering, she hung up her coat in the passage, then went towards the kitchen.

It was as she reached the threshold of a kitchen full of shadows and faint reflections from the moon, that a groan broke on her ears.

Immediately, she stopped, palpitant.

Had her Dad lost all restraint, and killed her Mam?

"Dad!" she ejaculated.

Then she half stumbled over a chair, and gave a faint shriek.

Which caused the second groan to fall on her ears.

It was in her Dad's voice.

Quite suddenly, the panic in Polly's heart passed from that which makes one to shake into the deeper panic which must find the matches — and *see*. She found them at last. Her hands were pieces of ice. The matches broke off. Then she struck them on the wrong side of the box. At last she found the lamp, lit it, and put on the glass.

She found him, laid on the floor, jammed between wash-boiler and his chair, which had been pushed aside in the struggle. There was blood. It made her sick. There was a lot of blood. Everything was spinning round now, for Polly. She wanted to scream, and scream and scream. But a hard, cold something would not let her.

"Dad!" she said.

He opened his eyes and saw Polly.

"I — didn't hit — her——" he said dogmatically.

Then Polly saw what had done it.

The one knife in the house that would cut lay near.

"Do you think you are killed, Dad?" asked Polly, despairingly.

There was a brief silence.

Then — Cherry laughed.

"I've bled a lot," he said. "Been here a hundred thousand years."

He tried to raise himself up on his elbow.

"Ooo, Dad," said Polly, "what a lot of——"

She shuddered again.

"About five stitches it'll need," said Cherry, dreamily. "I looked — then I lost the matches."

He rolled over dazedly again.

When he recovered again, he saw Polly's face.

She had been thinking harder than ever she had done in her life. "Attempted murder" for her mother — or "attempted suicide" for her Dad. Neither would do.

But she was not strong-charactered enough to act on her own initiative.

She managed to make Cherry understand, and give his assent to her plan. He wondered at her cleverness, in the way men wonder about things under the half-spell of an anaesthetic.

It seemed hours before she came again, after the dull sound of the door closing behind her.

"Well, what have you been trying to do to yourself?"

The words were spoken with a strong Irish accent.

The lamp was set down on the floor. It half blinded Cherry. He vaguely saw a young man, and guessed that this was the young, new doctor who had last week pulled Polly a tooth, and whom she had selected, with feminine cunning as most likely to keep his mouth shut, since he was a new doctor, just starting a practice.

Cherry lived up to the plan Polly had consulted him about. He murmured about life not being worth the living — and it was so near to his belief, just at present, that the young doctor never questioned but that Cherry had been trying to commit suicide. When he was got on his chair, Polly set the lamp near, and the young man put in the stitches, after Cherry had promised that he would *never*, however he was tempted, do it again.

Polly's teeth chattered as she beheld the operation.

Cherry made no sound.

The doctor was a little astonished.

For a degenerate, Cherry had stood it well.

"More blood than anything," said the doctor.

"But if it doesn't go on all right, let me know at once, else I'd get in a devil of a hole." He helped get Cherry to bed.

Then went out wondering why on earth he had promised the girl who had held his sleeve in the little waiting-room not to tell what her father had done, but to come to him. He had promised. But he was uneasy.

He decided that, hearing nothing for a few days, he would consider all was well.

Polly, meanwhile, got her Dad food and drink.

Cherry was drowsy.

"What about the door?" quoth Polly.

"Leave it unlocked," he said.

They were both thinking of the shrew.

Where she had gone they could not guess.

Polly piled up the fire.

She settled herself for the night

But the shrew did not come.

Polly sent word that she could not come to work next day. Cherry was very weak.

It was on the third day that he made the resolve to get out from that street, that house, that town. When Nan did come back she should find them gone. It was not that he had the intention of putting her away from him for good and all. But, for the nonce, he was tired. Within a week it was all settled. Moreover, he managed to sell the newly started business "as a going concern." Granny Harker had been written to. She only knew that Nan had left him. She answered that she had taken a house for him, suited to his needs. Cherry was going to start a fent-business and Clothing Club in Cherrydale, centre of a half-dozen villages that had to go to town for such things. He was setting up house with Polly.

Now that Nan had not come back for so long, he guessed that pride was keeping her away.

Perhaps, he thought, she was waiting for him to fetch her back, seek her out.

The thought made him smile.

Nan was a habit.

But a habit that he could temporarily give up, with very little inconvenience.

At least, such were his opinions as he followed the lorry that bore their household goods, on the road that ran to Cherrydale, where there was more scope for a fent-dealer, and more air. Polly he could see, perched up on the bedding on the lorry, her face every now and then turning towards the driver. She was flirting her way into Cherrydale.

Quite suddenly, he saw her start and grow demure.

Coming along the road was a milk-cart and a brown pony. Holding the reins was a handsome young man who was whistling, but broke off to look up at the girl on the throne of the bedding. He lifted his cap.

"Now, he'd a good head on him," called Cherry, from behind the lorry.

Polly laughed.

Her Dad *would* discuss the shapes of men's heads as if they were Airedales.

He was going to ask her who the young man was, when, coming to meet them, in her bonnet with the geranium looking redder than ever, was Granny. She stood full in the middle of the road.

"Welcome to Cherrydale," she cried. Then, "I know where *she* is. Sh — she's all reight. Nowt ever happens to nowt. I'll tell you, *after.*"

She winked, looking significantly at the driver, to tell Cherry it was too public a place to discuss Nan in, here. The driver winked back at her.

"Na, then. Noan o' that. We don't allow it here," said Granny solemnly. And everybody laughed.

Then, she pointed a fat finger towards the hills.

"Sithal!" she said to her son-in-law. "Th' good owd rainbow. Tha mun take that as a good omen."

She led the way to a lane that turned from the main road, and climbed up a hill. There, on the summit of the hill, just sufficiently removed from the hill-path to be out of way of dust, was a house — a whitewashed house, with a real porch whose top was cushioned with golden moss, and with a garden back and front. Granny told Cherry the price. He whistled.

"It's hardly," said Granny solemnly, "the price of the rosydandrum there, in the garden."

She took out the key and handed it to Polly.

Polly unlocked the door, giggling and important.

Then, remembering, she came back and helped her Dad through the doorway, into a place smelling of new whitewash — into a kitchen with mullioned windows, deep sills, and a window-seat.

In the corner was a man's big chair.

Cherry stared at this.

"It were *his*," said Granny Harker, in the tone she only used when referring to the Primrose Leaguer. "It's no good anybody falling out about who has *that*, when I can't say a word for mysel'. So I had it fetched up, Will. Here, mon," she shouted to the driver from the door, "come an' give a hand."

He came. They lifted Cherry into Pa Harker's chair.

Then Granny took off her bonnet and set to work.

"If there's owt I enjoy now and again," she remarked as she fetched and carried, "it's a flitting. Now, thee — lie back an' take it cool."

Cherry smiled.

But — it hurt to have to sit back.

121

He had left the drab house.

But he had not left himself.

There was one thing, though.

Here, in Cherrydale, he started in a house without the old, sad, bad memories. Here, in Cherrydale, he had not to live down the man who had been six foot one. Here, in Cherrydale, he started without Nan. It wouldn't be for long, possibly. But if she had to sue to come back, Nan was un-Nanned. Never again would it be the same.

She would have admitted the dominion of the mere male. He did not ask any questions about her. Like Granny, he knew that she was all right. Nan wasn't the sort they made angels of.

As he watched Granny and Polly together, the idea came to him that Granny might make a woman of Polly.

He decided, soon, to ask her about it.

Meanwhile, he watched the old things from the drab house going up on those new white walls, made rosy by a fire roaring in a wide chimney that let down its black throat shafts of sunlight, and the twitterings of birds.

Here, in the country, the furniture looked all right.

There, in the town, it had looked all wrong.

He began to wonder why they had stuck to the old, sad house so long.

Myrtle Cottage, Thomas Hill, was high up.

For the first time Cherry knew what the Psalmist meant when he spoke of the feet being set on a hill.

Chapter 11

Nan's return

The great struggle between Nan and Cherry began so soon as everything in the new house was in apple-pie order. It began, in fact, immediately the bustle ended, and the hole Nan had left in the domestic circle began to make itself felt, like a tooth that has ached yet leaves a mighty gap. Cherry knew where Nan was. He knew all that she was doing. He knew that sooner or later, her Lucifer-like pride would smash up. Nan living with another strange woman! Nan was not cosmopolitan. She would have to come back, because the savage in her would hound her back. But she was putting up a good fight, though Granny told him that she had it on good authority that she looked ill as a poisoned rat. It was this idea of Nan that bothered Cherry. Never in her life had Nan been ill. Granny said it was proud flesh that made her look so ill.

Nan was waiting to be fetched home, in glorious triumph, so that she could always tell him he couldn't do without her, and would act accordingly. Cherry was waiting till she came home, so that she would be forever un-Nanned. This invisible struggle, of soul with soul, need against need, was their most terrible and vital one. Sitting facing her empty chair, Cherry realised that in spite of everything he thought quite a good deal of Nan. More than that he would acknowledge, not even to himself.

He had started out in good earnest to map out the dale, and work it, week by week. But he found out early that whilst he had been right in his surmise, that Cherrydale was a good centre for a "Scotchman," there was also a real Scotchman, of the name of Sandy MacGower. Sandy had brought ill-repute on the "peddling man". Twenty-five per cent of the women in the cottages and farms were in his clutches. They bought things they did not want, lest he tell their husbands of their debts. He played up to their Eveish vanity like a very Mephisto, and — they fell. Only some few, stout enough of heart to confess to their spouses, or to eat dry bread and treacle until the debt was paid, wriggled themselves free. Tale after tale did Cherry hear, until Sandy began to appear to his imagination rather as a giant, holding souls in his hands, than a mere, common peddling man.

In some way this conception justified Cherry in the resolution he had formed, to oust any other pedlar from the vicinity of Cherrydale. Whilst the struggle was to prove the survival of the fittest, it had now the additional excuse of being an act of justice.

Sitting in the ingle-nook at night, in that kitchen whose poverty did not look sordid, as it had done in the drab, cramped house in Narrowfields, Cherry would alternately ponder how to get even with Sandy MacGower, how to bring Nan to her "scolden meat" — and, last and least, how to pay out Aunt Miriam for sending tracts from the Brand from the Burning Publishing House.

During this triangular problem, he received two letters from Billy Breeze, both saying that, very shortly, the Union hoped to see his case through. At which Cherry had smiled. Since that one awful ordeal, when he had foolishly thought it would be enough to fight his own case, he had no faith in law. He was going to give it a chance, however. There was always the ten shillings he could claim. Meanwhile, he was working out his own salvation, economically, and — domestically.

Slow day after slow day passed.

Every night as he came in, sometimes having done good business, sometimes having done little, he looked and listened for Nan's presence. His heart sank lower and lower. Nan, meanwhile, on her side had all the feeling of having lost caste that the savage she was believed in, since her husband could get on without her.

In the day time she washed.

Evenings she spent praying and singing in the Salvation Army barracks. Nan had been saved. Those nights following on the street's condemnation of her as unfit to be trusted with a little child, she had been what Cherry called "palling on with God." Hence she had told him he need not be jealous. But it was the great reaction of having left Cherry half-dead, as she thought, having struck him that mad blow in sheer desperation because he would not hit her in answer to those lesser blows, that had driven her towards the primitive religion that was eminently suited to her requirements. This reaction had come just at the moment when a famous Salvationist was setting county after county afire by sulphurous eloquence that made people afraid to die — unless they were saved.

Oh, Nan!

She could not surrender to anything but force, after all.

Whilst Cherry pondered his lesser problems, and the big one of hounding Nan home to himself and Polly, her flag lowered, if not pulled down forever, she was living in misery. Her jealousy was as a flame burning her. It was after Cherry had begun to deal with Sandy MacGower and Aunt Miriam, that a third idea presented itself to him as another good iron to have in the fire.

He sent up an advertisement to a local paper which he knew Nan would be sure to see.

It ran: —

"Wanted, by Elderly Widower (G.), a housekeeper, at once. Must drink only in moderation. *Must be one that will stay.* Religion no hindrance. Wages generous. — Myrtle Cottage, Thomas Hill, Cherrydale."

Nan, as Cherry supposed, knew his whereabouts.

After that awful moment when she came back to start at an empty house, whose dark, unshrouded windows looked at her with awful eyes, she had set her spies at work. For Nan had human communication cords around Cherrydale, that had known her in her youth.

When she read that advertisement, the world spun round for her.

Nan had to exercise more restraint than ever she had used in her life, to keep from running to Myrtle Cottage.

Cherry, meanwhile, was not having a gala day as the result of his plan.

The week following that advertisement appearing in *The Herald* he was besieged by all manner of "house-keepers." They engrossed his spare time from the poor soul who vowed if he took her in she would never leave him (he could quite believe her!), and said one bob a week would keep her going, to the ogling smart woman obviously out to catch a husband, with all the brands in between, Cherry had the pick of the market. It was all he could do to keep them at bay.

"Ooo, Dad, there's been another!" Polly would almost cry sometimes, when he returned. "She's comin' again, when you're in." Whereupon, Cherry would go out at the time she had to call. There was one fat woman who said she could cook anything but jellies and "entries."

In a deluge of housekeepers, in the struggle to oust the Scotchman, and between writing passionate letters of love to Aunt Miriam, which he posted at Thorn and signed by the fictitious name of Jerry Clin, Cherry said he was "working overtime." But under it all was the big hole that Nan had left. He weakened once so far as to say to Granny Harker that he had half a mind to go and fetch her back.

"Tha'll rue it as long as tha lives," Granny said, pointing a fat finger at him. He knew it was true.

Granny was generally right

He decided to hang on.

Polly was a very amateur housekeeper.

When her mother came home she was to go to Granny, to be made into a professional. Meanwhile — her mother did not come. The invisible struggle waxed keener and yet more keen. Cherry inserted the same advertisement for another week.

By which time Aunt Miriam's answers to Jerry Clin began to come back to the little shop where Cherry had it fixed up that they should come until he called for them. Oh, Aunt Miriam, hounder of sinful souls, how was thine then revealed to William Cherry. Aunt Miriam playing Juliet to the Romeo Cherry had invented was enough to make gods and men weep — and smile. He had not thought she had it in her. But oh, when Cherry imparted the joke to Granny, how she laughed. Every ounce of fat on Granny dithered like jelly. Tears ran down her cheeks. She coughed and held her hand to her side. Every time she looked at Cherry she started again.

"Man alive," she gasped at length. "What made thee call thyself Jerry Clin?"

Cherry said the name had trickled into his pate.

"Well, there is one," said Granny. "He's well-known in these parts. What will ta do now?"

"Married or single?" said Cherry.

"Single — except he keeps a hedgehog," Granny told him.

She gave him further particulars.

They pleased Cherry.

"To the bitter end, then," he said, which Granny interpreted to mean that he was going on with the joke.

Meanwhile, he was physically weak, mentally miserable, and Nan — sick.

Only Rag consoled him.

Rag was at Myrtle Cottage now, covering the chair-cushions with hairs, and barking at every housekeeper who applied and then licking their shoes before they went. He still wore the leggings.

It was on a calm, summer evening, approaching ten o'clock, as Polly and Cherry sat at supper, that Rag cocked his left ear in the way that made him resemble a cross between a gargoyle and a windmill.

Cherry looked at the dock.

He had that burst of hope which he had felt often — and which had dwindled away into despair.

Nan had been away three weeks.

Somebody knocked.

Hope died.

Nan would not knock.

Polly went to open the door.——*

She peered out into the blue dusk.

"Ooo!" she said.

Then all was silence.

She came in.

She was very white.

"It's — my Mam," she said in a giggling, hysterical whisper.

Cherry sat there outwardly calm.

Something had gone bust in Nan.

But — what was it?

They heard some one come in very heavily and slowly.

Then — she appeared on the threshold of the kitchen, cosy and quiet in the rays of lamplight and firelight.

It was Nan.

But — such a Nan.

She came forward with the faintest shadow of her old aggressiveness, looking to see she knew not what Then when she saw only Cherry and Polly — she flopped into the first chair. She did not cry. She did not faint. But her face twitched convulsively. Cherry believed that she must have lost a stone.

"Get thy mother a pot o' tea," was all he said.

This was his triumph.

But — it hurt him as much as it hurt Nan. Possibly more.

She took the tea and sipped it in the same dull way.

After a little while, she recovered sufficiently to say, "Settin' thysel' up for a widower! I could ha' thee up for bigamy."

Cherry was suitably humble. He explained that (G.) in his advertisement was a classification meaning "Grass."

When Polly had gone to bed, Nan cleared the table and washed up the dishes.

She sat down in the chair on the other side the hearth from his.

Her eyes had the same tortured look.

It would take her weeks to recover from the physical effects this soul-struggle of hers had entailed. Cherry could see that.

"After all," he reminded her, "it was thee 'at left me."

Her face twitched again.

"Shut thy daft face," she said.

He began to tell her about the housekeepers.

Her eyes blazed in their old way.

"House-breakers, tha means," she yapped.

She looked round the place jealously for any odd job that wanted doing. Then, when he intimated that he was tired, she helped him undress. Her hands were shaking. When she saw the lint peeping up at his shirt-neck, she pretended not to see. She lifted him on the bed in the corner.

It was when the cottage had only on it the rosy light of the fire that her voice came to him, long after he thought her asleep.

"Did I hurt thee — much, Bill?" she asked.

Cherry grinned in the darkness.

"Nay — just a bit of a scratch," he said with sarcasm. "It tickled me a bit, that's all."

She was not communicative about her conversion.

That led Cherry to believe in its reality.

But he knew it was only because Nan had been terrified by devils — that she was palling up with the Almighty.

"Put a good word in for me now an' again, Nan," he chaffed.

But Nan refused to be drawn.

Next day, she performed her household duties in a way that made Cherry remark she did things better for the Lord than ever she had done them for him.

There was only one drawback to Nan's being religious.

It entailed her going to Narrowfields every Sunday. That meant — cold dinners.

But Cherry did not grumble.

He was, as Grandma Cherry said he should be, thankful for small mercies.

In the new house he and Nan were beginning a new life. It was built on the old one, and bits would bust through, he knew. But still — it was a beginning. During the next week he did quite good business. He also got a bit of news that put him on the right way to oust his rival, the peddling Scotchman. His scheme against Aunt Miriam was at the second stage. He changed "Jerry's" address to the one that would find the real Jerry, still going on writing the Romeo-like epistles. The result came in two weeks' time.

A frightened-looking man going bald called to see Cherry. He had been inquiring at Granny's if she knew a Miriam Cherry, and Granny had sent him up to her son-in-law's.

"Is this Cherry's?" he asked.

Nan conducted him into the kitchen where Cherry was making out a great advertisement of the Invincible Clothing Club.

"Thy name Cherry?" quoth Jerry.

Cherry nodded.

He could not trust himself to speak, at first.

This was Romeo — this knock-kneed, bald-headed, timorous object!

"I've bin told you — know a Mir'am Cherry?" said he, stammering.

Cherry nodded.

"She's — she's under the impression I'm makin' love to her," said Jerry. "I — I've never heard tell on her. She's mad. But she'll not believe me."

Cherry did not understand.

So Jerry went into details.

"Got the address right, too," said Cherry, inspecting the envelope Jerry showed him.

Jerry winced at his look.

"Sure you haven't bin makin' love to her," said Cherry.

Jerry was emphatic.

"Me!" he said, aghast. 'I couldn't do it to save my life."

Cherry grinned.

"It isn't allus necessary," he said.

"But——"

"Legally," said Cherry, "you'd have hard work to disprove it. Seen that breach of promise case this last week?"

Jerry had.

He was fond of brass.

He went out from Cherry's in no wise comforted.

Nan looked at her spouse.

"What's ta bin doin'?" she asked.

Cherry hesitated.

He had ceased to confide in Nan since the third week after their marriage. But — he felt some reward was due to her, after the bruised condition of her soul in its utter defeat. Nan had half-hauled down her flag. But only half. She had made no open confession of surrender. She was yet quivering.

In a burst of the big softness, Cherry told her what he had done. Jealousy and a sense of the ridiculousness of the thing struggled for a moment. Then — she laughed.

She laughed in the way that she had laughed when little Rob punched the door.

It was at Nan's suggestion that Cherry began to send flowers, in the name of Jerry Clin.

"The plot thickens," Cherry would say sometimes. Or else, "It is dusty on the deep, Nan," mimicking the Narrowfields stage villains.

Polly was gone down to Granny's now.

In a way, Cherry was glad.

The weeks that followed made history for him and Nan. She was sitting on her old self, rather than having it for a stepping-stone as the poet puts it. And — its corpse would show galvanic signs of life at intervals. Somehow, Cherry felt that it was easier for Nan that Polly was away, that another female of the species did not witness her struggles. She tried very hard. At last he said:

"I wouldn't be too hard wi' mysel' for a bit, Nan. Yap a bit. The main point about havin' arguments, is not to carry them too far."

He didn't believe, afterwards, when he came to think of it in cold blood, that she would have been able to manage at all, but for the Sundays when she could let off the steam with the Army. Cherry was an apologetic sort of conqueror in these days. He brought her some roses one day, and he acknowledged that Rag was a bit of a nuisance.

Aunt Miriam did not trouble him any more.

It was taking her all her time to capture Jerry Clin, whom she was now accusing of altering his hand-writing to try and get out of it, and threatening him with breach of promise.

Cherry met the formidable Scotchman under rather unique circumstances. Sandy was drunk in the "Peep In," Cherry's favourite house of call (though the "Cold Well" and the "Black Mare" were also favourite houses of call. The Scotchman showed himself very human, in drink. He wept as he recited "The Mountain Daisy." He treated Cherry to whisky, and complimented him on Rag, which he took for a dachshund, in his dazed condition, though Cherry had distinctly told him it was an Airedale. He also, though he did not know it, paid for four mugs of nut-brown for Rag, who was certainly not a Rechabite. And — he let fall sundry hints as to the progress of his courtship of Widow Riley at Witch Gate.

They parted under the stars, swearing lifelong friendship, and Cherry realised that he had got MacGower dished.

He made it on his way to get round to Witch Gate with new summer dress materials. He called on Widow Riley. She was a prim, proud body whose great weakness was a dislike to being made in any way "cheap." When Cherry told her that MacGower had been boasting of the kisses she gave, in the "Peep In," she was scandalised. There was no chance of the wily Scotchman sitting in the dead and gone Riley's chair. She said that if she'd had a brother she'd have "shown him."

Which opened the way for Cherry's plan.

On a certain night, when MacGower was sure that the widow would meet him, as appointed (Widow Riley had made it a moonlight night) the unsuspicious MacGower, waiting under a great copper beech, saw her approach.

Widow Riley was very coy at this night when the Scotchman had decided he could not lose anything by marrying her.

She refused to say the word.

MacGower became ardent.

He embraced her.

At the same moment he was lifted clean off his feet — to a loud, masculine laugh that proceeded from the widow — and before he knew what was happening was dropped into a pond on the other side. MacGower knew a little of swimming, but when he did get out, he had four miles to walk before he got home. Whilst a band of young men, who dropped upon him a little lower down the road, suggested that it would help dry him if he were dipped in flour. Which they proceeded to do, despite his valiant struggles.

Of his progress that Saturday night over that four miles, scaring lovers who took him for the famous ghost that is supposed to appear as a warning to such foolish people, MacGower never forgot a single awful detail. But the most awful thing, on his next peddling trip was to find the whole story known. Women openly flouted him when he asked them to get the money quick, or he'd tell their husbands.

He had fallen from his tragic power to a farcical figure. In the pubs he would be twitted as the man who courted young Simms, the blacksmith, and folk would ask him how long it was since Widow Riley said "Yes" under the copper beech. He stuck it as long as he could. But the fact was — he was never the same man after that terrible night. Cherry got more and more of his business.

When autumn came he left the dale to his victorious rival.

By this time Granny had set Polly's worth as a domestic help down at "sixpence" a week and her meat.

Cherry was earning thirty shillings a week on an average. Rag was having bay salt baths, and Cherry was saying this was his last chance. But he had said that often. At the bottom of his heart Cherry believed he would never have the moral courage to put Rag out of a world that smiled at his short-comings.

Nan was gradually needing to sit less firmly on herself. Polly Cherry was beginning to flirt less promiscuously. When Cherry went back into hospital in October, for that painful operation that was to deal with the erring "narves" of that left stump, he went with considerable regret, but no real fear that on his return all would not be as he left it.

Nan yapped a good deal on the day before he went.

Now that the explosion of her pride had made the way free to her heart, Cherry had proceeded to make himself at home there. Polly at Granny's, himself in hospital, and his empty chair staring at her — would, he felt, do her a world of good. In which calculation he was not mistaken.

Chapter 12

Polly's confession

In the year that followed, nothing particular happened. The great change in the Cherry household was that things ceased to happen — though there were severe inward struggles of will against will, for both Nan and Cherry. Cherry's bluff in this year's course became fortitude. Nan's domestic virtues ceased to be quite so much iron qualities — things she set herself to do as a part of her religion. Sometimes Cherry fancied that a time would come when Nan would drop that crutch of the primitive religion and will by grace of sheer humanity and love of her kind.

But it was not yet. It might only be on the edge of the grave. Within Myrtle Cottage, which Bob Wild had newly papered, hung bacon flitches, oaten cakes on strings, and herbs from the garden. Outside, snowy whitewash made the house a shining patch of light set on the hilltop. Apart from extra cleanliness, nothing was changed. Moses and Daniel were still there. So was "Wedded Love." There was, however, an additional picture — one of Nelson, with his empty sleeve and his delicate face, with the brave eyes looking down always on Cherry and Nan. This picture was dear to Cherry. There was also a tiny bookshelf with the Southey's Life elbowing "Dickens." But Cherry knew that he would never be really a bookman. He had got on too well without books to worry about them. Eyes and ears had stood him in good stead of other men's ideas. But, occasionally, he passed an hour or so with them, generally ending by going to sleep.

Outwardly, the only mark of his intense struggle to survive in a changed world, was a little more grey in his hair, a more anxious look in the eyes, and a clear-cut manner that bespoke a man who knew what he wanted, and was getting it; who believed in himself, in his three ounces and laughed at difficulties. Economically, his position was about the same as before his catastrophe. But the pulling of Nan in the same direction meant a doubling of comforts, and of plenty. Domestically — he had realised "home" as he had not done in his palmiest days.

It was not a bad harvest that crowned the year of struggle. Polly was getting famed beyond her native county. She was not a nightingale.

But she was certainly a thrush — or "cock-throstle" as her Granny called her. She also knew her way about a house, now, and by extra baking for the shop made Granny no worse off than she would have been without her. So stood the world with these three, a year after Cherry had followed the lorry with his "sticks" going towards Narrowfields.

Cherry and Nan decided that a little house warming would not be amiss, to celebrate their having had a prosperous twelve months in Cherrydale. Accordingly, they asked Granny to invite the guests for them, by word of mouth. She was to be sure to include the two blind men whom Cherry had got friendly with — partners in a little newsagents' business at the end of the village. She was also to make pork pies.

Behold Myrtle Cottage, then, one Sunday afternoon, basking in warm sunshine, and a bluebottle droning sleepily against a window pane that was as a frame to Polly's garden (Adam Wild had given Polly lessons on flower-growing) — a garden in which flowers whose mere names sound like the Poet's Calendar grew in a burst of pomp that would have made Solomon's look poor. Within, as without, everything was spick and span. Polly had left Granny on her own in the shop and had come up to help her mother, the day before, for the great occasion.

Nan played the hostess in a white apron.

Nan in such a white apron always reminded Cherry of the third-rate actresses who take such parts in thirty-third rate plays.

Granny was the first arrival.

Her voice, speaking some comic philosophy, came from outside the porch, with Polly's giggling "Ooo."

"I've brought all Cherrydale wi' me," she said warningly, as she entered.

Granny had come in style, yet looking plain as a pikestaff.

"We shall want more chairs, Nan," said Granny.

Which would have been rude had it not come from Granny.

There was Ted the organ-blower, Bob Wild, Susan Thorpe, and the two blind men.

Mr. Gibbs and Mr. Moss, the two blind men, said they were rather tired, as they had been up all night, having been to see the sunrise from Bouldsworth.

Cherry felt that they were jesting at first, but Mr. Moss wagged his head in appreciation of his friend's apology, or of the sunrise.

"Bob allus tak's 'em up every year," said Granny.

Cherry wanted to laugh.

Fiction! It wasn't in it with fact.

"The grandest surprise I've ever seen," broke in Bob, enthusiastically. "We fairly enjoyed it." The two blind men nodded.

Polly led them into the parlour to take off their coats and hats. They wouldn't have them carried away. They were very independent.

"Does ta mean to say——?" began Cherry to Bob Wild.

Bob smiled.

"They enjoyed it as much as me," he said, quietly. "I told 'em about it. Moss lost his sight when he were twelve. He can remember. Gibbs — enjoys it in another way. He feels it." He ceased speaking as the two men came back, cautiously finding their way to their respective chairs.

"Here, tak' my bonnet away," said Granny, handing hers to Polly. Polly and Susan went into the parlour.

New chintz made into covers and cushions by Polly made it a pleasant place. Myrtle Cottage was looked on by Nan as her "duty," too, now. She cleaned it for God.

"Can I try it on?" asked Polly of Susan's hat.

Susan smiled assent.

"Do I — suit it?" asked Polly, anxiously.

She looked in Susan's face for the answer.

"Yes," nodded Susan.

"I don't think I do," said Polly, and took it off.

Susan was acutely conscious of Polly's childish charms.

"I don't think I do," said Polly, in a worried way.

Susan made a valiant attempt to like Polly, as she knew she would have liked her, but for her ironic position, as Bob Wild's mother confessor, the recipient of his year's confidences regarding Polly.

"Nice folk," said Jabez Thorpe's daughter, "look nice in anything." Polly blushed.

It was the first praise any girl had given her.

"Am I — nice?" she asked, archly.

"Very," said Susan, honestly.

"You," said Polly, "are the nicest girl I ever met."

Susan smiled.

A burst of laughter came from the kitchen.

It was Granny's, and was joined by that of the two blind men, and then, by Cherry.

Granny had just told a live joke about a little lad who came in her shop.

Polly set Susan's hat on the Siberian rabbit globe.

"Try mine on," she said.

It was an offer of friendship.

Susan accepted it — but not enthusiastically.

She was conscious of being at least ten years older than Polly, in reality. The freshness from Polly was the same as that she felt when near children.

It was this freshness the rollicking Bob was drawn by.

Susan was old, quite old, so she told herself.

And suffering in the deep, slow way of one so much older.

"Don't you like me?" asked Polly wistfully.

Polly was missing Becky — Becky who had not been to see her for months.

Moreover, she had taken a deep fancy to Susan Thorpe.

So that when Susan drew back from the touch of her hand she seized Susan's cold fingers, and said, "*Do* like me," with a lack of pride that amazed Susan, without touching her. Susan was trying hard to like Polly, who had demolished that dream of the little boy who had sat with her on the stone wall on those misty moors, and whom she had made to kneel down with her, and pray for the soul of the sheep they had buried.

"I — could tell you anything," said Polly, in her almost un-English way. "You have no sister. I haven't. Let's adopt one another." Her shaky little giggle told that she was ready to cry.

Susan gently pressed the warm hand in hers.

"Very well, then," she said.

"How cold your hand is," she said.

"Cold hand, true heart," quoted Susan.

They walked into the kitchen, arms linked.

"I forgot to introduce thee to Miss Thorpe," said Granny to Cherry.

Cherry looked at Susan.

"Not ailin' aught, I hope?" he inquired in a fatherly way.

Susan smiled denial.

"She looks like a beef-steak a foot thick with onions on the top would do her no hurt," said Cherry, candidly.

"She's allus her nose to th' grind-stone," said Granny. "But I never noticed before she were so pale."

Whereupon Bob looked at Susan.

Whilst he was amazed that they could think Susan pale. She was red as a rose. Her eyes smiled. But her lips trembled.

"It's nerves," said Granny. "That's what it is. Wait till I see Jabez. I shall tell him she wants a good sea-breeze."

Whereupon Susan said that nothing ailed her and her father mustn't be upset.

"Try dumb-bells, Miss Thorpe," said Bob. "First thing of a morning with the windows open — and deep breathing."

"Perhaps Miss Thorpe's in love," said Mr. Gibbs.

"I remember when I——" He went off into a fit of laughter, hearty, wholesome laughter at the young fool he had been.

"Well," said Cherry, "if she's aught like our Polly, she'll get o'er it an' be as bad again."

Which made Bob Wild cease wondering if a girl like Susan could be in love, and if she was in love with Adam — to look accusingly at Polly. Twelve months had made him more deeply in love than ever with Polly.

Polly was looking appealingly at her Dad, asking him to say no more. Cherry had served his purpose in turning the scrutiny from Susan.

"Well, when we get to our age," said Granny, "we want summat substantial. I'm feelin' peckish, so how other folk are. I believe same as the chap, it's hard work keeping the heart up when the carcase is down. Whatever comes, or whatever goes, we've got to keep on eating." Granny always quoted some mythical "chap" as her authority for such philosophy.

She had given the signal for tea-making.

Nan had all this while sat without a word.

She now got up and moved towards the scullery.

"Let me help," laughed Susan. "Do! Mrs. Cherry.

Nan melted under the readiness of Susan Thorpe.

"You can cut th' tay-cakes," she said.

Whereupon Granny began to tell a tale of two deaf folk who invited some friends to tea, and were kept cutting up, and whose audible remarks on that point were heard by their visitors. Which set Bob off telling tales about gamekeepers, how he had dodged them, and wonderful rabbit-chases, and then the two blind men got telling tales, and Polly sat, fascinated, her hands clasped around her knees, her eyes shining, until Granny said, "Tha lazy hussy! Help to get tea ready," whereupon she jumped up as if she'd been shot.

When they sat down Cherry said, "If anybody goes short, it's their own fault. It's there. Sam in."

Which — after a little time — every one did, except Susan, and — Bob.

"I'm glad you came," said Cherry twice, to no one in particular.

"We'll have to have another Cheer-up Party one o' these days," said Granny.

"Wait till our Polly gets wed," winked Cherry.

He was beginning to understand that young Wild's putting on the rose-sprigged paper on their kitchen wall was not just country kindness.

Whereupon Polly declared she should never marry.

And every one laughed and disbelieved her — but Bob became very gloomy all at once.

Until he caught Susan's eyes, smiling quietly, and telling him to believe no such wild statement. Whilst Granny, catching those meeting glances, felt bewildered. Was Bob going to fail her as a mate for Polly, also? Was Susan deeper than she seemed?

As for Polly, she was noting all Susan's ways.

No wonder Adam liked her.

After tea, they left Granny and the two blind men to be called for, after chapel.

Polly was soloist that night.

Bob had changed from a pagan haunter of the moors to a Methodist again. Susan had told him he could sit in their pew. Poor Susan! It had been what she called a "wicked year" for her.

Ted walked along with her to the hillside church.

Bob went ahead with Polly.

The sweetness of a blossom-scented world with a new moon gleaming through it, was all about them.

"I heard that Sagg Farm is advertised," said Ted. "Have you heard?"

"Oh — no," protested Susan.

"There were no name to it," said Ted, "but it sounded like it."

"Mr. Wild will be worried, won't he?" asked Susan.

Ted did not know that she referred to the careless Bob.

"He'll go potty," he said, cheerfully.

Susan was disappointed in Ted.

She had thought that he and Bob were David and Jonathan to each other.

She resolved to ask her father to help the Wilds out.

Which she knew was no light task. Next to her mother and herself, Jabez Thorpe was passing fond of his bankbook.

Polly sang, and Bob worshipped.

It was not hard to believe in seraphim and cherubim as Polly sang.

The Thorpes' pew gave him a fine view of Polly.

Susan found the hymns for him, and the chapters.

"Let's have a walk," suggested Ted, as Adam, Bob, himself and the two girls met outside, after service.

A walk they had.

Adam divided himself between the two girls.

It was a new experience for Adam.

A little awkward at first, the strain grew easier when they had climbed half a dozen stiles. Polly always influenced people towards the lighter side of life. Moreover, Adam had set himself to save Bob from Polly. He had set his hand to the ploughshare of Love, which he was going to drive through this light heart. She was trying to fool his brother. Adam Wild's brother must not be fooled. Adam's great fear ever since he was a boy in his teens had been that Bob would make a fool of himself. He was out to protect Bob, whom this girl was laughing at, just as he had protected him at school. That was his reason to himself. Your rational people have a way of persuading themselves that they do things for reasons. Adam, with his book-learning, and his science certificates, was sufficiently complex, to be able to lie to himself without detecting it, at once.

But whilst he set out ploughing the heart of this foolish girl, he took care not to estrange Susan.

It was Susan whom he asked to come up to help Sarah churn.

"Ooo," said Polly, "I should like to know how to make butter." Which frank invitation of herself to Sagg Farm made both Adam and Susan smile, their smiles meeting across her. Whilst Adam — looking from first one girl's face to the other, as the moon shone on them, for the first time realised why poets had written about women, and to women. Susan carrying her Bible, Polly exuding cheap scent, were admirable foils to each other. Susan's silences became demure, elusive things. Polly breaking into song, all at once — made the air flower with music. Adam Wild was conscious of a feeling of exhilaration, or triumph — a strong leaping of that old sex-pride of his. Susan he was sure of. Folly, he was going to teach a lesson.

Bob was a little angry at Adam, when he and Ted got up with them.

Polly was aware of it, and laughing in her sleeve, Adam knew.

"Do you think you can come, Miss Thorpe?" asked Adam, referring to the churning.

"I don't think so," said Susan. "We're busy with the chickens."

Polly was silent asking to be asked.

"Well, perhaps Miss Cherry will come?" said Adam.

He then gave way for Bob.

Bob walked on the stars.

The time he had wasted — knowing only men and dogs! Whilst as Polly led him on, her brain was busy trying to find out if Susan Thorpe really cared for Adam Wilde.

The blind men had departed when they all arrived at Myrtle Cottage. Granny had her bonnet on, waiting. Susan had some way to go. Adam proffered to take her on the way. He wanted to be moving cautiously with Susan, too, to let her see that he — needed her. More and more Susan became his ideal woman, the type that Swift depicted as the perfect wife, prudent, soft-answered, sacrificing, dependable.

"Let's all go," said Bob, at Granny's doorstep. "Come on, Miss Cherry."

Adam was thus foiled.

But he walked ahead with Susan.

"Is it true that — Sagg Farm is advertised?" asked Susan.

There was a little pause.

"I'm afraid it is," said Adam ruefully. "But — I think I shall be the one who buys it. Anyhow, it's safe yet." His optimism was a grim faith, considering the corner he was in.

This had been a wicked year for Adam, too.

"I — I will ask my father to give a hand," said Susan.

Her voice sounded a little nervous.

"That is kind of you," said the proud man.

Susan appreciated the compliment.

Adam had accepted her offer.

Susan was thinking how Bob would feel the hardship of hiring himself out on some other man's farm, if Sagg Farm went.

When Bob walked with Susan, Adam with Polly again, Bob was saying to Susan, "Do you think I've a chance, Susan?" Susan thought he had.

"But — do you think she likes me a bit?" urged Bob.

"It's just — possible," said Susan.

He saw that she was smiling.

Susan was copying a little of the lightness of Polly Cherry. For a moment she looked roguish, less like a demure mother confessor.

Acting on her advice, Bob procured the "Jewel Song" out of "Faust."

It arrived at Myrtle Cottage two mornings later. Polly had come up early that morning, to do her few daily tasks at "home" before starting work for Granny.

She tried to continue her task of whitening the doorstep that looked out on the "rosydandrum" in which the birds were singing gaily. But she made but a poor job of it. The "Jewel Song" engrossed her. Whilst as Cherry watched her at it — heard her fresh voice in the "Mirror, mirror, tell me truly" — he winked at Nan, saying: "Madam Albino there is having a good time."

When Polly went down from Myrtle Cottage to Granny's she passed Adam on the way to Narrowfields with the milk-float. He smiled down at her, stood up in the old cart, holding the reins over Jinny's back, and she smiled up at him — and blushed. The vision of her in her pink sun-bonnet, with that pink plush, haunted him all the way to Cherrydale. Whilst Polly — Polly was twittering: "Mirror, mirror, tell me truly," until Granny asked her what mak' o' rubbish she'd got on the brain this time. Polly was under the impression that Adam had sent this song.

When Adam called at Granny's cottage for hen-grit, late in the afternoon, he saw Polly in a new phase.

She was covered in one of the dead Primrose Leaguer's old shirts, as he entered, standing in the little scullery, taking lessons in washing from Granny. Just as he entered he heard Polly break off in her whistling from "Rigoletto" — and Granny saying, "Listen to what I'm saying, wilta? Drat the lass! Nobody'll ever teach her anything!" Which made him smile.

There was a certain play for his dominance in trying to break in the skittish soul of this town girl, just as there was a fascination to him in trying to save Sagg Farm.

When she ran out of the way on seeing him, with a horrified "Ooo," and Granny said grimly, "Eh, lass, tha'll do weel if tha'rt never sin no waur nor that," he realised that this lighter side of ploughing a girl's heart, instead of stubborn land, was a relief from that harder struggle that was now culminating.

"Choir practice up at our house to-night," he told Polly, when she came out of the scullery, still garbed in the shirt.

Polly nodded.

"Seven prompt," he called laughingly, as he went.

Polly was always late.

Polly lifted up the curtains that made the background for Granny's wares and peeped after him.

Granny's proud flesh in her gammy leg was troubling her to-day.

"Don't fa' in luv wi' yon mon," said Granny, grimly. "What he wants is a woman wi' buddin' wings, an' tha'rt a long way short, Polly. If tha could pop on a dook as wanted somebody to leet his pipe an' laugh an' sing — tha'd be a' reight. Well, happen. The chap for thee should ha' bin ordered, by good reights. Adam comes o' folk 'at warked their women folk to death, whilst they went up and down to cattle fairs an' sich like. He might weel crack on his grandfather. He's the spit on him — and he killed his wife — wi' wark. She starched for a' th' gentry, besides helping run th' farm. They laid her out on her own ironing board. Oh, they're grand 'uns are the Wilds. Either they don't care a brass button which end goes first — or they're like that."

Polly turned away from the window.

She was laughing.

"I'm not in love with *him*," she said disdainfully.

"I reckon naught o' folks at worships graven images," said Granny, returning to the wash-tub.

The keen-sighted old Calvinist had half seen through Adam's game lately. She did not like the way Polly grew tongue-tied in his presence at times. She was thinking of withdrawing her twenty pounds. After all, had it not been flying in the face of Providence to try help Adam keep Sagg Farm?

He was going to marry Susan Thorpe. At least, the Thorpes thought he was. She had heard as much.

The Thorpes stunk of brass.

They must help him.

In this spirit she worked all day, till the washing was done. Polly had been, as Granny said, "waur nor a bare place." She was glad to sit down, spectacled, and read Josephus, between the tinkling of the shop bell whilst Polly was at the practice.

When Polly got up to Sagg Farm she found three extra candles burning on the old harmonium top. Adam was dressed in his best.

Polly was all of the choir that turned up.

"Oh — don't go. We can run through a few pieces," said Adam. So they did.

They ran through piece after piece. It was Sarah, in Adam's old overcoat, and the muffler that gave her a mummified look, who asked Polly to sing "Come unto Him all Ye that labour." Labour! Sarah knew the full meaning of that word. Sarah had taken a wistful liking to the blithe girl with the lilting joy in her voice. She reminded Sarah that long ago she, too, had been feminine, and taken a little pride in putting her hair up. So few people came to the farm, too.

Polly singing that piece she had sung in the wheat-field had in her mind all the guilt of those kisses that ever lay, all this year since she had come to Cherrydale, a barrier between easy friendship with Adam Wild. Adam turning the music felt her fingers, going to the same task, draw back. The music fell on the sanded floor. Player and singer bent to pick it up — with a consequent bumping of heads. Then, Polly giggled. Whereupon Sarah smiled, then laughed — and Adam smiled, and old Wild woke out of his uneasy sleep, and murmured his old plea for this past week. "Oh — for a drop o' whisky."

"Take her and show her th' chickens," said Sarah, suddenly, when the playing was done. "An' — have a bit o' supper, Polly. I'm goin' to call thee Polly."

"Everybody does," said Polly.

She smiled.

She was in one of her honest, simple, seven-year-old phases, to-night.

"I don't think Miss Cherry cares about chickens — " said Adam.

But Sarah got the lantern.

"Let th' child see 'em," she said.

Adam wondered why Sarah was so eager to get them out of the kitchen. There was nothing for it but to go.

When they stood within the hen-house, there arose a great beating of wings from startled, sleepy birds. Polly clutched the arm of the man who held the lantern.

It was as she knelt down, looking into a box that held a fluffy-breasted Buff Orpington with her thirteen chicks, that Adam remembered this was a good opportunity for making his first furrow in Polly's heart. He was not altogether unexcited himself at this new hobby — playing at love. Bob must be saved, at all costs. Polly would not be a suitable wife for a — Wild. Thus did the rationalist excuse himself for laughing at Polly as Polly was going to laugh at Bob.

"How would you like to be a farmer's wife?" Adam asked her.

Looking up swiftly she saw a pair of Airedale brown eyes fixed intently upon her. Adam expected some of the wiles he had seen her use on Bob.

"It depends," said Polly candidly, "how much I liked the — farmer."

Then she fell cuddling a yellow chicken against her cheek. If he hadn't been there he thought she would have talked baby-talk to it.

"You can have — that," he said.

"What?" she asked.

"The chicken," he told her.

She looked at it, then at Adam, and said. "Oh — thanks." Then she asked, anxiously, "What shall I feed it on?" Adam pondered, then said, "Oh — beans."

"Beans?" she queried. "Really! Do they eat beans? I should have thought——"

Then, they both burst out laughing, at her innocence.

"You've a great deal to learn," he told her, "before you are fit for a farmer's wife."

She blushed this time.

The chicken squeaked.

"Ooo," she murmured. "Poor ikkle thing. I'm going to kill it."

Adam showed her how to hold it.

He held her hand and closed her fingers round it.

She was an utter little fool.

But, for the moment, he half hesitated at playing with her light soul. Wasn't Bob big enough to look out for himself? But even as he asked himself the question, he knew Bob was as irresponsible as Polly. They would be a couple of fools together — and Bob would have a fool tied round his neck for the rest of his life.

The only thing to remember was — to turn Polly's thoughts from Bob, without endangering his own chances with Susan Thorpe.

"I thought you'd got lost," said Sarah, as they entered the kitchen. Supper was ready. Sarah had made herself what she called "half-way decent". She had taken off the muffler and tried to put her hair up. She had also donned a blouse.

Polly had the same effect on every one.

She made them feel fossils and wiseacres.

"Some tay, father?" asked Sarah, as they sat at table.

The man on the settle groaned — thinking of whisky.

"Are you coming to-morrow, Miss Cherry?" asked Adam.

"Ca' her 'Polly,'" said Sarah. "'Miss Cherry* doesn't suit her. It's too owd for her."

Adam smiled.

"Polly, then," he said.

Polly dimpled — and blushed.

Looking at her across the table Adam thought, just for one fleeting moment, that had he been a rich man, he would have married Polly. As a working partner she was no use. She was just — a little, foolish beauty, with a throstle's throat. These were luxuries for the rich.

"Eh, our Bob'll be mad he worn't in," said Sarah once.

Adam and Polly were discussing music.

The foolish thing knew more about music than anything else — except lads.

"Art comin' to-morn?" asked Sarah.

Polly nodded.

"Tha can twine, then," said Sarah. "It gies me a pain under my left breast."

Adam started.

"You never said anything of it — " he began.

Their mother had died of cancer.

"What's th' good o' sayin' ?" she asked, a little nettled.

For a moment Adam saw a little of the tragedy of Sarah's overwork at the farm.

But — when he got out of this hole, she could have help. Besides — she would have Susan to help her. Susan who was young and strong, even as she had been when first this struggle began.

But it was not of Susan or Sarah he was pondering as he took Polly home to her Granny's through the splendour of a moonlit night. They both wished on the wishing-bridge. He held up the lantern to let Polly see a rose-bush in its glory and to hear her say "Ooo" in her foolish, rapturous way. He wondered what she had wished. There were star-ripples in the water below the bridge, and their reflected faces, looking down. Everything was scented. There was only the one rail. Adam held Polly's hand for safety. It fluttered in his like a foolish bird.

Starry silences all about them, plash of water on mossy stone, and the moon climbing up the sky, there was something elfin in the night.

As they passed from the bridge, a green hill came in sight — a little hill with a blue, moonbeamy sheen on it.

"If I saw fairies dancing in a ring," said Polly, "I wouldn't feel surprised. Would you?"

She looked up into his face like a seven-year-old.

The freshness from her that Susan had felt swept around the care-burdened man.

Perhaps the long, uphill struggle to keep Sagg Farm was telling on him.

He took off his cap, without answering Polly's remark, and stared up into the glory of the Milky Way.

"I like star-baths," said Polly's voice.

He was a little surprised.

"Mind!" he warned Polly.

It was another excuse for holding the foolish hand a moment.

The village lay sleeping under moon and stars when they came down to it. The little houses were like match-boxes against the hills.

Granny's light was burning, the inn had an illumined window. All else was — asleep.

"Oh — " said Granny, "tha'rt in good hands," and she closed the door after Adam with a "Good night, Adam." Granny had called in her twenty pounds. He would get the letter in the morning.

Before leaving the road, the inn light made Adam pause. He went back.

His father's misery, chained in that desert of Thirst, had made a human appeal to him. He did not realise it as a humanity in any way connected with that touch of that trembling, young hand.

He stopped on the wishing-bridge, listening to the water, wondering what Polly had wished. Then, he remembered that he did not mean to lose Sagg Farm.

"What's up with our Adam?" asked Wild, when Adam had gone to bed after pulling out the whisky bottle and handing it to his father with an ungracious look that said "Oh — take it."

Sarah shook her head.

"He'se not in love with that yellow-haired hussy, is he?" he asked. "An' gotten th' softenin' o' th' brain."

"She's a nice lass," said Sarah.

Wild enjoyed his whisky.

Then he said, in his dazed way, "I thought our Bob were after her".

Sarah said nothing.

"I wouldn't like yon lads to get across," said her father. Another silence. Then, "no, by G — ff, I wouldn't like them lads to get across."

In the morning Adam got up, betimes.

He had been awake before dawn.

He got up to carry out his intention to burn Polly Cherry's glove. It was somewhere in Bob's possession. Bob was yet asleep. His moor tramp of the previous night had been a long one.

Adam found it at length.

It was in Bob's breast pocket.

Adam carried it by the finger-tips — that thing with the impress of Polly's hand. It had cast a spell on Bob. He felt the spell of it, himself, as he carried it so. The fire was roaring up the wide chimney.

He pitched it into the middle of the flames.

It writhed, shrunk, and — he could not dispossess himself of the idea that he was burning that foolish little hand, one finger of which seemed to point accusingly at him.

After breakfast, he watched Bob feeling about in his pocket for it, looking in the deep shadow behind the door, looking questioningly at him, once or twice, too. But — a woman's glove was not a thing a dog-man could ask for.

Polly came that day to churn.

Bob leaned outside the door with the netting throwing shadows on the red tiles where the great pans of milk were set, and whereon Polly stood, a dainty dairymaid in blue muslin and exuberant youth.

Polly would not flirt with him, except very mildly.

She was busy, she said.

Adam was triumphant.

Whilst whenever Bob saw Polly staring in the direction of Adam, who took scarcely any notice of her, his suspicions about the glove grew. Though — he had taken it out of his pocket on Whitemoor, to be sure he still had it. For this was Bob's first passion.

It was quite late when Polly went down to Granny's.

The sun was gone down.

Granny had left Polly her ordinary tasks to do.

Granny saw that she did them, late as it was.

She was surprised that Polly did not grumble.

Half-asleep as she was, the girl went cheerfully about. Polly was moulding herself on Adam's lines. Polly had not the least doubt about it that some day Adam would marry her. She thought she would ask him to have a little churn for her — that could stand on the floor, not quite so difficult to keep going as this big one Sarah had put up with for so long. This was Polly's first affection. It had begun, subconsciously, on that night in the wheat-field, when she had told Adam she would sooner marry a monkey.

She woke, some hours later, out of a dream of Adam, to hear Granny making a strange noise.

"Ooo, Ooo!" cried Polly, shaking like a leaf. "What shall I do? What shall I do?"

Granny's heart had dotted and carried two, this time.

She got water — and spilled it over Granny.

After the second attack, Granny said: "Fetch Miss Thorpe. She'll talk less nor — anybody."

Granny was too ill to see that Polly ran out into the night with bare feet, and only a coat over her nightdress.

Through the dead stillness of the night Polly ran to the Thorpes', knocked them up, and came back with Susan. It was only when she got within the cottage that she realised the terrors she had braved.

Granny was better.

She had propped herself up in bed.

But Polly begged Susan to stay the night.

Susan did.

Whilst as she saw how little able the girl was to take care of herself — she shuddered at the thought of the irresponsible Bob having her in tow. Love is not always blind.

It was as they slept in one bed, in that moon-silvered room, Granny asleep, that Susan tried to keep her promise to Bob to do all she could.

Which left cunning Polly a way open.

"Do you like Adam Wild?" she asked.

There was a silence, through which the blind tap-tapped in a wind. It was like old Time walking along on a stick, because he was so very old.

"Oh, yes, I like him," said Susan, honestly.

"Do you like him a lot, I mean?" queried Polly.

She was peeping at Susan, Granny's white sheet up to her dimpled chin. She looked like an alabaster angel in the moonlight, her hair about the pillow, but too anxious for the comparison to hold quite true.

"Not — not in that way," said Susan.

She was watching Polly.

The little dream that had begun on that stone wall on the moors where the poor sheep was buried was building up, again.

"You do," accused Susan, swiftly.

The blind tap-tapped again.

"Ooo, — yes," said Polly, in her extravagant way. "I could — die for him — I think."

"You foolish child," said Susan.

They fell asleep with their arms round each other's necks, and the blind tap-tapped the night through.

"Think on," said Granny, in the morning. "Nobody has to know I've been ill. I'll not be messed an' mucked about wi' folk — whilst I'm wick. They can do what they like wi' me when I'm dead."

Chapter 13

Bob Wild leaves home

At the turn o' the year, Bob Wild made fewer confessions to the girl he had made into his adviser and the sharer of his great romance! Something in Susan herself may have accounted for this; or it may have been the odd hallucination that sometimes seized him, when raving to her of Polly — the hallucination that he had seen eyes like Susan's a thousand years ago, somewhere in a time he could not remember. It bothered him more and more. Moreover, when talking of Polly, he often stood near enough to Susan to see himself mirrored in her grey, quiet eyes. Sometimes he went to have a chat with Jabez—and if Uncle Nat was over, took a hand at Ludo. After his moor walks, too, if he saw a light, he sometimes called in.

But the full reason of the hallucination only dawned on him one Sunday, when he accepted Mrs. Thorpe's invitation to tea.

"The sheep," said Bob, suddenly, in triumph, and stared at Susan, his hand suspended over the plate of currant-cakes.

His memory had given up the mystery, at length.

Susan was the little girl who used to mind with him — the little girl whose very name he had forgotten. He saw the moor, the stone wall, solemn covenant of the finger across the throat, and Susan — praying for the soul of the sheep.

Moreover, as Susan's eye met his, he saw that she *had never forgotten*. And he wondered if she recalled the kiss. He remembered the touch of her rain-wet mouth yet. That little girl — was — his mother-confessor.

He was fond of Polly.

He was very fond of Polly.

But—Polly was irresponsive all at once.

Bob's affections weren't the kind to stand too much of an ice-refrigerater.

But that night, when Polly sang, and he saw her from the Thorpes' pew, her mouth a rosy O — flooding the place with melody, the old spell was on him, with this difference, it irritated him, and caused some conflict with that innocent memory of the sheep-incident. When the choir sang "All we like Sheep," his mind was again back with Susan, little Susan, whose Dad had been poor then, on the moors. Sometimes, lately, he had wondered what kind of a child Susan had been. As she had listened to his confessions about his feelings for Polly, she had looked so pale, quiet, and crystallised. That had been Susan, that child mate of his childhood, to whom he had once given a sandpiper's egg. As he knelt by Susan in the pew, he could smell the violets at her breast.

He went straight home after chapel.

Adam, however, had got in before him.

Adam was busy book-keeping when he hung up his hat.

The accurate man, his face set in the look that said he would go down fighting to the last to save the farm, was trying to find a sixpence that eluded him in the accounts. His grandfather appeared to him from the dark-framed picture on the wall. A square-jowled, deep-lipped old fellow in swallow-tails, knee-breeches and buckled shoon.

Sarah, who had neuralgia, was bathing her face with camomile. Old Wild was in bed. Sarah retired after setting Bob and Adam their supper, at the other end of the long table.

When she had gone, Bob remarked. "Where's that glove, Addy?"

The repressed anger that had seethed in him since he missed the glove that morning was stamped on his face. Perhaps the knowledge that Polly was scarcely likely to make him a contented man, made him more angry. It was the moment when he was trying to convince himself his passion for Polly was deathless. There is no more intense moment.

Adam Wild looked up.

"What glove?" he asked, casually.

The silence that followed was sinister.

Adam went on trying to find the sixpence.

The hunt had occupied him the night before, and the half-year's rent was due.

"*Her* glove," said Bob, at white heat. "Where is it?"

Adam went on trying to find the sixpence.

"Give it up to me, Adam," said Bob, thickly. "Tha'd best."

Adam looked up.

His brows were knitted.

"What art talkin' about, Bob?" he asked dispassionately.

"Give me her glove. Tha'rt jealous on me, Adam," said Bob.

Adam stared for a moment, then broke into laughter.

"She's my sweetheart," said Bob.

"She's everybody's," retorted Adam.

He went on hunting the sixpence.

"What! Doesn't ta want her?" queried Bob.

Adam laughed lightly.

"But——" began the younger brother.

It was difficult to accuse Adam of having laid siege to Polly's heart. Yet gradually, for a year, and latterly, almost openly — Adam had paid attention to Polly.

"Get out o' my light," said Adam, impatiently. "I'm reckonin' up."

Then Bob Wild struck out.

Adam fell like an ox.

When Sarah and her father came down, Adam was just picking himself up. His best coat was covered with yellow sand, from the floor. His eye was bleeding. And — the Wild demon was awakened in him.

He rubbed his hand across his eye.

"Lads!" said old Wild, appearing. "Lads! Eh — this would ha' put your mother in her grave if she hadn't been there."

Bob Wild's passion was gone.

The sight of the blood on his brother's face had shocked him into sanity.

"Whatever is it o'er?" asked Sarah, trembling.

Adam approached Bob.

Bob suddenly collapsed — mentally, before that look.

"Hit me, Addy," he pleaded, humbly. "Hit me. I deserve it."

Sarah pushed herself between, looking up at Adam's face.

"I'm not goin' to hit him," said Adam, quietly. "But one of us two goes out of here to-night."

"I'm sorry, Addy," said Bob.

The slow apology from a Wild might have moved some.

"He's struck his own blood-brother," said Adam, bitterly, "o'er a wench!"

The tribal code was logical from the man trying to keep a farm, because his ancestors tilled it.

"Lads!" said the old man, quaveringly. "Lads!"

But the fiat was gone.

It was Bob who went down the hillside, Sarah's tears warm on his cheek, his father's eyes following him. At the foot of the hill, before crossing the wishing-bridge, he turned and looked back at the farm.

He understood a little of what Adam had felt for it now, as he was leaving it. Homeless! And the sight of his brother's blood hung guiltily before him, through the darkness of the night. He had struck Adam who had fought for him at school — over a wench. He had struck Adam, with whom he had slept in his childhood, fighting on the bed till their mother came and thrashed them both, and left them in the dark. Never had they dreamed of this — then. He wandered aimlessly to and fro about the village for an hour and a half. People were then going to bed. There were shadows on the blinds.

There were people who would have taken him in, but he could not ask them — to-night, meet the questioning glances. Shame was on him. It was only chance that he had not killed his brother — or, blinded him. No two passions so conflicting could live in one breast. In that hour, when Bob Wild struck over the Clouds, black under the ghostly veil of mist lowering down from Fouldsworth, his passion for the singing-witch went under. Never in his life had Bob Wild been so like his elder brother, as an hour after he had struck him, a guilt which he felt he could never forgive himself if Adam did. Whilst Adam — Adam in the proud misery of his heart threw the blame on this light girl, and if he had wavered in the punishment he was bringing on her, the revenge for the lads who had danced to her pipe, he hardened again — now.

Chapter 14

Adam speaks

Seven moons, one after another, peeped through Cherrydale's trees that broke the bareness of the land about. It was going to be a white Yule; such as Christmas cards are made from. Every step of Cherrydale's lanes, now, would have made Christmas vignettes. Every bush was a blossom with puffs of snow, as though trying to mimic May. White roofs, window-ledges, gardens.

Dawns came up over the dumb, sheeted hills with torch of gold blazing over a world in its winding-sheet.

At noon the village would be trying to shovel itself a path from each one of the little doors, and a path down the one street, only to have it covered again in the night-time. Afternoons had sapphire and emerald skies against which hips and haws that had managed to poke through tumbles of snow, burnt blood-red. The brooks, wandering in all directions, were lamp-black. When the sun sank the moon came up. The bills changed from blinding white to lavender and rose-pink, then — into silver, under that moon, after the sapphire of the sky had faded into that wash of Iceland green that heralded night. Every stone wall was snow-blown. Some were entirely hidden.

The rough, broken landscape was buried under a soft graciousness without one single line of ugliness. It was a super-beauty that had in it something almost uncanny.

Cherry had not been out with his pack for a whole week.

But he was not worrying.

He was pedlar monarch in the dale.

A year and a half had given Cherry a good grip on the feminine heart of the little villages.

His success as the Little Pedlar was becoming as assured as had been that of the Big Porter.

Nan had as yet had no relapse.

There was peace in the Cherry castle.

But Cherry had one care. He was not satisfied about Polly.

The making of her into a woman appeared to have put a strain upon her. She was thin. She never sat down in the old easy, adolescent way. He missed the foolish lightness of her giggle. She had let all her frocks down.

She was working hard, of course. Every week she was singing somewhere. The religious bodies found that fresh Harker voice an asset — and a cheap asset.

Even Nan noticed that "our Polly" was altering.

It was "our Polly" now — not "that bitch."

The fear of God, in Nan's case, had worked out on the side of greater politeness and the scrubbing brush.

Nan was Christmas-decorating, though it was yet eight days to Christmas.

She was mounted on a pair of squat wooden steps, hanging Moses and Daniel with fancy paper trimmings, in a kitchen that had red firelight and lamplight.

Tea was spread — waiting for Polly.

"She's here!" said Nan.

She was.

Rag went into his usual delirium.

For a pedigree dog Rag was a demonstrative, uncontrolled savage. He began to lick Polly's boots as she came into the range of firelight.

Polly had indeed changed.

But the blurred softness ensuing from her plumper condition had hidden some of her beauty, it seemed, now. Even the slight look of strain that had grown into her expression had added that touch of character without which any face fails to attract for long.

"Anything from Becky?" she asked.

She asked it as she had never failed to ask. Without rhyme or reason Becky had suddenly stopped writing to her.

"There's a letter there from Narrowfields," her mother told her.

Polly flew to it with a touch of her old lightness.

"Is it from Becky?" asked Cherry.

"H'm," said Polly, excitedly.

She knelt down on the fender to read it.

"Summat up, Polly?" queried her Dad, watching her face.

"Ooo," she murmured. "Ooo," and broke into a passion of tears.

Nan picked up the letter and read it.

"She's come to a misfortune," said the shrew. "She says she goin' to the workhouse——"

Polly sobbed again.

She sat sniffing at intervals over her tea. But the attitude of her parents towards Becky did not encourage her to follow the course she had thought to take — to ask Becky to come there.

Polly was not built to beat things down.

After her second cup of tea she ceased to cry.

Apparently she regarded Becky as lost.

"Pansy laid an egg this morning," she told her parents less sniffily after a while.

"Good lass, Pansy!" said Cherry. "Tha didn't think she'd lay paving-stones, did ta, Polly?"

"Ooo, it was such a nice little egg," said Polly.

"A *little* egg?" said Cherry.'

"There's a lot of strength in first eggs," Polly informed him. Polly as an authority on food-values was too comical. Cherry burst into laughter.

"Bring it for th' lad," he said. "I need all th' strength I can get."

"Eh — tha art a greedy swine!" said Nan.

"If everybody looked after No. 1," said Cherry, amiably, "there'd be no No. 2's, would there?"

For a generous man he had the old passion of liking to appear a selfish brute.

"Granny's cough any better?" asked Cherry.

His week of snow-bound martyrdom had kept from him the doings of the village.

Polly nodded.

Granny had impressed upon Polly that if ever she told of her "ill doos," she would cut her off with a shilling.

"She'll live to be a hundred," said Cherry. "Well, here's health to the best mother-in-law in the world, and to my wife's husband." Something glug-glugged out of a bottle, into his cup. It was sufficiently near Yule for the action to be justified.

"Want some, missus?" he asked.

Nan hesitated a little.

Then — the vision of the devil made her turn her back on temptation.

"Well," quoted Cherry, "one in a house is enough."

"We'll have a goose," he said, dreamily. "One o' them big, bumping-weight fellows wi' yellow feet an' fat as creases your chin. We'll have open house. We'll——"

"Tha doesn't know what'll happen afore Christmas," Nan told him, grimly.

Nan was always sitting on coffins to survey the world, now.

After tea Polly went upstairs and Nan went down to see Granny.

Polly had reached a crisis in her life. Polly was burning up love-letters, valentines, photos. Adam Wild had asked her to meet him before choir practice and walk with him to Witch Gate and back. Adam had indeed ploughed his furrow deep.

"Music?" queried Cherry, as she came down, her portfolio in her hand.

She nodded.

Music! All life was music, to-night. Forever and forever, and forever, she was going to be happy. Music! The world itself was music, as she stepped out into it, a huge, spreading blossom of crystal purity, lying under a white moon, in a great silence. She sang as she went down the hillside. It was an old French gavotte. Adam had told her how brocaded dames and fine beaus had danced to it. As she lilted it they seemed to trip along with her, down the white hillside, dancing, dancing. Then, she recalled Becky — just for a moment. Becky was sad. Should one friend be glad when another was sad? But — Oh! How could she be sad? Adam Wild had asked her to walk to Witch Gate and back with him. *Walk with him.*

She became fey.

She danced down the hillside, changing her song.

It was Tartini's "Devil-Dance," now. Little imps seemed to trip down the hillside with her now, dancing, dancing, rig-a-jig, jig, under the light of the moon. She stopped and began to gather handfuls of white snow and to toss it away, watching it sparkle. But — the cold made her hands ache. Her hands that she had been so vain of were chapped now, always. Sometimes they bled. But always she had the ecstasy of knowing that she was getting a little nearer to that ideal woman of Adam Wild's — strong, hard-working, *useful,* "hodden, grey."

To-night he was going to ask her to be his mate.

She was sure of it.

He had made love to her in every way but that of common speech — ever since Bob went away, especially. He had endeavoured to mould her mind, and the giggling Polly had painfully plodded through books she did not like. Always he had given her to understand that he did this because her destiny was mixed in with his.

When she had showed him the pats of butter she had made — all by herself — when Sarah was sick, he had told her she was going to be a fine little wife for a farmer, and his Airedale brown eyes had said which farmer.

At the bottom of Thomas Hill were two flat fields, intersected only by a low hedge. No foot had trodden their whiteness. They sparkled fairily under the moon.

What fantasies are not hidden in the heart of girl-hood?

Down the glistening track of the moonbeams on the first of these white fields Polly waltzed, whistling Tartini's "Devil-Dance," up and down, down and up, from one end of it to the other, her shadow dancing with her, whilst she drew all that glory of whiteness into her very soul, and the memory of those days when she had felt sick, and lost, and up against bars, in Narrowfields, was danced under her feet. A strong man, a good man, a man who could take care of her — cared for her, foolish, joy-loving, peril-daring little Polly.

"Ooo!" she said.

She floundered into a bush.

Snow was powdered over her.

She looked dazedly at the moon.

The fit of ecstasy was over.

She walked demurely towards the place where she was to meet Adam.

She saw his shadow on the whiteness of the snow.

The boys that had waited for her like this!

But — never one whose shadow she had loved.

He saw her coming.

She tried to walk steadily.

But her knees shook under her.

The foolish heart was glad and afraid.

To think that a man like Adam Wild should care for a foolish creature like Polly Cherry! She couldn't quite credit it, yet.

"Which way?" he asked.

Adam's voice was not quite steady, either. He had come out to punish this girl who had meant to fool his brother. Her face, looking in his direction, as he waited — had unnerved him. He had done his work well.

"Up the hill," chose Polly. "Right up into the stars."

Her giggle was tremulous.

It was funny to choose the path for the high-handed Adam.

Before them rose an upland field of white. A little path was trodden up its face. A dog had rolled down it. Polly's feet tripped along. Their two shadows went before. They kept almost guiltily apart, those two shadows. Adam's looked like a Cossack's, for his hat was exaggerated on the snow. Polly's hat took the shape of a poke bonnet.

"A penny for your thoughts," said Adam.

"I was thinking," said Polly, "about Becky christening you 'John Willy, from heaven'".

Adam laughed.

He stopped to show her Orion.

Then they went on again.

The world seemed trying to dissolve itself into light. Stars overhead, and underfoot, drifted snow flashing like powdered gems.

The singing of snow-frosted rushes was the only sound about them as they topped the slope, walking towards Witch Gate, going by the golf-links, white, smooth and with only the shadows of the barriers upon them.

They discussed Handel — set him above all others.

Then they got on to Grieg — and quite suddenly, Polly was singing one of Grieg's cradle songs, exquisite as it floated between snow and stars. Then they discussed cradle songs in general, and Adam sang what he thought was the finest one in existence — an outlaw's cradle song, about being rocked in the heather, and defying the world. They had really to keep on talking.

At last they stopped.

The path went downwards.

Witch Gate was in sight, a white village set by a black sheet of water. They could hear dogs barking from its road far below them.

Adam leaned on a gate, Polly stood beside him.

Adam went into the history of Witch Gate. So long as they kept talking — talking, they did not feel the awkward silence. They stood so long by the gate that Polly's feet got quite cold.

"We shall have to go back," said Adam.

He had meant to tell her by the gate, but his courage had failed.

Between the gate and reaching the downward slope they fell back on music, once more.

It was as they began to ascend the slope, with Cherrydale going to burst on them at any moment, that Adam nerved himself for the actual confession.

"We can rest here a little," he said.

Polly stopped. She was in a dream.

"I suppose," said Adam, making himself hold on to that ploughshare of justice, "you will wonder why I asked you to come to Witch Gate with me?"

"H'm," she nodded.

Her voice was almost inaudible.

She was looking down at the snow.

"I thought — you and Miss Thorpe — were very friendly," said Adam. "Do you think she would marry me?"

He had told her now that he just thought her a little fool — that all this fooling of his had meant nothing.

For pity's sake he did not look at her for a moment.

But her long silence made him fear she had gone dumb.

She was holding on to a fence, staring at him.

If she had gone into hysterics he would not have been surprised. She was struggling. She was so white he recalled a pink blush and pink sun-bonnet on a far away morning and felt sick.

"I thought you might know if she liked me," he added.

"I — I — don't know——" said Polly.

If there had not been Sagg Farm!

Her cloak blew out from her listless grasp.

He had a fool's impulse to fold it round her.

But the older passion held sway.

Set yourself to do a thing, and do it.

That was the creed of the Wilds.

None of the Wilds had held it as more of an iron law than this last struggler to retain the old soil that had grown round the roots of so many of them.

They walked back, down to Cherrydale.

Polly walked with difficulty.

The world was one huge blur of white that hurt her eyes. Her eyes smarted with tears she did not dare to shed. The moon was a leering, idiotic face.

"I think Miss Thorpe will make you a good housewife," she said once.

Her attempt to speak brightly hurt Adam.

He felt sorry that he had dealt her this blow before the choir practice. She would have to sing.

If only she had not been such a little fool.

If only there had not been Sagg Farm.

They entered the little chapel.

The others had arrived.

"Are you sick, Polly?" whispered the little mezzo.

Polly shook her head.

"You look so white," said the other.

"Do I?" asked Polly. "I'm a bit cold."

Music! She had never, never dreamed music could be so awful, that she could hate it so much. There was an eternity of it. Every note was like a funeral wail.

Fancy the "Conquering Hero" sounding like that. It was all wrong. Something was the matter with it. When she had to stand up and sing the nightmare reached its height. It *was* a nightmare. She was sure of it. She was singing, and had made two mistakes and the others were staring at her, and she was trying to laugh.

But at last it was all over.

They came out into the moonlight.

The great smarting behind Polly's eyes was fire now.

The trees they passed weren't real.

They were dead images of trees with awful weights of snow on them.

The others went to make a great snowball and roll it down from Witch Gate slope.

Adam said he would walk "agate" with Polly.

"Are you going to see Miss Thorpe, now?" asked Polly.

They were walking under the shadows of two elms, white, ghostly things.

Adam nodded.

He had half done his task to-night.

He would go on to the Thorpes'.

"Well," said a hard little voice, "you might go and ask Susan for her money and her life, but you're a little late. Your brother Bob is going to marry her. So — Sagg Farm is gone."

Adam stared at Polly in the moonlight.

He received two concurrent shocks.

The first was — the news of Susan, the sound of Sagg Farm falling. The other was — Polly's fixed, scornful look, in which he saw himself a madman, with a mania, who had set all things after that mania. Blind bat!

Susan had been in love with his brother.

He recalled that walk to Cherrydale Fair.

He looked dazedly at Polly.

He half stretched his hand out to her — appealingly.

She drew back.

Her look was unutterable.

Polly had found herself.

The pride of that long line of Cherry dames had awakened.

"Not," she said in that hard, frosty voice, "if you crept on your hands and knees."

With which she left him.

A door closed.

She had passed into Granny's.

In the vernacular, Adam had lost the halfpenny and the cake. Strangely enough, he was most bothered about the cake, now. He felt afraid of going up to Sagg Farm, Sagg Farm that had stood between him and the sunshine of youth, of care-free manhood — and this foolish girl whom he had only considered from a point of view of usefulness — as a housekeeper.

He struck up towards the Clouds.

An hour's steady walking over the crisp snow made him feel a little less demoralised. At some moments he felt he could win Polly over. At others the memory of that look of hers burnt in his brain. It was like having one's inner meanness discovered by a child.

On and on, until the glory of white hills rose around him into a sky of moonshire blue, drifting clouds like other snow mountains.

Then — across the snow something bounded towards him.

It was the Thorpe dog.

Even as he stopped, to pat it — he knew whose were the two figures coming along, lover-close.

Susan and Bob had been to look at the spot where they had buried the sheep.

They came up to him.

The brothers had never spoken since that night of the quarrel. Sometimes since Bob had worked for the Thorpes, Adam had passed him on the road.

The dog gave a glad bark to draw their attention to him.

Mean!

That was what Polly Cherry's glance had said he was.

"Good-night, Miss Thorpe," said Adam.

The two lovers stared, recognising the man in the shadow of the stone wall.

"Good-night," said Susan.

She was giving Bob a little nudge with her elbow. Adam saw her. She was reminding him that he was youngest.

Then — to Bob Wild's utter astonishment, his proud brother spoke.

"Forgi'e me, Bob," he said simply.

And then the two hands had met and Susan was smiling.

There was nothing for it but that Adam should go with them and have some supper at the Thorpes'. He went.

Whilst his wonder grew that he could ever have thought Susan in love with him.

Moreover, in that strange reflection of himself that had looked at him, from Polly's eyes, he didn't feel that he had been fit to tie Susan's shoe-laces. The fact that he would have married her — for her domestic virtues and the pot of brass — covered him with shame. He tried not to look like the criminal he felt.

Jabez, full of winks, Mrs. Jabez between tears and smiles, Ned Thom, looking and laughing very loudly, would have told Adam the truth, even had he not met the couple over the Clouds.

He learnt that Uncle Nat was very poorly.

"Tha wants to go an' keep him warm, Adam," Mrs. Thorpe told him. "I shouldn't wonder but he's a bit o' money."

Adam smiled. "Uncle Nat is as poor as a crow," he said. "But I'll walk over and see him, to-morrow, maybe."

When he passed Granny's cottage on his way home, he saw Polly's shadow cross the white blind.

He stood to watch it pass again, that girlish shadow, of the floating hair, and candlestick in hand. But the window grew dark. He climbed the hill after crossing the old wishing-bridge. Sarah was sitting up. The light came from the two windows and the gap under the door. It was the old demoniac grinning face that had struck his childish fancy as a child, when he hung on to his mother's skirts, and she had told him tales of that grandfather of his, ingraining into his mind the idea of the awful thing it would be if ever they had to leave it.

"Father in bed?" he asked Sarah, on entering.

She turned an anxious face.

"I thought — it were him — now," she said.

"Is he out?" asked Adam.

For the inn was closed.

They sat an hour waiting.

But old Wild did not come.

"Get the lantern, an' we'll go out look for him," said Sarah, tearfully, at length. —— "Eh — Adam — it's bin a mistake, lad, hangin' on here. We ought to ha' got out on it, when mother deed. The place has gotten on his nerves. Some men is like that."

"We shall ha' to get out, now," said Adam, grimly. "I'll tell that town-chap to do his worst — to-morrow."

Even yet — he clung to some foolish hope of saving Sagg Farm.

He crossed the yard, and into the mistle.

He was worried about his father.

But the worst thought that entered his head was that the old man, half-drunk, had slipped in the dark, hurt himself, and could not get up.

He groped his way into the mistle.

Adam knew every inch of the place, even in the pitch dark. The lantern hung on a hook in the farthest corner. He went straight to it. As he went he collided with something between himself and the lantern-hook.

"Dad?" he queried.

He thought that his father had lost himself, in his drunken state; got into the mistle instead of the house. His hand went out He touched something cold. He shrank back. The hair of his head stood on end as he struck a match, then his voice went out in a yell of appeal.

"Sarah!"

When Sarah arrived on the scene Adam had cut his father down.

The woman with the taper saw him with the old man, trying artificial respiration.

"I have killed an old man — an old man," he was saying. "For bricks and mortar — I have killed an old man."

Sarah, with a long breath, lit the lantern.

No change took place in the empurpled countenance.

From the roof of the mistle the suspending rope, cut by Adam's knife, swung to and fro.

A little scrap of paper caught Sarah's eyes.

It said so little, yet so much.

"Sag Farm has killed me. Forgive me, Addy. I couldn't stick it."

"We mun burn this," said the ghost of a woman, bent also with her struggle under Sagg Farm.

"Nay," said Adam.

The policeman arrived eight minutes later, and the doctor.

Life was extinct.

The crazy old farmer had been dead over an hour, even whilst the children sat anxiously over the supper table. The fact that they had not heard him come in was explained by his having left his boots at the foot of the hill, where they were found next morning, half-full of thaw rain and snow-broth from the dripping trees.

After that first outburst in the mistle Adam said no more. The publication of the message in the local papers, the discussion in the village, the eyes that followed him, Adam bore without outward token of emotion. He had lost Sagg Farm. Indirectly, he had killed his father. Polly Cherry flirted with the bass in her old way. Nay, divers strange youths appeared in Cherrydale that very week-end. The Celt in Polly was roused. People began to ask Cherry which of the lads was *the* one. He winked a knowing wink. He also had a little conversation with Polly, which left him just as much in the dark as before. Whilst Polly — Polly with over-bright eyes, a hard look that gave her a stronger resemblance to Belle Harker, covered up the paleness of her face with rouge — and covered it very badly. A few people said she ought to be expelled from the choir. But after all, her voice was a cheap asset, and no one could say anything definite. Whilst the anomaly of the human nature that could render "I know that My Redeemer Liveth" in angelic sweetness, and turn its back on Adam Wild, in his black clothes, to laugh with the bass, became one of those things only to be explained by a great inward conflict. The more the strain told in her face, the more rouge Polly used, the harder she laughed, the more she flirted, the more locks of her hair she sent out, calling back to her those devotees who had not forgotten her.

As for Cherry and Nan — they sat and looked at one another more than they had ever done in their lives.

Granny talked in vain.

Polly sat and smiled in a cold, tired, remote way.

All that she would vouch was, "Ooo, I'm tir't of good people." The Harkers were on top, now. And the Harkers, when once they got going, were a lot that didn't know when to stop — till too late.

"Dear Polly, forgive me," from the proud Adam, whilst Sagg Farm furniture was ticketed, had not the slightest effect. Pansy was carried back to him, by a small boy, also the dry books that had made her head ache.

Cherry was laying stuff in for Christmas.

He was also trying to think round the problem of — Peter, Peter who had been the last to answer the call of the siren's hair.

If he had had feet he would have "punched" Peter till he had to stay in bed for a few weeks, by which time Polly might have been expected to have become normal. Something, said Cherry to Nan, "had thrown the lass off her trolley." She would get back again. Maybe — if Peter could be kept out of the way. As he sat in his nook, he was very busy using his "three ounces."

Adam Wild went to see Uncle Nat, who very thankfully took the five shillings Adam offered him for nourishments, whilst the idea that the poor old man was thought by the Thorpes to be worth "keeping warm" on the score of brass amused Adam — as far as he could be amused, in this black hour. Every day that he spent at Sagg Farm, now, was begrudged. It weighed on him like a black shadow of troubled conscience. A bill appeared on the farm walls, by the roadsides, on gable-ends, advertising all stock, household goods, utensils, farm implements, to be sold by auction in the yard behind the "Peep In."

His graven image was gone.

Sometimes he walked about in the road looking up to see Polly's shadow fall on that white blind. He realised now that that irritation she had made him feel that night, in the wheat-field, had been the beginning of *this*. He had looked down on her as a feather-brained, feather-hearted fool. The tables were reversed now. Some men see themselves as others see them in one moment. Adam had been such. Intellectually his inferior, physically weaker, she had condemned him — by the simplicity of a childish heart that regarded him in the light of a liar, a thief, and a coward, to have thought to walk to Susan Thorpe, take her money and her life, when it was her foolish self he liked.

That this hardness lay under the softness of the nature she had hitherto revealed, made him realise that the same comity had bred her.

Christmas — the last Christmas in the old place, drew near. Bob Wild and Susan Thorpe were asked out for the first time in Cherrydale Church.

And the spectacle of Polly Cherry, in a great white muff and fur that made the rouge more noticeable, walking out with first one lad, then another, was close to him always — allied hauntingly with the memory of that cut rope swinging in the draught in the old mistle. His lips closed more firmly one on the other. Adam — was taking his medicine.

He took it like a hard Wild.

But the cup was not yet drunk to its lees.

Chapter 15

Polly's despair

When Peter arrived at the Cherry castle twice in one week, Cherry realised that something must be done. Peter was so obviously a young man in a hurry. Worse than that, he was also the wrong young man. Polly had apparently selected him as one most suited to rile good Cherrydalers. "Goodness," temporarily at least, since that night when she saw Adam Wild's soul, was to her another word for meanness.

She was seen by divers people leaning against Peter, looking, as the cobbler's wife said, "like a deein' duck in a thunnerstorm." She smoked a cigarette, one evening, in public view of four persons.

After that Cherrydale was prepared for anything, and — Polly was so sick, Cherry recommended a milder brand of cigarette.

He and Nan had a miserable Christmas, eating the goose alone, Granny being bad with asthma — Polly forgetting to do more than walk up there to meet Peter.

Cherry was watching Polly now — from his inglenook, with its recently added ledge that could serve as a writing-table on which ever stood ready a pile of printed forms headed "The Invincible Clothing Club".

Six new members had joined that day.

He was getting used, at length, to the idea of himself as the Little Pedlar. He had even dreamt of himself, in this new identity that had thrust itself upon him.

Now — here was the problem of Polly.

He surveyed it — a white-faced problem, of antagonistic look, and chaotic soul, in which revolution was going on — sensible Cherries against the mad Harkers.

Polly was cutting out something from her new muff and fur.

Candlelight shone on her face.

It struck him that she was near a nervous breakdown. The resolve to banish Peter became a vow.

The youth appeared that very evening.

Cherry asked him to have a "walk," and winked.

They went down to the "Peep In." There was no one in the little parlour. Peter sat down, and Cherry admired the finished artistry of Peter's handling of a pint pot, with a reservation that a man with a face like Peter should never get drunk — as he would be sure to bring disrepute on good drinking. It was Cherry's steadfast opinion that only a gentleman, with inlaid morals that would not wash off with beer, deserved to get drunk.

It was after Peter's tenth pint that Cherry said suddenly, "Well, lad! What's this cock-an'-bull story about thee weddin' *my* daughter?"

Peter was not drunk.

But he stared at the reflection of the ram's head through the mirror advertising Pale Ale, as if he imagined, for a moment, that this strange observation came from the ram.

"Pardon!" — he said, at length.

Cherry was smiling.

"Tha can't be serious about weddin' yon lass o' mine," he said. "What tha wants is summat tha couldn't punch out o' shape — summat 'at'd stick to thee whatever tha did. Yon lass o' mine — she's as monny moods as a fiddle, an' needs as much care."

Peter's black eyes stared at the laughing blue ones.

"How much to call it off?" queried Cherry.

Peter leapt up.

For a moment he had forgotten that Cherry could not leap up.

Cherry jingled his money in his pocket, and gave Peter time to cool down.

Then he repeated, "How much?"

"I'm marryin' Polly," said Peter, doggedly.

Cherry's look said they'd agree to differ.

"I shall do right to her," said Peter.

"Eh?" queried Cherry.

Peter winced away from his look.

"I could do wi' chaps like thee," said Cherry genially, "if you didn't want to take a woman aboard. I've known some knew theirsel's well enough not to do. Anyhow, my lass isn't bookin' a ticket."

Then he saw George peeping in at the doorway.

"Fill us up, lad," he said.

George filled up their pots.

"Ten pounds," said Cherry, meditatively.

Peter sneered.

"It'd buy a hen-pen," said Cherry. "Well — fifteen, then. That'd take thee to America."

Peter started at that.

Cherry realised that for some reason or other he had touched the right button.

An hour later they left the inn, Cherry with a written statement from Peter that he would neither see nor communicate with Polly Cherry, after receiving the fifteen pounds.

"Where's Peter?"

It was Polly who asked her father this on his return.

"Gone home," said Cherry.

She looked weary surprise, yawned, bundled up her sewing, and departed for Granny's.

When Cherry saw her, in the morning, she had evidently passed a sleepless night Now that she had left the rouge off, Polly's pallor, the strain on the young face, was noticeable. Granny had tried to make the girl eat and behave herself, but was now, as she told Cherry, saving her breath to cool her porridge with.

Cherry winked.

His wink said he had the matter well in hand.

"Tha'rt goin' to have another matter in hand," said Granny. "For *that* Jerry Clin came here yesterday, axin' me if I knew a Miriam Cherry 'at were writing him letters threatening him for breach o' promise."

Which Cherry would have enjoyed mightily, <u>had</u> he not had this weight of Polly on his mind.

"Send him up to me," he said.

Granny said she would.

The little pedlar went up the road.

Soon afterwards Polly Cherry went up the road, also. She went on until she saw the carrier. Something passed hurriedly between them. Polly put it in her pocket, until she could read it.

It was a message from Peter.

Peter was asking tax to moot him at Narrowfields Station, on the following Saturday afternoon, and emigrate with him. He told a wonderful tale of a fortune left by an uncle.

He asked her to be sure to burn that letter. Polly never did the thing she should. She carried it in her pocket two days. After which she forgot it, owing to a strange, uncanny feeling she got whenever she went out, that Cherrydalers were watching her with a something in the feminine eye she could not understand.

Strange fancies about seeing rats run up the blind — cats run across the shop and vanish through the middle of the yellow-stoned flags in the scullery, possessed her, and odd fragments of music she had not heard or thought of for years, came up in her mind. Sometimes she would be unaware of what Granny was saying, listening to this music — until the old woman repeated the question two or three times. She would be dog-tired on going to bed, and be suddenly alert, unable to sleep, as soon as she lay down.

All this while she tried to ponder whether or not to "run away" with Peter. Running away appealed to Polly's romantic heart. All the nicest heroines "ran away." She was engrossed, at times, in thinking of Adam Wild's feelings, if told she had gone away. But she could not decide whether or not to do it.

Cherry came to the cottage and borrowed five pounds of Granny.

Two days later he came again.

If Polly had not been too engrossed with her own sick fancies she would have noticed the pain-graven look on the pedlar's face. She went out to sweep the cobbles in the yard.

"I heard to-day," said Cherry, to his mother-in-law, "a terrible lie. I know it's a lie. But — oh——"

His voice broke.

His look was terrible.

"Here, ha' a sup o' reviver," said Granny and gave him a nip of whisky.

"I heard," he said, "'at it's all over Cherrydale 'at our Polly is in trouble."

Granny stared like a Cheshire cat.

Then that remarkable old woman, with one staccato-like "What?" yapped rather than spoken, made for her bonnet.

"Goin' out, Polly," she said, as Polly came in with the broom.

Poor 'Polly!

Her strained smile, her subdued look, the revolution going on within her, gave her a sadly changed look that lent colour to the story going about.

She watched the two go out, sat down and tried to read a love-tale. They were dreadfully unreal, now, these love-tales. Moreover, she couldn't read long, or sit still long anywhere — there was a buzzing in her ears, and always she struggled with a temptation to set off and walk and walk, right up into the snow of those hills around, away from everybody. Sometimes she thought she was going to be ill.

She began to stitch at the baby coat Susan Thorpe had finished cutting out for her. She was making poor Becky's poor baby a lovely suit. As Polly's heart had hardened against good people, it had softened towards what those good people call "bad" ones.

Mrs. Jay came in to be served.

Polly laid the coat down on the counter.

She served Mrs. Jay.

Mrs. Jay was fat, and wore a virtuous look — a look downwards from the height of a British Matron's Respectability.

When she pocketed her change and took the article she remarked, pityingly, "Eh — I am sorry for thee, lass!"

Polly stared.

She didn't understand.

But a colour leapt like fire into snow.

"Oh — I don't want anybody to be sorry for me," she said, with a proud look Mrs. Jay defined as "brazent" afterwards.

"But — I am," said the matron, and went out sorrowfully shaking her head. Polly rubbed her own, trying to solve the problem.

She was still trying to solve it when Granny came back, Granny with a high colour, excited eyes, and a warrior-like look.

"Granny——" said Polly.

"Eh, lass," said Granny shortly. "Tha doesn't know what folk are sayin' on thee."

Polly looked dazed at her.

The buzzing in her ears was growing louder.

"They're sayin'," quoth Granny, "that tha'rt in trouble."

Polly stared.

Then — she laughed.

Quite suddenly the world appeared as one monstrous joke.

"It's summat to laugh at, isn't it?" said Granny wrathfully.

"Gran," said Polly, "you don't believe——"

In this monstrous joke of a world, she held out her hands to Granny.

"No-a," yapped Granny, dearly.——"But — thy father — it's meeting him all over th' place. If I could only lay my hands on where the lies started. Eh — yo' can lock th' doors against a thief, but not against a liar."

She sat down and rocked.

When she looked up, Polly was crying. The Harkers were under. The Cherries were up.

And — Granny did the most foolish thing in her life.

She crossed over to Polly, lifted the limp figure up, sat down with her and rocked the big young woman as though she were a baby.

"Tha mun get summat to eat, cock-throstle," she said. "Or tha'll be ill."

She made bite and sup, but Polly would not eat. It was seeing the girl trying to sew the baby coat gave Granny her clue as to how the gossip began. A little conversation with Polly clinched the idea. She went out to see Mrs. Jay, and came back, after telling half the village on the way of the libel on Polly. She went to see the minister, an admirer of hers. After hearing her tale he promised to preach a special sermon on Sunday, when Polly was to sing. Then she went to report to Cherry that she had half pulled back what evil tongues had done.

It was on the edge of dark when Cherry returned to his castle.

When he saw that Granny sat by his hearth, toasting muffins as Nan buttered them, he smiled. His heart had been a coal all day — sometimes against Polly.

Granny related what she had done.

"You're an angel, mother-in-law," he said. "Well — th' lass'll never need to know."

"She knows," said Granny, "an' — she's come to her senses. By Goff! Will! It's more luck nor management. Or else — there's stunmat looks after silly persons like our Polly."

"She knows——" said Cherry.

Granny nodded.

"An' — what did she say?" he asked.

"She said at first," quoth Granny, " 'at she'd never go out no more. She looked scared. Then she said she would. Anyhow, she's to sing, Sunday."

The days that followed were a nightmare to Polly. She went out into the village, with uplifted head. Once she met Adam Wild. His whitened look, the wincing of it away, made her see that he, also, had heard that rumour.

Women's eyes peering out on her from the little cottages — to turn round suddenly and find the fixed stare of gossips, while pretending to sweep their flags — began to obsess her. She began to think of Becky, poor Becky, and to cry with a new, tender sadness for the hard joke of a world. There was nothing she could say to nail this lie down — only — to come out, and keep her head well up, and stare them out.

She did this for three days.

By that time people were not sure of the accuracy of the rumour.

When she did sleep, she would wake to find eyes watching her, curious, feminine.

A girl who couldn't fight her way out of a sugar-bag nailing down this type of lie was conscious of the strain. Above all things, nature had not meant Polly for anything heroic.

"I can't go an' sing, Gran," she told Granny, whimperingly, on Friday night.

*It's the only way of provin' it's not true," said Granny. "They'll say tha's bin expelled out o' th' choir."

Polly wrote a note to Peter, saying she was not coming Saturday. But she forgot to post it. She forgot things strangely, now. Granny put it down to "upset." Whilst the ordeal of having to stand up on Sunday and sing, with all those eyes and that thought to beat down in them, became a terror, magnifying with each hour.

But the iron-strung old Calvinist held her to it.

All Saturday, until dinner-time, Polly helped in house and shop. She had sent her love and the coat and bonnet to the erring Becky — at least, to the old address, begging it to be forwarded. Also, four and sixpence — all her worldly wealth. Sometimes, as she stood at the counter, she grew quite dizzy. John Milton seemed to stare at her in a very peculiar way with his sightless eyes, from the opposite wall. Granny said there would be a blizzard before night, or she was no judge.

Granny was tired with all the excitement of fighting Martha Jay, of trying to unravel the lies, and fell asleep after dinner.

When she awoke Polly was gone out.

Granny thought she was gone "up home." But when the second hour passed and the girl had not returned, she sent a small boy to the house on Thomas Hill.

He returned with snow on his coat, and the news that Polly had not been near.

Nan came down soon afterwards.

She had to wait until Granny's shop emptied.

Nan was "dressed up."

"That lass has gone an' done summat," she said to Granny. "An' now I'm goin' to that Martha Jay — to give her a hidin', first of all — an' then — I'm goin' to seek our Polly."

Granny stared.

" 'Vengeance is Mine,' Nan," she quoted.

"I were told to go an' see her, an' hide her," said Nan calmly. "An' I'm goin'."

She went.

Whilst Granny mused on the folly of setting out to seek any one when you didn't know where they had gone — and at the earliest opportunity searched through Polly's pockets. She found the two letters — read them — looked at the clock, and started. The lass had been gone two hours. The train for Liverpool left Narrowfields in another hour and a half.

Ting-ting!

The shop-bell worried her.

Sometimes — only sometimes — it seemed that she would not mind "liggin' low an' sayin' nowt" in Cherrydale Churchyard. If only Cherry would come. Then — it began to seem a long time since Nan went out to Martha Jay's. Granny put on her bonnet and cape, left the shop to Providence, and went towards the Jays'. There was a side window to the Jay house which school-children loved to tap, and run away. The blind was not pulled down. Granny peeped in through this window, and saw a remarkable thing taking place.

Mrs. Jay was sitting writing, evidently under compulsion. Her hair and dress were very dishevelled. She had evidently been pulled about. Nan stood like Nemesis, took the paper, dried it at the fire, and — came out.

"Tha didn't lick her, Nan," said Granny, in a tone that said she hoped she had done so.

"She'll not use her tongue so ready again," said Nan. "She's written an apology."

"I'll pay for the printing," said Granny. "Well — an' tha licked her."

The wind was playing hurly-burly with the sleet now.

"Yon's Cherry," said Nan.

There was welcome in her voice.

"Nay" — said Granny.

"Just by the bush," said Nan.

The little figure on wheels came on through the blinding sleet.

"Bill," called Nan, "I've licked yon Jay woman. She's written a public apology. An' — our Polly's run away. I'm going to seek her."

Cherry blinked snow from his eyelashes and stared.

"Run away!" he said, at length.

Granny's shop was full. So she opened the door of what she called "the room," for Cherry and Nan to talk things over there.

"Like looking for a needle in a haystack," said Cherry. "We can't get there by the train starts. But I'll go an' wire em to stop her gettin' on the boat. She's a minor."

"It'll be another name," said Nan.

They went back, up to Tom Hill.

It was as much as Cherry could manage to get up the hill — a whitening hill.

The wind was gathering in the valley, making a hollow roaring.

They ate.

"There's nothing for it but to wait," said Cherry. "Besides, she mightn't have gone."

"If she hasn't — where——?" began Nan.

Cherry shook his head.

Through two hours in which every rattle of the door made them hope it was Polly's hand on the latch, they waited.

"It's only eight o'clock yet," said Cherry.

Nan went down to Granny's.

"Has she come?" asked Granny. Then, "She's not gone on that train to Liverpool Bob Wild has bin in, an' he says he met her ower by th' Clouds — walkin' steady along, like she knew where she were goin'. He said she didn't see him, though he passed close enough to touch her. Ay, it were her. She were humming, he said — quite happy."

Granny looked disturbed.

Nan looked fear.

"Tha has it as I got it," yapped Granny. "Oh, Lord — if I could see that lass sattled — I could dee content."

Then she said, "Whear arta goin'?"

"To get a search party," said Nan.

"At half-past eight?" quoth Granny. "An' happen she'll walk in, whilst they're seekin'. Happen she's gone to walk things off. But — out on them lonely places——! Well, we'll bide another hour."

They bided.

Then Nan went to report to Cherry.

"She's not gone, then," said the Yorkshireman. "But where——?"

At nine o'clock the blizzard leapt down in all its strength.

Polly had not returned.

Adam Wild sitting up in the big kitchen with Sarah, in this their last week in Sagg Farm, heard a knock on the door.

It was Nan who came in, a snow-shape of her, with her eyes looking in on them.

"There's a party goin' seekin' our Polly ower th' Clouds," she panted. "Cherry said, wilta come."

Adam did not answer.

He moved mechanically towards the door through which the snow was blowing.

"Adam — thy cap an' coyt," Sarah reminded him. "An' you'll want as many lamps as you can get."

Then she said, "Let me come, too."

Her brother did not answer.

Sarah became a dark dummy, carrying a huge lantern, the same lantern that had shed its light on the swinging frayed rope.

The party was gathered up at Myrtle Cottage.

There were a score of folk, Mrs. Jay's husband amongst them, with Bob Wild, who took the Thorpe dog. Nan and Sarah were the only two women. The party went out and left Cherry sitting in the ingle-nook, alone.

At the foot of the hill Nan Cherry found she would hinder the party.

She went back.

"Polly!" said Cherry.

Then his eager look faded into disappointment.

"It's only me," said Nan.

They sat waiting together.

The voice of the wind was like the roar of a white panther now claiming the countryside.

Cherry's heart was striding about in the blind whiteness of the hills around — seeking, seeking. His body sat still on the chair.

"It's a punishment on me!" wailed the woman opposite him, once.

He did not move.

"Bill!" said Nan, once.

He looked at her.

"Say summat," she said.

"If she comes back," he said, "I don't care for aught else. Not for aught else. But I've to sit here. Just to sit here — like an old woman! — an' *wait*."

It was as though his pent impatience hurtled itself against his body. His face was ashen, his Cherry-blue eyes blazed.

Nan drew her chair up to his, and sat down.

Another hour went by.

The two hands clasped one another.

They were waiting together.

And, little jerking confessional phrases were spoken by Nan — such as, "I wanted to be boss," "I didn't like to let thee see I cared

— it looked daft——" to all of which Cherry listened, saying nothing. Nan had hauled down her flag for good.

Cherry said nothing.

Nan got up from the chair and built up the fire. If Polly came, it might be needed. *If.* The agony of the clock grew intolerable. They ceased to look at it. They only listened.

"There's summat," said Nan, at midnight.

"A sash rattling," said Cherry.

But — it was the latch.

Sarah opened the door.

She was like a snow-woman.

"They've found her — " she gasped. "But——"

"Dead?" came Cherry's voice.

It had the old falsetto note born of striving against emotion.

Sarah shook her head.

"Jesus wept!" cried Nan, and burst into a loud fit of sobbing. Then she ran out down the hillside — only to stand, caught in the teeth of the storm, unable to get a step further.

Adam Wild strode past Nan, without seeing her.

He carried Polly — wrapped in his topcoat, which in its turn was wrapped in snow.

The rest of the party had stayed at the foot of the hill endeavouring to shelter behind the hedge of that long field down which Polly had danced not long ago.

Nan followed Adam, tearing herself savagely towards the door left open, its light streaming out.

She helped to pull away the frozen coat.

"She's dead, Bill!" she said.

At that moment Polly Cherry opened her eyes.

She saw Adam Wild, felt that he was holding her.

"Go away," she said, childishly. "Go away," and endeavoured to thrust him from her. They were the last coherent words she spoke for several days. The doctor pronounced brain-fever, when he arrived.

Sarah stayed to help get her to bed, in that bed in the kitchen corner, and to tell how Adam had saved her from walking into White Moor Reservoir. She had been stepping out blindly, unconscious of anything, singing, and somehow fighting her way through the storm, with a mad strength. Her voice, shrieking out "Kyrie Eleison" uncannily, had led them to her. The long strain was over. She would not need to sing in Cherrydale Church to-morrow, and the sermons preached on keeping one's tongue from bearing false witness against one's neighbour would have an added eloquence from that empty place in the choir.

Half way down the hill Adam turned back. The doctor passed him.

Adam had left his lantern.

Polly was babbling again — incoherencies about music — singing out of tune, but with that euphony of tone nothing could destroy. Nan was warming blankets.

"If there's anything I can get," said the man with the lantern, "or do——"

"That French gavotte," said Polly, "they don't play it right. I say — they don't play it right. It goes——"

She la-laed all out of tune.

"Or fetch from town," proceeded Adam, calmly.

Cherry nodded.

"I'll call in — every morning," said Adam.

He waited, for leave to do so.

Cherry nodded.

"Wrong, wrong, all wrong," said Polly.

Cherry looked at him.

Adam understood that just at present he was not wanted.

"By the way——" he said blunderingly, and stopped.

"If she gets better," he said, "have I your consent to come here often, Mr. Cherry?"

Cherry eyed young Wild.

"If tha likes," he said, shortly. Then, "But — hast heard all the gossip?"

Adam nodded.

Then he mumbled something about it making no difference if she were in the gutter, he'd have her. Cherry did not undeceive him. He had arrived at his own conclusions before Adam — believed it was he who had thrown the lass "off her trolley." He let Adam Wild have those few more hours of uncertainty before the minister's sermons would clear the little singer in the sight of Cherrydale. But as a man Adam's fumbling's words had placed him in the right place in Cherry's heart.

It was next morning, as the church bells rang, that a weary figure trailed up Tom Hill.

Nan saw her first, out of the window.

"There's a woman hangin' on our gate," she said to Cherry.

Then she said, "It's that Becky!"

But — what a Becky!

Becky, draggled, verminous, dragging foot by foot painfully through the snow, come from that doss-house and unable to get to the Workhouse. A green velvet bow hung down over her hat — half hiding her features.

"Polly — she said, 'Come' — " said Becky. "I haven't anybody."

"Get upstairs wi' thee," yapped Nan.

Becky dimly perceived that Polly was sick, on that bed in the corner.

"I'm not fit to sleep in a right bed," she said, miserably. "I'd no idea. I got a bed for fourpence, an—— "

"Go on," said Nan. "I'll find thee some clean things."

It was quiet after the blizzard.

Sunshine lit up the white village.

Cherry went out on his wheels to ask the cobbler's wife to come and stay with Becky, and inform the doctor.

When he got back Nan said, "Look here! I found this in her pocket."

It was a note from Peter, in which he declared he didn't believe the child was his, and that he would not pay for it.

"Every chap as is born ought to be strangled at birth," said the Amazon fiercely.

Two hours later she brought a pink atom down, wrapped in "swaddling bands" that had been used by all the cobbler's children.

"Look at its hands, Bill," she said. "Look at 'em."

She spread out a pink pair with almost invisible nails.

"What is it?" asked Cherry.

"A lad," she said. "An' look at th' collops o' fat behind its neck. Well, it's happen a good job it's a lad. An — it's as fit to live as onnybody else, for aught I can see."

There were moments when Cherry perceived that hooliganism had its bigness. Nan's calm acceptance of the child was so unashamedly Nan-like. Her sympathies were still with folk who were not "born in chapel vestries."

Meanwhile, Life had entered the house on the hill. Death stood hovering near. Against the doors stood two stubborn souls — Nan and Cherry. Never had they been as one before, but they were now, when they fought to save Polly, Polly who never rested day or night, and perhaps would never rest again until——

But of that they would not think.

At last, these two differing souls had a great common impulse.

Chapter 16

Nan's fight for Polly

Cherry sat in his ingle-nook during the weeks that followed, watching the drama of Nan fighting death. His own part was necessarily that of an onlooker. Sometimes he stretched his hand to lift a little pan from the hob, when it boiled too quickly. Occasionally, he went out and came back restless. To all inquiries as to when he would visit farms again he sent diplomatic postcards. Tear himself from that agony-hope of watching Polly he could not. It seemed to him, now, that all the work of his life was in danger of downfall. Always it was Polly the child — who lay there. In the lucid seconds that came between hours of raving Polly's ghost-like "Mam, I want a drink," or "Is my Dad there?" came as moments of heaven in a hell-like nightmare.

Nan's "Yes, luv. He's there," was a miracle of revelation, but it had the absurd effect of making him want to laugh. Polly dying, as the doctor had told Granny she was, it only being "a question of time," was treated with almost grovelling reverence. Nan lifting Polly's head and letting her drink, and laying her back again, was so like a big, horror-stricken savage in charge of a broken doll, it had a weird ludicrousness. Whilst in between was the attending on Becky, and the pink baby, who was, said Cherry, "a most awful drinker."

The cobbler's wife came every morning at nine and what she called "saw Becky right" in that little room upstairs, and each time argued with Becky on the reasons why she should call the boy Saul, after an uncle of herself, the cobbler's wife. To all of which Becky would only reply, "How's Polly?" Which the cobbler's wife told Cherry (a safety-pin in her mouth) showed a lack of motherly feeling.

After her outcast misery Becky had seen in Polly an angel, whose influence had brought her to a clean bed, and a window that looked out on hope.

The strange way in which the Cherry castle, once the stronghold of individual selfishness, had been turned into a port of rescue, was another of the things that amazed the boss of the castle.

But the most amazing feature was — Nan.

It seemed as though Nan's astounding vigour of body, tenacity of mind, even her very savagery had been given her for this one supreme struggle. It was not the tender patience of the average woman appealing to Omnipotence. It was the unreasonable, super-human efforts of a hooligan struggling against deity. Always, in her blue-checked apron and the gaudy little shoulder-shawl that was Cherry's Christmas present, he saw her, fighting for the life of her cub, in this flowering of motherhood that made her a cactus rather than a rose. She was never tired. She never seemed to sleep. She was jealous if any other woman took a turn for even an hour. If some one would be almost dead always, Cherry saw Nan with a pair; of wings budding.

It was Cherry who did the wincing when Polly's head was shaved.

"What's a bit o' hair? It'll grow again," she yapped.

Her maternity was almost an iron thing.

But the only attribute in it of human pathos was her endeavour to surround her daughter with those foolish trifles they had known to give her joy. Polly, with shorn head, dwindled body, her eyes fixed unseeingly on the rose-sprigged wall opposite, had on her bed a counterpane with bright-coloured birds and flowers, specially chosen by Nan from Cherry's selection. Every day, too, on the little table sacred to the medicine bottle, berried sprays had fresh water given to them.

But it was each morning, as the dawn came up once more, and a small, fat, round-eyed little boy said "Milk" very quietly, just outside the door, that Cherry felt the mother's softness make him want to cry — like a woman. Always he watched Nan hold the jug and the boy pour it in (how gravely and with what purpose!) with a feeling that Polly had lived through another of those black, endless nights — that she was here for another morning.

One morning the fat little boy brought a pigeon, held head downward.

His face was yet smudged.

"Who sent this?" asked Nan.

She was on guard against Martha Jay trying to salve her conscience by sending food for the sick girl.

And — the fat little boy blushed, saying the pigeon was his, and he hoped Polly would get well. He had had his pet killed because he heard they were strengthening. He had used to hear Polly sing — his eye at a crack in the blind of Old Fiddlestick's parlour.

"Oh — she'll mend when she's eaten that," said Cherry.

The fat little boy ran out to hide a new rush of tears at his pet being eaten — and stumbled against a chair, which crashed over.

Polly, who had lain making little groans, sat straight up in bed.

"Take the snow away," she screamed. "Take it away," and her thin hands made a motion to throw it off the bed.

The obsession about music, and the taking of her father's ribbed coat for a mass of writhing eels, magnified by her feverish sight, the whim that always a little black lion stood on the bed-rail looking fiercely at her — all gave way before this new craze about snow.

Startled by the noise, the poor brain went back to some sensation that had worried her. Day and night, night and day, there was snow on the bed, which she shrieked to have taken away. It was as he watched whilst Nan tended Becky that Cherry heard a name linked up with this snow idea.

The little brass knocker was muffled and the milk-boy kept outside the door, now. But Polly became wilder.

"There's one thing," said Granny, "she'll end or mend soon, Will."

All day there was coming and going from the village to the house on Tom Hill.

So many fair things were now remembered about the giddy girl. Nan kept the people outside, gave them to understand they hadn't time for them.

The doctor advised strapping Polly down in bed.

It was Nan who fought with the girl, remorselessly laying her down, again, again, again, until, worn out, the automatic action of springing up ceased. Susan Thorpe came every other night, to let Cherry sleep.

Sometimes, Cherry dozed in the corner. Always he found Nan with wide-open eyes. Sometimes he thought she prayed. He fancied sometimes she thought this a punishment for her past blasphemies. Nan had never been the same woman since the voice in the night.

As Polly became worse Nan became more of an Amazon — withal a christianised Amazon.

She lifted Polly in her arms like a baby whilst Susan drew on the clean sheets.

It was as though she had set herself by sheer strength, bodily and of will, to save her daughter's life. Nothing in the house was neglected. Always, in between tasks performed silently, Nan sat — watching, pouring drops of nourishment between the girl's lips, or fixing the ice-bags, or giving medicine. The doctor found an iron disciple in Nan.

As she watched, Cherry knew that Nan was promising the Omnipotent to be a saint, if He'd let Polly live. Funny, he mused, how some women had to see devils before they believed in an Almighty, or did what they should by men.

There were three intolerable days and nights in which Granny Harker so far broke down as to accuse them of being keeping the poor lass in misery, when it was plain that the Lord wanted her, and advised that they take her off the feather-bed, as folk couldn't die in beds full o' feathers plucked whilst the geese were wick, as everybody knew.

But Nan did not offer to let Polly go out of her misery.

Cherry and she were more in harmony than ever they had been in their lives.

Cherry sat in his ingle-nook, waiting — moving the little pan sometimes when it didn't need it. Nan sat watching and keeping the spoon going — little drops.

"I'm afraid she's rather worse," said the doctor, as he came and went "Two in the morning, I should say, will see the turn."

He went out quite cheerfully.

Nan refused to have any one stay up that night. Cherry settled himself down in the nook.

Again they went through the drama of the snow — and she would leap up, and Nan firmly made her lie down.

At nine o'clock the striking of the hour disturbed her. She became conscious for a moment.

It was the old cry.

Her gaze fell on Nan.

"Mam! I want to drink," said' a weak child's voice.

These were moments when Nan found strength to go on battling. She looked around the place after drinking.

"Susan Thorpe was here a bit sin'. Where is she?" she asked.

Susan had called at four in the afternoon.

Polly had lost consciousness again when Nan was going to tell her about Susan.

"She's going to get better, old girl," said the man in the corner.

Nan said nothing.

Cherry tried to read, to while away those dreadful hours before two. Hamlet's Soliloquy, Mark Antony's — Oration — but they failed to grip.

Always the fascination of that hour drawing near, whilst Cherrydale slept, made all other things less than nothing. He could see Polly's thin cheek, the big eyes that dwarfed her face — the thin hands doing what old wives called "weaving their winding sheet". There was Nan — more little drops — fresh ice — watching the clock for medicine.

"Nan!" said the Yorkshireman.

She looked at him crossly.

"If I had my time to do again," he said, "I'd wed thee again."

She dropped more liquid nourishment. She hadn't heard him. The ticking of the clock became an awful thing.

"She's changin', Will," said Nan, at length. "There's summat. Her breath's slackenin'!

"Wheel us up," said Cherry.

Nan came and wheeled him up to the other side of the bed. She stood for a moment, behind his chair. Then she said, "Bill, if she gets reight, I'll — give the Army up, except once a month. Cowd dinners isn't nice on Sundays." She passed her hand over his hair. It was the first caress she had given him.

Then she went over to the other side of the bed.

The flush, the excitement was dying out of Polly's face.

It grew pale and peaked.

How the great chin-dimple made a hollowy shadow, now.

Nan looked across at her mate, in terror.

Nan was breaking up at the last minute.

"Bill! say summat. I'm flayed," she said.

"Howd thy din," said Cherry.

He had taken control now.

It was the rational manhood of him, that placid strength she had used to try and shatter.

She was mum.

She was subjugated by the strength of the male.

Cherry was watching.

"Go on spooning," he said.

Nan gave more little drops.

It was half-past one. The fire was a little low. Upstairs they could hear the future Saul carrying on a small revolution for more drink.

Polly moved restlessly.

Her hands were ceasing the motion that had got to be a haunting picture.

She slowly turned on one side, face towards the wall, with a weary little sigh.

"Bill!"

"Shut up."

Cherry's gaze went back again to Polly.

She was quietening down.

The hands had ceased the restless motion altogether, now.

The house grew a still thing, save for the importunities of the infant upstairs.

"Leet a cannel, an' shade it so's it doesn't shine on her eyes," commanded Cherry.

Nan did so.

"She's asleep," she said, with tragic hope.

There was another half-hour in which life battled with death. Then Nan said, "She's breathin' nice, Bill. She's — comin' back, Bill," and went upstairs to console the infant Saul, and astounded Becky by wrapping her shoulders up.

Whilst outside, in the snow-slush, stood Adam, keeping watch until the blind went up, to say Polly lived, or remained down, to say the sun had gone out for him.

A week later, Polly was sitting up in bed, wondering how she would face the world without hair. For the rest, she was taken up with Becky's baby. Sarah Wild came to see her one day, bringing a bag of rosy-cheeked winter apples, from Ashdale, where Adam was working for Uncle Nat — a proud Wild become a hireling. When Sarah tried to find out Polly's attitude towards Adam, she was nonplussed. Polly the transparent had become Polly the enigma. Without being aggressive, Polly was not encouraging — nor discouraging. So far as Sarah could see, it was worse. But she wrote to her brother that she believed he had a chance.

"Where's Rag, Dad?" asked Polly, suddenly, one day.

She had thought of him before — but imagined some one had been keeping him to "train."

Cherry stammered a little — then decided to make a clean breast of it. He looked sadly at Polly, who was sitting up, and then at Becky, who was also sitting up, for the first time, very humble and white, but not utterly unhappy. "He made such a noise — barking, an' pullin' th' bedclothes," he said, apologetically. "So — one neet — when I'd had eight pints, Polly, and it seemed as if his legs would never be straight — well, there were a chap wi' a gun came into the 'Peep In' an' we gave Rag four pints an' he mopped 'em all up — and fell, like a soldier an' a man."

By this time Polly burst out crying — and Cherry, almost crying too, said consolingly, "He's buried yon under a little sycamore tree behind the 'Peep In.' Poor old Rag." The thought of all Rag's idiosyncrasies was too much for him. He began to laugh. Rag had left a humorous ghost behind him.

But Polly cried for some time.

She did not know how he could have done it, she said. And Cherry said he didn't either, but he believed it was kindest. The dog that couldn't fight didn't have half a life.

In two days Polly came to be less certain that Rag had enjoyed himself as well as any one. By this time Adam had got Sarah's letter, written from her place in "service" — her place that was breaking her heart.

How it came about that shortly afterwards, as Polly and Becky sat in the parlour, Polly sewing for the baby (who had actually been hawked round Cherrydale in the identical coat that had caused such heart-burning, with Granny not forgetting to point it out and laugh), a knock came to the door.

Nan answered it.

She saw Adam by the light of the lamp Cherry had bought for the porch.

"Oh — come in," she said.

Cherry had given her instructions.

Adam entered.

He was a long time wiping his feet on the mat.

Then, "Can I see Miss Cherry?" he asked.

Nan had to ask him what he said. He repeated the query.

"Oh — " she said. Then, "Ay."

She went into the parlour.

"Becky," she said, "I think it's time that child went to bed."

Becky took the hint, and came out.

"Go on," said Nan, and gave Adam a push.

Holding his cap very tightly, he crept in.

Polly looked up to see him standing there.

"Ooo!" she exclaimed.

He gripped the cap a little tighter.

"I came to see if you would marry me," he asked, humbly.

She was staring at him with those big eyes.

That close-cropped head gave her a nunnish look, further carried out by the candle at her side, the worn look of the face that had been so blurred and soft.

Then — she shook her head from side to side.

"Polly!" he appealed.

"No," said a hard little voice.

He did not move.

"No," she repeated.

She had been to the gates of death and back and had come through with that same kernel of hardness he had realised that night.

No Wild ever asked a woman twice.

He went out.

He walked about quite a time, then swung over to Witch Gate. The Wild pride that hemmed him in was a thing that riled him tonight. He had lost all, by wisdom. Wisdom tired him to-night. The cheerful stamping of feet on a sanded inn-floor to the strains of a concertina seemed the wisest thing in the world to-night. He cast off the self-esteem that had divided him from other men, and crept in humbly amongst them.

When he left it was quite dark.

He never remembered much about that night, excepting that a man he had never seen before invited him to sleep in his bed, and that his refusal hurt the man's feelings, so that eventually they were fighting. Somebody — he didn't know whom — parted them. He fell down a bank near the river, scrambled out again, and somehow blundered along to Cherrydale, going by the links. There was a moon — which he was sure was drunk. It was as he went by the path that led to the Cherry castle that it seemed nothing to ask a woman twenty times, if you wanted.

Somehow, he remembered that Polly had once told him, oh, a thousand years ago, that she wouldn't have him if he crept on his hands and knees. It became a ludicrous thing. He refused to believe that any woman could refuse any man who crept on his hands and knees.

When he got up the hill again, he could hear supper pots clinking, a baby crying, and Cherry's voice, and Polly's giggle — weak as it was. There was so much talking they did not hear him open the door.

With the stealth of a madman he came along the passage, and then — dropped upon hands and knees.

"Ooo!" said Polly, upsetting her tea.

The thing that had wambled in looked up.

"P-ple-ease, Miss Cherry, will you marry me?" it said.

It was an indescribable scene that followed.

Everybody laughed — except Polly.

"Get up," she kept saying, angrily. "Get up."

"Ay. Stand on thy hind legs, Wild," urged Cherry.

"P-ple-ease, Miss Cherry, will you marry me?" asked Adam.

"Ooo, yes," said Polly. "Get up."

She was tugging at his collar.

Adam got up.

He was so drunk that he could scarcely stand.

But he got hold of Polly's hands.

He gazed at her very fixedly — in the way of a man seeing two, though, and not quite sure which is the right one.

"I love you," he said, with dignity (staggering a little) "better than I love the Clouds, better than I love the heather when it's purple — better than I loved Sagg Farm."

Then, putting his cap on his head, back to fore, he went out — rather uncertainly, but on his hind legs.

"You never know a man till he's drunk," said Cherry, afterwards, of the event, "an' I never liked Wild so well as when I see how he made a fool on himself. He's a gentleman."

Chapter 17

Polly's wedding

Cherry engaged the room in which Polly's wedding was to be "held up" a month before the time. The only thing in its favour against the homeliness of Granny's cottage was — it would hold a hundred and fifty folk. The clan was going to be gathered to be merry, at last Cherry was very anxious that Polly's wedding should be no "dry affair." It was to be a regular cheerful, northern wedding, with lots of eating, some drinking, and Granny agreed with him that a "bit o' musick wouldn't be out on it" — that on such occasions a bit o' summat like that helped things on.

Nan refused to write out the invitations to the wedding. She had suddenly discovered that Polly didn't ought to want to be married, after all they'd done for her.

As for Granny — she avowed that the age of miracles was not gone by, since Polly had thus lit, like a cat, on her feet, despite all her invitations to destiny to ruin her.

Adam kept his head pretty well.

Perhaps the fact that he had deserved neither the half-penny nor the cake, yet was getting both, humbled him a little, or perhaps he fully realized the responsibility he was taking with Polly Cherry.

For Uncle Nat, who had lived in what appeared poverty, and accepted stray half-crowns very graciously, had died and left him eight hundred pounds. Adam had taken a little farm on the opposite side of the valley, right away from Sagg Farm. Sarah was coming to help them with the work. He had bought a little churn for Polly.

The great day arrived at length.

It was a wet morning Cherry saw out of the window — from his bed.

Polly and Nan were making breakfast.

"Changed thy mind about not going?" he queried of Nan, as she helped him to dress. "After all, I've spent five pounds on thy outfit. It'd be a shame for Mrs. Jay not to see it."

"Tha's no nateral feelin's," yapped Nan.

But when he was pushed up to the table and observed a gaudy new pair of stays airing inside the fender — he knew Nan was going.

Polly sat at table, her short hair in "wavers."

There was a trembling in her manner.

"Cheer up, Polly," said her Dad.

Whereupon she giggled tremulously.

After breakfast Mrs. Bob Wild arrived — to see the wedding-dress, Adam's present. It was one of those foolish things meant to wear once — and once only.

"I hope you'll be as happy as we've been," quoth Susan, with the air of a century-old wife.

"Ooo, Susan!" said Polly, suddenly, "if only I was a bit — wiser."

"Adam," said Adam's sister-in-law, "has sense enough for two." But even as she said it, she wondered what Polly would think had she known that Adam had been out, roaming the moors all night, in the crazy way some wise men have when once they definitely settle to make fools of themselves.

"Yes. He's up," she told Polly.

Adam was staying with them for nearness to the church.

"I'll go down to Granny's with Susan," said Polly.

Polly was afraid of a scene on her leaving that cottage. So was Cherry.

Polly was being married from Granny's.

This was the last private appearance of Miss Cherry at Myrtle Cottage.

She got ready. Susan packed the wedding-frock. Polly never could make a decent parcel.

At last there was no more excuse for lingering.

"Well," said Polly.

She looked from her mother to her father hesitatingly. Susan went out and walked slowly along.

"Tooraloo, Polly," said Cherry, cheerfully.

He had a little of the Cheer-up Party smile.

Polly walked up to his chair, put her hands round his arm.

"I've — given you a lot o' trouble," said Polly, stumblingly.

"Don't mention it," said Cherry, winking.

"An' — I've been happy here, too," said Polly, a dim surprise at the fact shining in her wet eyes. "I — I don't think I want to leave you both."

It was Polly all over.

She sat down and cried.

The hundreds of times she had wished herself well away — and now — to find she didn't want to go. At least, not for five minutes.

"If ever he doesn't do right by thee, I'll kill him as dead as a herring," said Nan, with her high colouring ebbing, her eyes ablaze.

And — Polly giggled, dabbing her eyes, and said, "Well, I'll have to go, I suppose."

Nan's good-bye, thought the man in the corner, might have been worse.

Polly only turned back three times before really joining the patient Susan.

The last time she ran, sobbing openly.

Behind a scented briar-bush Susan put her into apple-pie order, before they went into the road that ran past the little houses.

"Just an hour to get ready," said Cherry.

"Chaps doesn't need much gettin' ready," yapped Nan.

He watched her struggle into a twenty-six inch circumference — gave a victorious hurrah when she got the clasp fastened.

"Here," he said at length, "what about me?"

Nan proceeded to get him ready.

They set out, a quarter before the time, going down to Granny's through the now sunshiny village.

"Th' weather-clerk knows it's our Polly an' is doin' his best," he told Nan.

Nan, in a dress of Irish green, and a blue hat with ears of wheat (what Cherry called a you-can't-go-wrong hat), went on with her head up. Cherry, on his wheels, in blue coat, with yellow jonquils, white gloves, and white bowler, looked like a tomtit beside a grim paraquet.

"Well, you do look weel," was Granny's verdict, as they came through the door.

She sat on a chair by the open door, dressed in her best, her bonnet on ready, only the strings wanting tying.

"Out o' puff, mother?" queried Cherry.

"No — full on it," she smiled.

Granny was breathing badly. She was more than a little excited.

There was another brand-new geranium in her bonnet. She wore, corner-wise, a cardinal silk shawl, which Susan admired and did not recollect having seen her in before.

Granny took a pinch of snuff.

"I were wed in this," she said, slowly. "When Harker were drunk he used to talk about this shawl. T'were th' only thing he ever bought me, barrin' th' ring, an' I used to wish he'd not bought that. But — but for me there wouldn't have been our Polly, would there? We serve our purpose in this world. An' — she's goin' to be happy. So — I put on th' old shawl, by way o' lettin' by-gones be by-gones. It'd suited Harker. He were soft in some ways. An' — he were a good-lookin' chap, when he were washed. Our Polly owes her good looks to him. I reckon him an' me came together for summat, an' has our bit o' share in this day. I'm fain to ha' sin it, Will."

Cherry was touched.

In all his life Granny Harker had never struck him as a pathetic figure before. She had been both too droll and too grim.

On Polly's wedding-day she had squared her account of the "gammy" leg, had forgiven that Primrose Leaguer who had given her that painful souvenir to carry to her grave.

"There ought to ha' bin some fiddlers," said the cobbler's wife.

"Oh, them'll come later," said Cherry, grinning.

"Polly!" yelled Granny. "Tha'rt goin' to be late!"

Granny was most impatient this day, for a calm old Calvinist.

Susan went upstairs to help Polly.

There were already a trio of neighbours, quarrelling as to which hook went to which eye of the puzzling dress, with Polly very pale and helpless amongst it all.

Susan set the puzzle straight, and they all flocked downstairs.

Polly in a shimmer of satin and soft lace and mock-orange blossom, was a sight for sore eyes. Even in the upheaval of this her careless life she enjoyed the sensation she created. The little milk-boy who had come in to look at her, didn't really believe it was Polly.

"Eh, ay," said the cobbler's wife, "some o' th' aristocrats can't hold a cannel to poor folk for looks. Now — who'd think to look at her, she'd ever done a day's wark in her life ?"

"She takes after her dad for bein' handsome," said Cherry, which made the women smile at male conceit.

Polly sneaked into his corner, and gave him her little finger.

"Adam's here," said the cobbler's wife.

Adam was in a grey suit.

His eyes sought for Polly amidst the throng, and found her in that dim corner — a white satin mouse, whose bright glance asked him if he was satisfied.

"Well, tha ought to be proud on her," said a neighbour.

He smiled awkwardly.

The Wilds didn't wear their hearts on their sleeves.

Even Polly had found him the most silent, undemonstrative lover she had had.

He looked at the clock.

"There's Grandma Cherry to come," said Granny. "An' — I wonder if that owd musicker as is to giye Polly away is *up* yet. An' them cabs — cabbies is th' carelessest folk born."

Granny was plainly afraid of any hitch occurring.

"Bob's gone to see the old man up," said Adam.

Steps sounded on the cobbles.

A shadow fell across the doorway.

"Becky!" said Polly.

Becky it was, Becky with the fat baby trying to eat her shabby hat, Becky thinned and humbled out of knowledge, Becky living with a respectable aunt in Narrowfields, who didn't forget to let her know how good she had been to take her in.

"Sit thee down, lass," quoth Granny.

Adam got her a chair.

Becky had lost a day's work and carried a fifteen pounds baby six miles to see her friend in her hour of glory.

"Make her a sup o' tay, Nan," said Granny.

So Becky sat eating and drinking tea in the way some people do eat and drink with others there — nervously, but glad of the tea.

Polly came out of the corner and forgot her self-consciousness and poured Becky a second cup.

She stared at Polly with eyes that filled with tears — glad, yet conscious of her forlorn lot.

"Come an' see us, any time — any time — for weekends — when you like," said Polly, and looked towards Adam.

"It's Polly's home," said Adam.

"Oh — here's *one* cab," said Granny, in relief.

Out of it stepped Grandma Cherry and Billy.

Billy had laid out in a new suit for Polly's wedding. His look said that Adam had all the luck. Nan was almost gracious with her mother-in-law.

"Fancy havin' a chap to give yo' away as can't get up!" said Granny.

Bob marshalled in Old Fiddlesticks.

He had helped to dress him.

He sat down near Adam, and hoped Adam would let Polly go on singing, just as if Adam was shutting her in a cage. Adam answered appropriately.

"I never knew that clock miss cuckooin'," said Granny, "but — happen it's wrong."

Three folk looked at their watches.

Granny's clock was "Greenwich, dead," according to her son-in-law.

They waited for the moment to strike.

"Cuckoo!" sang the clock.

Granny rose up, rustling and relieved.

"I reckon nowt o' havin' to push," she said.

The other cab had come along.

What a business it was.

The cobbler's wife insisted that the bride ought to enter the cab with the bridegroom, and quarrelled with all convention because she didn't, but went in on the arm of the best man.

"Poor Becky!" whispered Polly to Adam, who cut across.

He was quick to understand.

Becky was "pushed in" the third cab, and shared in the glory. The Cherry clan was waiting in, and almost filled the little church.

It was all over, as Cherry said, "in no time." Adam it was who had to be asked to "speak a little louder, please." Granny it was who greeted them as they came out of the vestry with, "Well, you've teed a knot wi' your tongues you can't undo wi' your teeth, an' I hope you'll never rue it!"

Cherry, meanwhile, invited the new parson to the feast. Cherry was master of the ceremonies now. He had taken a fancy to the parson — who had a quaint resemblance to a well-fed monk.

Cherry being lifted in and out the cab and set upon the wheels again, felt it had been a "big job" for him, but that the fun was now commencing. Bob and Adam carried him up the twenty steps to that long room. Even yet, he always gritted his teeth a little at having to be carried. But when once he was wheeling himself about the huge room, as M. C. — the man who was going to make this feast a success — he had got over it.

He had sent out a hundred postcards to the clan.

Ninety had been answered — in person. Their ages ranged from ninety down to nine. There were also "Pontius Pilate," Jane, the charwoman, Tim, her husband.

"Well, by gum! There's enough to eat," said Uncle Silas, in amaze, as dish after dish was carried on the table.

Cherry wheeled himself along past that array of chairs, holding the clan — the clan that was going to eat his stuff in return for that they had brought long ago.

There was no patronage, pity, nor charity in the eyes of the clan, now.

Nothing succeeds like success.

It was man to man now.

How the great room rang to the singing of the old-fashioned "grace" started off by Uncle Silas! What a hush was that which followed, wherein every one was at an awful pause, not liking to be first to begin, until Uncle Silas broke the ice by saying in a seriously meditative way, "I think I can't do better nor start wi' sausage-rolls." Whereupon every one fell on sausage-rolls.

"Now, folk," said Uncle Silas, "don't be shy."

He winked across the table at Polly.

Adam handed Polly the dish.

"Get plenty down tha," advised Jane, the char-woman, sitting by Tim, who was eating sausage-rolls "wholesale." Then she said by way of explanation, "For tha doesn't know what tha'll ha' to go through."

Whereupon, getting scared or embarrassed, Polly made a grab at the sausage-roll.

Something slipped.

It had gone on the floor!

Polly, scarlet, looked beseechingly at Adam.

"The sausage rolled," said a waggish voice.

It was the merry, red-nosed parson.

And everybody laughed.

Adam rescued the sausage-roll from under the table, and it was the universal opinion that in any case it had lost nothing. Such eating, such laughing, such talking, with Adam and Polly too delirious to eat, and so ashamed to be delirious that they must make martyrs of themselves and appear sane.

Whilst little fragments of conversation crossed each other comically.

"Dinah couldn't come. She's morphy in her cheek three times a day, now. But she's a rare plucked 'un. She'll not dee on purpose——"

"Ay. Them were gradely weddin's, when they had fiddlers walking afore, an' posies thrown under their feet."

"Muvver, can I have a pickle-onion?"

"An* I said to him, well if I have lived afore — I were a Brussels sprout."

"Give me a mongrel dog — wide between the ears——"

"Please, Adam, I can't eat any more," in a whisper from Polly.

Round about Cherry was the sound of a bottle clinking.

The parson was a very human man.

Aunt Miriam was about to refuse anything in her tea, but seeing Mr. Roecome accept, she thought better of it.

Aunt Miriam had watched the door in a way no one could fathom.

"Here's to my lass," cried Cherry, proud as Punch, and lifted his cup.

Granny jinked hers with him.

"Hear, hear!" called Bob Wild, tapping the table with his knife-haft. Only Susan restrained him from another partaking of the bottle.

"Then," called Uncle Silas, standing up, "to everybody's lasses. They're all somebody's, aren't they, exceptin' them as is nobody's, an' they're somebody's, too, an' God bless 'em — every one."

Which started off a series of applause.

Cherry's eye missed nothing, as its glance roamed the length of the table — Becky, letting the infant Saul suck a bit of jam from her finger, when she thought no one watched; Aggie, flirting madly with Ned Thom, whilst her husband raged and lost the flavour of the crab; Granny, elate and gay; Susan keeping her eye on Bob; Captain Brown, telling his lovely lies about his army career, and with a manner that made women believe him; Nan, unbending to Billy Breeze's amiability and quite nice with Grandma Cherry, who was talking to Mr. Moss and cutting up his meat for him — he missed nothing of it all. This was his day. Jane and Tim. How they ate. It made him a little sad. Pontius Pilate was on thought forces.

When a little, bald-headed man sneaked in through the door, it was Cherry who called out, "This way, Jerry," and saw Aunt Miriam flush and grow pale — Aunt Miriam dressed in pink, the colour Granny called "old maid's last refuge."

He knew all the tumult of Aunt Miriam's soul as Jerry Clin sat down, and began to cut. For a writer of burning love-letters Jerry Clin was pathetically nervous. Perhaps it was the effect of Aunt Miriam's answers, and the threat to have him up for breach of promise.

After Jerry came the five fiddlers, who dined in a little room behind, and no sooner had they sat down than in came Sandy MacGuir, with his pipes, and sat down also, in the little room.

Uncle Silas was the last man to cease eating.

They waited patiently for him.

"Any more, Silas?" quoth Granny.

Silas touched his neck with his hand, sideways — to assert that he was filled to the top.

"Well, then——" said Granny.

There was a great shuffling of chairs.

At the far end sat Jerry Clin, casting glances at the door, now the feast was over. Cherry, on his wheels again, trundled towards him.

"She's here," said Cherry, in a confidential whisper.

Jerry looked like bolting.

"Which is her?" quoth Jerry.

Cherry pointed out Aunt Miriam.

"She's religious, too," said Cherry. "Tha might go further an' fare worse. Come an' be introduced."

But Jerry would not.

Aunt Miriam casting sheep's-eyes at him had scared him to death.

Cherry conducted him into the little room where the fiddlers were now tuning up their instruments. The fiddlers and Jerry said they didn't mind if they did, and the man with the pipes said that was a fine brand o' whiskey, though he'd known a better at two shillings would burn a man's guts out.

Jerry was quite courageous when they left the little room.

Half a dozen people were waxing the huge floor; the tables were pushed back against the wall; everybody was talking; Aunt Miriam was sitting, heaving great sighs.

Cherry introduced Jerry and left him to Aunt Miriam. He made a half-move to follow the man on the wheels — but Aunt Miriam was not to be thrown off.

The five fiddlers sat themselves down, and struck up the lancers. The big room was suddenly filled with people eager to make up "sets."

Great was the astonishment of Polly to find that Adam could dance, nay, that he was one of the best dancers in the room. Here, they were, they two, in heaven when the dance brought them together, when they touched hands in the "chain" or went down the middle. Polly's paleness was gone, now. It was the dream come true. After all, had Adam not rescued her? She giggled as some of the dancers missed each other — and at the face of one man which appeared to be set on another man's shoulder, wearing a look of stony horror. It was Jerry Clin — dancing for the first time.

Uncle Silas was what he called "pushing Granny through the Lancers" — and that set they danced in laughed too much to dance really, laughed until everybody got with the wrong partners and "chained" out of order, and what Granny called "blundered through it," and found themselves at it when the five fiddlers had stopped.

But it was when the barn dance came on that Granny shone.

She led off, with Uncle Silas, going down the middle with a broad, beaming face, and all the others following — whilst the good humour spread. The dancing only stopped when the five fiddlers went to "wet their whistles" in that little room. When they came out, and played a hornpipe the young folk stood abashed. But the older ones danced the hornpipe and two of the five fiddlers got so excited as they watched Granny that they yelled "go on, old girl," "keep it up, mother," — and Uncle Silas said he wouldn't be licked by Betsy, if he knew, but had to retire after all.

It was Adam and Polly who led off when the waltz music struck up, and danced so beautifully together no one else got up, and the cobbler's wife cried, and they only found they were the cynosure of all eyes half-way through the waltz, and Polly said "Ooo," but Adam said, looking down, "Nay, let's dance it out, Polly."

Soon afterwards the little platform was filled with the Concert's Committee, Cherry being one.

Unanimously he was elected Chairman, and perched at a table, which held a glass of beer.

"The next dance," said Cherry, "will be a song. Mr. Silas Cherry will oblige. 'Roses Underneath the Snow'". Thus began the entertainment, where people had to sing whether they would or not.

"Sitha — I'll kill thee, Will," shouted the first singer on the programme.

"Eh — we all know tha can sing," called Betsy.

Four picked men escorted Uncle Silas on to the platform, nay, pushed him up the four steps, and saw he did not run away. Whilst the piano player vamped to Uncle Silas trying to get the pitch, and people tried to look as though they couldn't hear him.

Uncle Silas fronted the audience.

"If I forget a bit, yo' mun excuse me," he said, before beginning.

Cherry could see Adam and Polly sat together — both pair of eyes on Uncle Silas, and Adam having taken one of Polly's hands in his.

"Turn around in brave en-dev-hour,
Let your vain rip-pinin's go —
'Opeful harts wfll find fur-rever,
Ro — oses underneath th' snow."

Uncle Silas managed a verse and the chorus and sang the chorus twice, and again with the audience, and went down the four steps to a thunder of applause and a "We don't know what talents we've got!"

Cherry was in his element now.

There sat Uncle Bob Rimmer, unconscious that his was the next name down, waiting delightedly for the blow to fall on somebody else.

"Mr. Bob Rimmer will oblige with 'Bite Bigger, Billy,' " — called Cherry. Mr. Bob Rimmer said he would see Cherry somewhere, first. The whisky had upset Bob. There was quite a scrimmage before *he* was hauled upon the platform. But once having got thereon he recited with a fervour that surpassed himself, a warmth, and a delightfulness that made his audience see the little scene of the two urchins in the dimness of a snowy morning, finding the apple, the faded flower, and sharing.

"If tha has'nt no luck o' thysel',
Tha can share all th' findings wi me."

Which made his audience expand, and grow moist-eyed and shake their heads as to say what a different world it'd be if that spirit prevailed.

But the star of the entertainment was Grandma Cherry, singing "The Kerry Dancers." It was the ghost of a sweet old voice singing a song of a youth passed away — a thread of a voice, quivering the sad, sweet words — and Cherry noticed that Adam's hand gripped Polly's more closely. Song after song, piece after piece. The sun was going down, the room filling with gloom — and the five fiddlers were almost drunk. It was then that James MacGuire gave his exhibition of the pipes, going down the aisle between the chairs, coming back again, skirling away. Then when the lights were lit, Cherry called out "Mr. Adam Wild will oblige with a song".

The end was felt to be approaching.

Adam faced the platform, though he had his own ideas on a bridegroom singing at the bridal feast.

Polly found to her delight that Adam had quite a fine baritone voice. She sat seeing him through the eyes of the audience — her hands clasped.

It was the man with the pipes who accompanied
"O, wert thou in th' cauld, cauld blast"

The tenderest of love-songs rolled through the big room.

"A gradely song," applauded Uncle Silas. Then he said to Granny, "Who's that chap our Miriam's picked up?"

It was at this moment that there arose sounds of a conflict from the little room. The five fiddlers were fighting, and with difficulty disentangled, and set to playing again. After this, it was almost time for Cherry's speech.

He knocked upon the table for order with the beer-glass.

"The last song," said Cherry, almost sadly. Then, turning again, he said, "*By request.*"

Everybody waited.

"Mr. Tim — over there — will oblige with 'Young Kate', he said, pointing at the sand-hawker, who was almost drunk, so drunk that he wanted to kiss Jane.

They carried the last singer up on the platform. Jane had said he had a good voice.

Supported by a man on either side, Tim managed to keep a swaying sort of balance. Then, he began to sing that old, old song, with its crooney, monotonous tune that any one could sing, whether they knew it or not.

Tim realised that it was up to him to "shine," so began. He had not a bad voice, but he had taken a lot of whisky.

"Young Kate, she was a flower gjrl,
Young Kate, she was a flower girl.
Young Kate, she was a flower girl,
And ofttimes she did say —

*Will you buy, will you buy, will you buy,
Will you buy, will you buy, will you buy.
Will you buy my posies?
I've cowslips and primroses,
And I've lilies, daffydowndillies,
Daisies, honeysuckle and wild roses."*

It was one of those songs where the audience sing and the soloist chips in. In fact, Tim found that they could do very well without him. "Will you buy, will you buy, will you buy, my posies?" The room rang with "buy, buy, buy." Cherry saw Nan singing it! Christopher Columbus! Nan was singing. But then — everybody was singing.

"Here, come back," said Tim's supporters, who had forgotten to support him, in singing. "There's another verse."

Tim wobbled forwards, scratched his head, and saw Jane prompting him with her lips, and looking happy to see him such a big man.

After some reflection he recalled the second verse.

"And Kate became the squire's bride,
And Kate became the squire's bride,
And Kate became the squire's bride,
And no more will she say — "
——Chorus: "Will you buy?"

The chorus was sung, every one applauded their own share, and Tim came down, in a halo of glory.

Cherry knocked soberly with his beer-glass this time.

When he had succeeded in getting order, which took a little time, he looked down on the upturned faces.

"Ladies and gentlemen——" he began, smiling.

"Cheese it, Will," came a voice.

"Well then — Foak —!" he addressed them.

"Ay — that'll do."

"Order — order."

"Shut up!"

"Fill his glass up."

"Foak — " said Cherry, meditatively, "I'm glad to see you here, and believe you've enjoyed yourselves."

(Some furious hand-clapping.)

"The merry-makin' is drawin' to a close. Everything draws to a close. Sometimes it's a good job. But I believe in bein' happy, if possible — despite what the parson says. It's easier bein' happy wi' some one to share your happiness, an' double your sorrows. It's a bit hard, sometimes — but is anything easy in this world? I sit here and lift up this glass——"

He lifted it and eyed it with beneficent look.

"And drink to the health of the bride and bride-groom."

He drank, amidst a dead silence.

He set the glass down.

"May they be happier nor anybody ever was before," he said, "though I don't think they will — there's a lot o' happiness in th' world — an' allers will be——"

"An' when they're not — let em' stick it —"

"Hear, hear!"

"I'm not in favour of month-old contracts —"

Loud applause.

"You don't get the best out of friendship in a month. It's stickin' does it — just stickin'. Here's to them 'at has stuck it, an' kept to th' bargain, an' grinned an' borne wi' one another, like a mother bears wi' her child, like a dog bears wi' its master — like the Boss o' th' Great Show bears wi' all on us. Here's to our Polly again, an' to our Adam. An' now, before we break up, we'll just push th' chairs to one side, an' sing 'Auld Lang Syne' — after which I declare this meeting closed."

The climax was reached as the clan seized hands in the great room and sang the immortal song, swinging hands vigorously. Then a travelled person suggested the outlandish custom of sending up "rockets." This was merely a hand movement, coupled with a mouth-noise as of a rocket bursting, and calling out the name of the person. A "rocket" was sent up for Cherry, Polly, Adam, this body and that, however, until it began to feel delicate to leave anybody out, so everybody had a rocket sent up for them — even Becky — Becky whose baby was asleep in the cloak-room. Even Nan — Nan, who looked touched to receive this public mark of esteem.

"He ought to have a do like this every week," avowed Uncle Silas.

There was a great to do in the cloak-room finding garments. They also found Mr. Roscoe, quite sound asleep, and quoting Scripture when he was roused — with a whisky bottle in his hand.

Cherry trundled up to Miriam and Jerry Clin.

Granny was talking to them.

"They're going to be asked out next Sunday," he said.

Jerry gasped.

"I've sin the letters he's written," said Cherry, to Aunt Miriam, "they'd read well in a court o' law. A hundred poun' damages it'd be."

Jerry groaned.

A hundred pounds!

"It's a forgery," he said.

Cherry laughed.

He took Jerry off to have another nip in the little room.

"I don't — mind — if I do," said Jerry, desperately, and offered to kiss Aunt Miriam.

"So you're engaged?" said Cherry.

Jerry looked hopelessly at him.

"Ay, I suppose we are," he said.

Aunt Miriam and Cherry and the whisky combined were too much for Jerry.

"I hope, Miriam," said Cherry, "tha'll fix him up well on Brand from the Burning stuff. It'd be a pity for owd Nick to get *him*. An' if I were thee, I'd never show him them letters. He mightn't have written 'em."

Aunt Miriam stared at Cherry.

Then — a light dawned in her eyes.

She took the arm of Jerry Clin — and saw him safely home.

"I suppose there'll be another weddin' to dance at, son," said Granny.

She was peering about.

"Th' trap came just after I made my speech," said Cherry. "I saw 'em go. They've gone home."

He referred to Polly and Adam.

Nan came out of the cloak-room just then.

"Darby and Joan, now," he said, comically. "Left all alone in the cottage by the sea!"

Granny looked at him.

"It's me 'at 'll fed it," said Nan, chokily.

But Granny was staring at Cherry.

"All flesh is but grass, Will," she said. "She's gone th' way o' all flesh — except that as is hay wi' havin' a' th' human nature dried out on it. Well, he has a trap. You'll see her a lot."

They took Granny home.

Then went up to Myrtle Cottage with Grandma Cherry, who was staying overnight And there — waiting "innocent like," as Cherry said — was a letter, bringing the great news that Cherry had won his case. He had a pound per week for life.

Across the valley, in that little white farm, Sarah was waiting, with a big fire, for Polly and Adam.

"We're not stayin' in," said Adam.

"Eh?" she gasped.

Adam was off to harness the new brown cob, and drove Polly to Narrowfields, to start her honeymoon week of Grand Opera. "Faust" was first night — the wonder, the glory of it, with a star company; "Rigoletto," "Il Trovatore," "Maritana," "Lily of Killarney," with Polly scarcely breathing through it all, and afterwards the drive back under the low moon in a spring night, with the trot of the brown cob setting itself to music, and Sarah awaiting at the other end to mother Polly as she had never been able to mother Adam. Polly was in clover.

"We'll go down to Granny's to-night," said Polly.

This was on Sunday.

They called, after chapel.

"I'm fain yo' called to-neet," she said, repeating the statement twice.

Granny had not been herself since that jig in which she out-jigged Silas.

They were glad, too, three days later.

Granny died, sitting in her chair — whilst laughing with the cobbler's wife.

She had gone as she wanted to go, "like the crack of a gun" — giving trouble to no one, and on her own hearthstone.

All that she was possessed of she left to her granddaughter Polly. It consisted of the household furniture and some forty pounds. Conditional on the household furniture was the clause that if ever

Belle Harker came to Cherrydale, she should stay as long as she liked with Polly. She also begged that the weather-vane should cause no bad feeling — but that one or other of the two who had asked for it should "give way" if necessary. She asked that there should be no flowers, a sad waste of good money, and ended this Grannyish will with the remark that none should miss any sleep over her going, *as she'd had a good innings.*

The funeral took place just a fortnight after Polly's wedding — the clan gathering in the same room.

So genial a ghost had Granny left behind her that no man ate with a sense of shame.

Only Polly did not eat at all.

And was remonstrated with by the parson. But really comforted by Adam and her Dad.

"She's left such a memory behind," said Cherry, "we shall never believe she's right gone from us. An' it's not th' sort of memory you can cry off."

Which was perhaps all the flowers Granny needed. It was very appropriate that the minister forgot his glasses, and, therefore, could not read the burial service, laying Betsy Harker back into the earth with a few human words spoken as a friend. Only the cobbler's wife thought *she* wouldn't like to die *laughing.*

But, as Granny would say, "In this world it's hard to suit everybody."

After a life with its full innings of mirth and sorrow, she "ligged low and said nowt".

www.ingramcontent.com/pod-product-compliance
Lightning Source LLC
Chambersburg PA
CBHW052128270326
41930CB00012B/2804

* 9 7 8 1 8 4 9 2 1 2 3 6 6 *